To Ali and Susie

With love,

A Tradition Reborn

BOOKS BY DOV PERETZ ELKINS

Worlds Lost and Found (With Azriel Eisenberg)
God's Warriors: Stories of Outstanding Military Chaplains
Welding the Old to the New: A Biography of Rabbi Abraham Isaac Kook
So Young to Be a Rabbi: The Education of an American Clergyman
Rejoice with Jerusalem: Prayers, Readings & Hymns for Israel Observances
Olamot She-Ne-Elmu Ve-Niglu (Hebrew translation of *Worlds Lost and Found*), Tel Aviv
Treasures from the Dust (With Azriel Eisenberg)
A Tradition Reborn

AS CONTRIBUTOR

Best Jewish Sermons—1966
Best Jewish Sermons—1968
Best Jewish Sermons—1970
Best Jewish Sermons—1972
Sermons for Special Occasions
Sermons on Jewish Holidays and Festivals

A Tradition Reborn

SERMONS AND ESSAYS ON LIBERAL JUDAISM

Dov Peretz Elkins

FOREWORD BY ROBERT GORDIS

SOUTH BRUNSWICK AND NEW YORK:
A. S. BARNES AND COMPANY
LONDON: THOMAS YOSELOFF LTD

© 1973 by A. S. Barnes and Co., Inc.

A. S. Barnes and Co., Inc.
Cranbury, New Jersey 08512

Thomas Yoseloff Ltd
108 New Bond Street
London W1Y OQX, England

Library of Congress Cataloging in Publication Data

Elkins, Dov Peretz.
    A tradition reborn.

        1. Sermons, American—Jewish authors.   2. Sermons,
Jewish—United States.   I. Title.
BM740.2.E43   1973   296.8'346   73-2772
ISBN 0-498-01381-2

PRINTED IN THE UNITED STATES OF AMERICA

For

ELAINE

"Blessings rest on a man's home because of his wife."
—Talmud

Contents

7

Foreword

In our age, when automation and computerization threaten to blot out all sense of personal identity, the human dimension refuses to be destroyed. Much, if not most, of the chaos and confusion of our age stems from misdirected efforts of some of our youth and their elders to follow blind paths, basing themselves on the illusion that they will thus achieve personal significance. The drug culture of our time, the various patterns of sexual aberration that are glorified as "alternatives to marriage," the growing resort to violence and crime in all forms, even the graffiti that disfigure our buildings and make our cities nightmares of ugliness—all these are pathetic and perilous routes that different segments of society have been adopting in order to "find themselves," or, to use the current phrase, "do their own thing."

Fortunately, increasing numbers of men, women and young people are discovering that these much touted "life styles" are really highways to death. A significant and growing minority of our most sensitive and potentially creative men, women, and young people are seeking to discover their identity as individuals and their significance in society by exploring the historic experience of their specific group and the potential values in their own heritage.

No tradition in the Western World has richer sources of

guidance and insight to offer than Judaism, which is the oldest living religion in the world today. No people has amassed a wiser understanding of human nature, both of its limitations as well as of its potentialities, than the Jewish people.

Two and a half centuries ago, the French philosopher Voltaire was engaged in a philosophic discussion with Frederick the Great of Prussia regarding the possibility of miracles. The King of Prussia challenged the French thinker to cite one authentic miracle. Voltaire's now famous answer was, "Sire, the Jews." Our age offers the best evidence for the truth of Voltaire's response. In this, the last third of the most brutal century in human history, when men and nations are beset by an all-pervasive sense of hopelessness and defeat, one great authentic miracle has occurred that is capable of reviving the crushed spirit of man—the survival of the Jewish people. This miracle is exemplified most dramatically in the birth and progress of the State of Israel, and, almost equally significantly, in the growth and development of the American-Jewish community. In spite of small and unpromising beginnings, American Jewry has become the largest, freest, best-integrated Jewish community in history.

To be sure, American Jewry is beset by a variety of major problems, and these need to be faced with integrity, intelligence and courage, as does Rabbi Elkins in the present volume. Problems are inherent in the human condition and major achievements are inseparable from major perils, and in this respect American Jewry is no exception. Nevertheless, it remains true that the future of the Jewish people lies before it, not behind it. The brutal extermination of six million Jewish men, women, and children, who constituted six-sevenths of European Jewry, an act which the Nazis could not have perpetrated without the silent acquiescence of "the free world," should have marked the end of the Jewish people. Instead, it helped fan into a mighty flame the spark of Jewish loyalty and identification, which gave birth to the State of Israel. Not only has it now survived twenty-five years of unrelenting hostility from its neighbors, but it has made significant contributions to every phase of human life and culture. Not only the Jew, but all men can find in the tragic history and the heroic saga of the Jewish people in the twentieth century the source for a clear-eyed, courageous faith in life and in man's potential, which are the manifestations of God in history.

But faith needs always to be articulated anew, particularly in our generation. It is good that among the spokesmen for religion in our time there are at least some young, idealistic spiritual leaders like Rabbi Dov Peretz Elkins, whose roots are deep in the Jewish tradition, whose eyes encompass the human situation, and whose hearts are responsive to the needs of their fellow Jews and their fellowmen.

According to the Talmud, "God desires the heart." In ancient Hebrew psychology, the heart was the seat not only of emotion and desire but of intelligence and understanding as well. In this wide-ranging volume, Rabbi Elkins brings his mind and his heart to bear on all aspects of the life of American Jewry and Judaism, particularly the difficulties confronting them in achieving vitality and meaning. These same attributes are evident in his discussion of the plight of Soviet Jewry, and in his analysis of the achievements and problems of the State of Israel.

All the timely issues of the day are illumined by the timeless insights of a great tradition. Rabbi Elkins speaks in clear and straight-forward fashion directly to his generation. The theme of the discourses included in this volume may well be described by borrowing and expanding the words of the Latin poet Terence, "I am a Jew and nothing Jewish or human is alien to me."

Deep calls unto deep and youth to youth. So long as young, vigorous, dedicated voices may be heard in the land, there is hope that our youth—and their elders—will hear the call, see the light, and walk the road of life.

Robert Gordis
Professor of Bible
Jewish Theological Seminary of America

Acknowledgments

I am grateful to Mrs. Alfred Hart for making possible the publication of this volume. I am also indebted to several cherished friends for their support and encouragement: Kivie Kaplan, Jack Becker, Ben L. Friedman, I. Irving Mandel, and Robert P. Abell.

My appreciation goes to Pearl Ostroff, who did much of the typing, for her ambitious and devoted assistance, and to Howard Crane and Jill Vigdor for reading the proofs.

I am grateful to Rabbi Marshall Maltzman for permission to use a sermon, "What a Congregation Expects from its Rabbi," which we have jointly written; to Mrs. Muriel C. Margolis for permission to quote her poem "Tale of My Temple"; to Rabbi Samuel H. Dresner for use of his beautiful translation of Agnon's introduction to the Kaddish; and to the *New York Times* for permission to quote a brief poem by Brian Lang (© 1969 by the New York Times Company. Reprinted by permission).

Dov Peretz Elkins
Rabbi, Temple Beth El
Rochester, New York

A Tradition Reborn

The feeling of Jewish communality touches
every Jew, across generations and across
geographic boundaries. Some Jews accept it
and comply with it, others rebel against it,
and still others deny or ignore it. Yet no
Jew can escape it.

> Dr. Mortimer Ostow
> *American Journal of Psychiatry,*
> November, 1972

The victory of the Six Day War created pride
and a stronger determination among the Jew-
ish People the world over to stand by the
State of Israel. It will be no exaggeration to
say that those six days opened a new chapter
in Jewish history. . . .

> *Ha'aretz* (Israel's daily newspaper),
> May, 1972

Part I

AMERICA, JUDAISM, AND THE JEWS

1
Social Action—Whose Business?

MANY PEOPLE FEEL THAT THE FUNCTION OF RELIGION, JUDA-
ism included, is to offer soothing balm to our spiritual
wounds, to comfort the afflicted and disturbed and grieving
members of society—a kind of palliative. This is indeed one
function of religion, but certainly not the only one. Another
equally important function is to declare war on evil and
injustice in society, not only to comfort the disturbed, but
to disturb the comfortable, the complacent, and the apathetic
souls among us.

The group of people who emphasize only the first function
of religion often are heard saying that we have no business
meddling in politics and social action. Let religion stay in
its own bailiwick, and not intrude into society. After all,
doesn't America insist on separation of church and state?—
meaning that religion should keep its nose out of political
issues.

Now this is a delusive slogan which really means, "I'm the
kind of person who doesn't want to get involved, and doesn't
want to be disturbed out of my complacency. Let religion

comfort the disturbed, but not disturb the comfortable status quo.

This reminds me of the story of the Negro woman from South Carolina who came into a large church in New York, where the ushers were boutonniered and befrocked and the atmosphere was quite cold and formal. When the preacher was delivering his sermon this lively, vibrant lady enjoyed a certain point, and yelled out in this quiet, formal church, "Amen!" One of these boutonniered and befrocked ushers came running up and said, "Lady, are you ill?" "Ill, man," she answered, "I got religion." The usher then said, "My God, lady, not here!"

Somehow or other so many people feel that churches and synagogues, whose roles in society should be to foster social change and social action, should be their refuge from the prods on their conscience that they sometimes find outside.

Well, that's not my idea of the role of religion, and I hope it's not yours. Christianity is just getting around to the notion that religions should be concerned about *this* world more than the next, but that has been our view all along. The non-Jewish theologians are talking about religion going out of the church and into the market place and the secular city; and instead of hiding behind their stained-glass windows, they should come out and feed the hungry, clothe the naked, and free the oppressed. These are things which Judaism has been saying all the way from the time of the Prophets and the Talmudic rabbis until our own time.

Jewish Law (Halacha) has always dealt with the most specific of moral and social issues, including peace and war, social injustice, poverty, housing, discrimination, and all the rest. It is ironic in light of this humane social tradition to find people today closing their eyes to the need for social justice in the Jewish community. Some Jews insist that their rabbis only talk about Judaism, but not about race and poverty and peace and fair housing.

You may have heard the story of the minister who visited a small rural church and preached on the Commandment "Thou shalt not steal." The congregation was thrilled with this brilliant sermon, and asked him to return the following

Sunday. He was so pleased that he announced that he would speak about the same subject, only this time he must make it a bit more specific: "Thou shalt not steal chickens." Whereupon the congregation ran him out of town.

This is the kind of person who would divorce society and social issues from religion. As long as you are talking in generalities about love and motherhood and God and other abstract terms, you're on sure ground. But if you dare add that one extra word which makes it specific, like "love black people" or "God who demands justice from landlords," then you're in trouble.

One of the best definitions of religion I ever heard appeared in a local newspaper on the Main Line, and was headed "Religion Is Not a Hobby." I'd like to quote part of it to you:

"Religion is not a hobby that can be neatly tucked into a pigeonhole that is opened only on Sundays. It is not an insulated refuge where creamy-voiced clerics pour mental soothing syrup over harassed psyches. It is not a magic formula whereby congregants who do what they damn please the rest of the time can obtain instant redemption by dozing in a pew once a week (except in good golfing weather). It is not an insurance company that guarantees salvation and eternal life to all dues-paying members of the flock, regardless of how they conduct their daily lives." (*Main Line Times*, April 18, 1968.)

Neither can we listen to those people who are so boxed in by their liturgies and their rituals that they cannot see the essence of religion. That's not the way Hillel saw it when he was asked by a pagan to define Judaism while standing on one foot. You know his famous answer: "What is hateful to you, do not do to your neighbor." He didn't say go to shul on Shabbat, or eat matzah on Pesach, or say kiddush on Friday night. He said love your neighbor as yourself. All the rest, he told the pagan, is only commentary on that one ethical doctrine of caring about the guy next door. Going to synagogue, and eating matzah and making kiddush are all part of the great commentary of caring about the guy next door.

There is a wonderful story told about one of the great ethical teachers of the nineteenth century, Rabbi Israel Salanter. He used to supervise the baking of matzot before Passover to see that they were completely kosher le-Pesach. One year he took sick and could not supervise the baking himself, so he gave instructions to the head of the community about what to do in his place. He didn't say anything about the flour or the water, but said only this: "You know the women who go to the well every day to bring the water for the matzos? They get paid every day, so make sure that they get paid before they leave."

The best thing one can say about Rabbi Israel Salanter is that he had perspective. He knew that the baking of the matzot was a meaningless act if it were done in a way that exploited those who were engaged in it. The baking and eating of matzot is all only part of this commentary on the Golden Rule, and if it violates that rule, that it undermines its very purpose.

Someone once compared a person who performs all the outward rituals of Judaism and says all his prayers and doesn't practice being an ethical Jew, to a man who mistreats his wife all year and on her birthday each year buys her expensive presents. He is only using that present to soothe his conscience and try to absolve himself of his sins. It isn't a sincere gesture of affection. But if he really loves his mate and treats her like his queen all year, then a nice birthday present is a beautiful topping to a delicious cake. So in ritual. Rituals are dramatizations of great ideals and values. When these values are present in our lives, then the rituals are very meaningful and add a special flavor to our lives. They are not just dressing for a cake which is sour or spoiled to soothe our consciences.

What I am saying is that in living the religious life we have to have perspective, and we have to order our priorities very carefully.

A society, in order to create a great messianic future, a world under the Kingdom of God, must order its priorities and establish its values very clearly. If it is a society which spends over half of its budget on guns, and pitifully little on

curing the social ills of the day, then it is a sick society, and
as Jews we must scream as loud as we can when this happens. The rabbis of the Talmud used to warn their Jews not
to go to the public amphitheatres because immoral things
took place there. But one rabbi, Rabbi Nathan, said it is permissible to go there if you scream out in protest. That's the
same thing Edmund Burke meant when he said that for evil
to take place all that is needed is that all the good people
in the world keep silent.

A German survivor of the death camps was once quoted
as saying: "When they went after Jews, I didn't protest
because I wasn't a Jew. When they went after gypsies and
Communists, I didn't protest because I wasn't a gypsy or a
Communist. When they went after labor unions, I didn't
protest because I wasn't a unionist. And then when they
came for me, I couldn't protest because it was too late."

If we are to be God's partners in this operation called
human existence, then all mankind has to be united into one
family. If you sit back and adopt the philosophy of the German who minded his own business until it was too late, then
it will be too late for all of us. The world is too small today
and forces of destruction are too powerful and swift for us
to sit back and watch anybody be treated unfairly. I say
this for very selfish reasons. For whenever there is injustice
in the world, it is bad for us as Jews as well as for us as
human beings. Somehow we're always next in line when
punishment is being meted out. So if we sit back and say,
"Let them go after the Negroes, because we're not Negro,"
and "Let them go after the Biafrans because we're not
Biafrans," or "Let them go after the Puerto Ricans because
we're not Puerto Rican," then by the time they get to us it
will be too late to do anything about it.

If we are to establish a messianic society, then we have to
set our goals very clearly *today* as to what this era will be
like. Plato said that man's highest good is the attainment of
a state of inner peace and harmony. Aristotle claimed that
a life of intellectual contemplation achieved through moderation in all things is man's greatest goal. The Epicureans

said that the wise enjoyment of pleasure is best of all, and the Stoics argued that life's finest fruits are to be found in a noble emotional detachment. But Hillel said that the essence of life is loving your neighbor as yourself, that the pursuit of justice and the practice of lovingkindness surpasses all of life's goals. At every moment in our lives we have to ask ourselves this question: Whose burden did you lighten today? What human suffering did you alleviate today? How much closer are we to that Kingdom of God on earth because of what I did during the last twenty-four hours? Or you might ask yourself the question I saw once on a church bulletin board: "What on earth did you do today for God's sake?"

Our tradition has a lot to say about the Kingdom of God, or the age of the Messiah, which is our theme this weekend. Rabbi Yochanan ben-Zakkai once said that if you have a plant in your hand when you hear the news that the Messiah is coming, go and plant the plant and afterward go out and greet him. (*Avot de R. Nathan*, 31.) That is as practical and down-to-earth advice as you can find anywhere in any literature. We Jews are not supposed to sit back and wait for the scientists and technologists to serve us a good and peaceful society on a silver platter. More important than sitting back and waiting for the Kingdom of God is each little act that we perform which will help speed it along its way, and assure its future once it arrives.

Another story in the Talmud relates how one of the sages had a dream and saw a beggar dressed in rags sitting at the gates of Rome.

A voice then said to him, "Do you see that man? He is the Messiah dressed as a beggar." The sage was at the time planning a trip to Rome from Jerusalem, and when he reached his destination there he was—a beggar in rags at the gates of Rome. He asked, "Are you the Messiah?" The man nodded affirmatively. The rabbi then asked the beggar, "What are you doing here in the gates of Rome?" And the man answered, "Waiting." "Waiting!" answered the sage. "In a world full of misery and hatred and war, in which the Jewish people is scattered and oppressed, and the Torah neglected, where children go hungry and innocent people suffer, you sit here waiting! Messiah, in the name of God, what are you waiting for?" The Messiah answered, "I've been waiting for *you*, so that I could ask *you*, in the name of God, what were *you* waiting for?"

I guess we could ask each other the same question. What is America waiting for to eliminate the poverty and the racism, and the hunger and the sickness and the slums? Are we waiting until we can send ten men to the moon and back safely, and until our country is filled from border to border with antiballistic missiles, before we can spend some money in the right places where God's partners think it ought to go?

You all remember the section in the Haggadah we read two weeks ago at our seders about the four sons? What was it about the wicked son which made him wicked? By saying "What is this service to *you*?" he excluded himself from the group and therefore, says the Hagaddah, he violated the cardinal principle of Judaism. The wicked son said, "It's none of my business; I'm not concerned about society, about the group," and that certainly is a violation of the most important principle in all of Jewish ethics.

Isaiah tells us (63:9) that when people suffer even God suffers. How much more so must we mortals suffer wherever another human being suffers! Jeremiah phrased it this way (8:21–23):

> For the hurt of my people I am seized with anguish; I am black, appallment has taken hold of me. Oh that my head were waters and mine eyes a fountain of tears, that I might weep day and night for the slain of my people.

The Torah admonishes us thirty-six times to practice justice and mercy toward strangers, assuming, of course, that to native citizens it goes without saying that the same treatment is to be afforded.

To the prohpets, our task in life is to "seek justice, relieve the oppressed, judge the fatherless, plead for the widow, open the eyes of the blind, free the prisoners from the dungeon." These are the paths toward the kingdom of God.

With a tradition like this, how can anyone possibly ask, "Is it our business to be involved in the community? Is it the business of the synagogue and the Jewish community to fight for the black man and the hungry man and the homeless man?" If we are descendants of men like Isaiah and Amos and Micah and Jeremiah, and if we are Jews who believe in God and in our role as his partners in this venture on earth, and if we truly mean what we say when we recite in the Alenu the phrase about refashioning society under the Kingdom of God, then that *is* our business. And may it always be our most important business!

2

Jacob, Conscience, and Amnesty

TWO INCIDENTS IN THE LIFE OF JACOB, AS PORTRAYED IN THE
Sidrah of Vayishlach, describe a little-known characteristic
of the great patriarch: that he was a man of deep conscience.

The opening verse of the Sidra finds Jacob returning home
to Eretz Yisrael after twenty years of sojourning with his
uncle, Laban. He now has a large family and has accumulated
much wealth. Realizing that his twin brother, Esau, will
still be angry at him over the birthright and blessing taken
from him, he becomes frightened. To handle this potentially
dangerous situation, Jacob employs three vehicles for self-
protection: a gift offer to Esau, a prayer, and preparation
for self-defense.

What prayer did Jacob offer? The ancient rabbis put into
the mouth of the patriarch two separate prayers: *May I not
be killed by my brother* and, secondly, *May I not kill my
brother*. The second prayer is of special interest to us.[1] It is
natural to think about self defense. But it is less usual to be

Delivered Shabbat morning, November 25, 1972, Temple Beth El,
Rochester, New York.
1. I am grateful to Rabbi Jack Riemer for this quotation.

concerned about the role of our own conscience, our own brutality, the possibility of our becoming callous to human pain and destruction. Jacob prays to control his strong impulse to violence, inherent in human nature. He fears for his body, but also for his soul. This is the role of conscience in human life.

A second incident further develops Jacob's sense of conscience. After bringing his family across the ford at Jabbok, he remains alone, confronted with a strange challenger who wrestles with him until dawn. Winning the battle, Jacob limps away with a new name, Israel, he who struggled with creatures divine and human, and prevailed.

Who was this angel? What did he symbolize? Maimonides (1135–1204 C.E.) suggests that the encounter was with Jacob's own *yezer hara,* his impulse to do evil. He struggled with his lower self, and his higher self won. He came away limping, but he did not surrender his better self. His conscience was victorious.

Amnesty Today

This brings me to our situation today. Thousands of young Americans are now facing the same crisis that Jacob did. They have struggled with the angel of their conscience. Could they permit themselves to kill their brothers? In today's global village, they see Vietnamese, Communists, all men, regardless of color, creed, nationality or ideological persuasion, as brothers. Their prayer has been, *May I not let myself kill my brother.*

Men who were about to be drafted, and men already serving in the Armed Forces, had to decide this question of conscience. It was an inner war deep inside the fiber of their being. Who should prevail? National duty or the call of conscience? Perhaps for some it was more of a question of merely protecting their own skin. Their prayer was *May I not be killed.* But for most I sincerely believe it was the second prayer, *May I not kill my brother.*

What shall we do with these young men, draft resisters and Army deserters? This subject has been debated this

year (1972), and will be debated even more strenuously in
the year to come. It seems to me that the voice of the synagogue should enter this debate with vigor and sincerity.
There are now some 100,000 of these young men in exile and
in jail. Senator Edward Kennedy has said that instead of
being a nation that is a haven for refugees, we have become
a nation that has created refugees and political exiles. With
the POWs not released, most statesmen have agreed that
amnesty cannot be granted. Now, however, it appears that
the war will end very soon and the prisoners freed. The
decision of granting amnesty or not will soon become more
than an academic one.

Let us take the case of one young Jew, Burton Weiss.
Mr. Weiss was involved in the peace movement, student
politics, and civil rights at Cornell University. He was denied
the status of a CO (conscientious objector) and refused in-
duction into the military. On the day he was to appear in
United States District Court for arraignment, he was invited
by eighteen rabbinical students at the Jewish Theological
Seminary to enter their synagogue to "reaffirm your right
to refuse to be forced to kill." Weiss wrote to the presiding
judge: "I have committed no crime. . . . I would not step
into that murderous machine because, quite simply, . . . I
do not belong there. I decline to shed blood. This apparently
is the extent of my 'crime.' It makes no sense."

What Weiss is saying is this: Like Jacob, I cannot shed
my brother's blood. How shall we treat such a person? Like
a criminal? An anarchist? Or a man of deep convictions and
of conscience?

To me there is only one fair way. Once the war is over,
and the prisoners freed, we must grant unconditional and
total amnesty. Historians find ample precedent for such an
act. The first amnesty was granted in 403 B.C.E. to Athenians,
to patch up their rebellion-torn city. In our own country, in
more recent times, George Washington, in 1795, proclaimed
a "full, free, and entire pardon" to all persons who participated in the Pennsylvania Whiskey Rebellion. In explaining
his action to Congress, President Washington said: "For
though I shall always think it a sacred duty to exercise with

firmness and energy the constitutional powers with which I am vested, yet my personal feeling is to mingle in the operations of the government every degree of moderation and tenderness which the national justice, dignity and safety permit."

Later, John Adams granted amnesty to Pennsylvania insurrectionists. Jefferson, Madison, Jackson, Lincoln, Andrew Johnson, Grant, and Coolidge each made amnesty proclamations. One historian counted thirty-seven different instances in American history of the granting of amnesty. It does not seem, therefore, that the "national justice, dignity and safety," to use Washington's words, were jeopardized, if amnesty was granted so often throughout American history.

Yet, there are many who object to total amnesty, and some to partial amnesty. It would be an insult to the memory of the 60,000 men who gave their lives in Vietnam, they say. On the other hand, among those in favor of amnesty are many Vietnam veterans and parents of Indochina victims. One father who lost his son in Southeast Asia asked the President to grant amnesty, with this explanation: "These refugees are our sons, and we need them back. They did not deserve what we have done to them." Many such parents only wish they had advised their sons to go to Toronto, instead of letting them go to Quang-Tri. Because they made an error, why should others suffer?

A New York lawyer raised this objection: "They broke the law, and should take the punishment due them. Their heroes, Gandhi, and Martin Luther King did and so should they." I don't know if it is fair to ask every young man of conscience in America to play the part of a hero. If they have committed no crime, for what should they pay? For breaking the law? But most Americans now feel that it was the law that was immoral, not the resisters and deserters. If that is the case, why should they be punished? Rabbi Abraham Joshua Heschel recently stated: "Something precious will have been lost by the American people if they should regard amnesty as a matter of mercy. Much of the hope of the future depends upon a clear recognition that resistance to an unjust cause is a sacred right of man."

Some propose a partial amnesty, only to draft dodgers, but not to military deserters. But is there really a substantial difference? Is it not merely a matter of timing? College educated boys knew how to avoid the draft. Others did not realize until they entered the military what was happening to them and their conscience. Why discriminate between the two?

For the same reason, I am not in favor of Senator Taft's proposal of two years of service to the country in order to be exonerated. These men have acted out of conscience. They have paid a penalty of jail or exile. Their only crime, in the words of Burton Weiss, is that they refused to step into the murderous machine. Why must they be exonerated?

In a statement published a few months ago by a group of Protestant, Catholic, and Jewish religious leaders, the following position was taken: "Amnesty is a belated recognition of a right they should never have been denied. It is a blessed act of oblivion, the law's way of undoing what the law itself has done."

It seems to me that the place of individual conscience is being forgotten and sadly neglected in American society today. Had the law provided for the possibility of selective conscientious objection in the first place, most of the resisters would not have had to become exiles. It seems that as each day passes, more and more of our civil liberties and fundamental human rights are being cynically disregarded by the courts and the administration. Now we hear of young reporters and teachers, university professors, going to jail for doing their work and following the dictates of their conscience. This nation desperately needs an act of reconciliation! *A full and unconditional amnesty is the only way to completely close the book on this bloody and nasty horror of Vietnam.* Dr. William Gaylin, a prominent psychoanalyst, was quoted as saying: "Without amnesty this war will never end in our own minds."

Even as conservative a cleric as the late Cardinal Cushing of Boston said in his Easter sermon two years ago: "Would it be too much to suggest that we empty our jails of all protestors—the guilty and the innocent—without judging them;

call back from over the border and around the world the young men who are called deserters; drop the cases that are still awaiting judgment on our college youth? Could we not do all of this in the name of life, and with life, hope?"

It seems that we all agree now, including the President and Dr. Kissinger, that this war must end immediately, and can only end diplomatically, not militarily. Why penalize those who prematurely took the same position two or five or eight years ago?

It seems to me that there is a loyalty to God and conscience that was important to our father, Jacob, and that must be more important to us than any temporal loyalty. And we must never lose sight of that highest loyalty, because it is that which ultimately makes us human.

3

A Tu Be-shevat Sermon on Our Environment

"NOW OR NEVER." THESE WERE THE WORDS OF PRESIDENT Nixon just two weeks ago in signing into law a measure which created a special commission on our environment, to check the pollution of our air, water, and soil. "We are all concerned," said the President, "with our environment—everywhere."

Indeed we are concerned. Judaism has set aside a special day to express our concern for our physical environment. It is one of the so-called "minor" holidays of the Jewish calendar, but it is a festival to which we should all be paying more attention in future years.

In the Mishnaic tractate of Rosh Hashana, the very first statement reads as follows:

"There are four Rosh Hashanas (New Years): on the first day of Nisan is the New Year for Kings and for Festivals; on the first of Elul is the New Year for the tithe of animals. . . . The first of Tishre is the New Year for the

Delivered January 16, 1970.

years. . . . On the first of Shevat is the New Year for trees, according to the School of Shammai. But the School of Hillel says on the fifteenth of Shevat."

Scholars conjecture that the School of Shammai, which represented the wealthy classes, chose the first of Shevat because the rich had better fields and gardens and their fruits matured earlier than those of the poor. The School of Hillel, which represented the poorer classes, chose a date two weeks later, on the fifteenth of Shevat, Chamisha Asar Be-Shevat, which has become the fixed day for this Festival of Jewish Arbor Day.

Our ancestors were extremely concerned about not exploiting our natural resources, and so they set aside one special day on which to pay homage to the importance of soil conservation, tree planting, and beautification of the landscape of Eretz Yisrael. The Talmud declares emphatically that "Any city which does not have greenery, a wise man may not dwell in it." In making this statement the ancient rabbis, I am sure, had more in mind than the mere absence of greenery in the natural environment. Any community that does not concern itself with greenery and its physical resources, in which a spirit of selfishness and lack of vision prevails, is one that will ultimately destroy itself.

Such a community, the rabbis felt, which did not see into the next generation, or even the next century, was narrow-minded and did not deserve having in its midst one of Israel's distinguished citizens.

A beautiful story is recounted in the Talmud of an eccentric teacher named Honi the Circle-Drawer, a miracle-worker who lived during the first century. One day Honi saw a man planting a tree and he asked him, "What are you planting?" The elderly gardener answered him: "A carob tree." "In how many years will it bear fruit?" asked Honi. "Seventy years," responded the old man. "But you are very old," continued Honi; "will you live to see it bear fruit?" The old man answered by saying, "When I came I found trees planted by those who lived before me. I am doing for future generations what they did for me."

There is a very important message in this story. It challenges us with the question of the old gardener: When we were born we found clean air to breathe, clear water to drink, clean earth to walk upon. Will we bequeath these same clean natural resources to those who come after us?

Professor Claude Levi-Strauss, the famous French anthropologist, recently stated in a dramatic, apocalyptic tone how important the problem of our environment will be in the next decade. To solve this problem, he said, will take a spiritual revolution.

It would require that man, who since the Renaissance has been brought up to adore himself, acquire modesty, and that he learn the lesson of all the atrocities we have experienced for thirty or forty years. He would do well to learn that if one thinks only man is respectable among living beings, then the frontier is placed much too close to mankind and he can no longer be protected. One must first consider that it is as a living being that man is worthy of respect, and hence one must extend that respect to all living beings—at that point, the frontier is pushed back, and mankind finds itself better protected. (*New York Times*, Dec. 31, 1969.)

Judaism has always had great respect for living creatures. It is one of the cardinal principles of our tradition that whatever lives was created by God for a purpose. The Midrash states explicitly, "The Lord God has not created a single thing that does not have a function."

We are enjoined never to destroy any useful thing in the entire world. "Whosoever destroys something useful," say the rabbis, "is violating an important biblical principle, 'Thou shalt not be destructive.' "

Leaders of the automobile industry have just declared that they will attempt to create within ten years an automobile that has no dangerous exhaust. This is commendable, but some feel that even that much time is too long. A recent analysis has shown that merely by walking in the streets of New York City for a solid day, a person will breathe in the toxic equivalent of two packs of cigarettes. At the present rate of increased level of carbon monoxide, we may have to walk around wearing an oxygen mask right here on earth, not only on the moon.

Rabbi Levi declared some fifteen hundred years ago that for every breath a man breathes he should thank God, because the Psalms say: "Everything with the breath of life within it should praise God." One wonders, if Rabbi Levi were walking the streets of Manhattan day in and day out, whether he would make that statement today.

The destruction of the soil is no less serious a matter. An ancient rabbi said: "Those who cut down good trees are reckoned among the sinners who will never see any good in their lifetime."

Those who have violated this rabbinic injunction during the twentieth century have caused two million acres in twenty-eight states to crack, subside, and sink into the ground, sometimes swallowing houses and automobiles with them.

And what about the monstrous automobile graveyards, often many layers deep, which we find on our American roadsides wherever we travel. Talmudic law forbids a man from moving his boulders from his own field into a public place. It is the responsibility of the individual, of industry, of the community, and of the nation as a whole, to see to it that these wastes are not piled up into huge masses of refuse to pollute our countrysides and our rivers.

A news item a few months ago reported the results of an expedition in India by the Department of Archeology of the University of Pennsylvania. The archeologists found the remains of the ancient civilization of the Indus River Valley, which was apparently at one time a prosperous center of civilization. This civilization disappeared without a trace of its language or culture being preserved for posterity. The reason for this, the scholars discovered, was not that the community was destroyed by fire or sword, but by *mud*. Slowly but surely the overflowing waters of the Indus River laid successive layers of mud on the cities and villages of this civilization, until the mud completely choked off all of its life.

It is becoming more obvious every day that we are in

danger of choking out our own lives with the mud of pollution of our soil, water, and air. In President Nixon's recent
State of the Union message (1970), he said:

> The great question of the seventies is: Shall we surrender to
> our surroundings or shall we make our peace with nature and
> begin to make reparations for the damage we have done to our
> air, to our land, and to our water?

Our young people are beginning to see this danger even
more quickly than the adult generation. Many of them cor-
rectly see this problem as having even more serious long-term
implications and dangers for American society than the wars
of the races and the wars in Southeast Asia. They are beginning to devote themselves to this issue on the college campuses in ever greater numbers, according to recent surveys.

It seems to me that we are lacking several important elements in our program for ecological balance and conservation
of our environment.

The first of these is the *will* to do something about it.
Former Secretary of Health, Education and Welfare John W.
Gardner recently wrote: "We know our lakes are dying, our
rivers growing filthier daily, our atmosphere increasingly
polluted. We are aware of racial tensions that could tear the
nation apart. . . . But we are seized by a kind of paralysis
of the will. It is like a walking nightmare."

At the recent White House Conference on Hunger, Senator
Walter F. Mondale of Minnesota made an angry speech in
which he said the following regarding hunger in America—
which applies equally to environmental problems: "The problem is not that we lack facts . . . the problem is that we lack
the will to eliminate it. . . . The job requires unrelenting
public pressure."

The second thing we lack is the *recognition* that our problems at home are becoming far more serious than any threat
from abroad. In the report of Milton Eisenhower's Commission on Violence, the authors warned us that "the greatness
and durability of most civilizations have been finally determined by how they have responded to the challenges from

within." "We believe," said the Eisenhower group, "that we can and should make a major decision now to reassess our national priorities by placing these objectives in the first rank of the nation's goals."

This is the challenge that Tu Be-Shevat presents us with for the 1970s. One of our most important tasks as human beings today will have to be to help get man off the list of endangered species as quickly as possible—or else we may all be buried, like the ancient civilization of the Indus River Valley, in the mud of our own complacency. May we be worthy of this important task. Amen.

4
Power Corrupts, Poetry Cleanses

"One small step for man, one giant leap for mankind."
"The Eagle has landed."
"Tranquility Base."

THESE ARE PHRASES WHICH WERE ALMOST MEANINGLESS combinations of words with no particular relevance to things real just sixty days ago. Yet now, they immediately conjure up a dramatic image. When we hear these words we immediately think in our mind's eye of that Sunday evening on July 20, sitting before our TV screens watching man for the first time in history set his foot down on a body in space other than earth. Our lives, our communities, our nation and our world will forever after be different because of this gigantic leap into space by three men representing all humanity.

What meaning is there in this event for the religionist? What lessons are there wrapped up in this voyage of man bursting out of his atmosphere, "stepping out of the womb of nature," as Jacques Lipchitz put it, and exploring new

Preached Rosh Hashana, 5730 (1969); published in *Best Jewish Sermons of 5729-5730*.

worlds? What relevant message is there which can make of this technological achievement one which enhances and illuminates our spiritual lives as we gather to greet a New Year, and take stock of our lives and our world on this festival of the birthday of the world and of the creation of man?

There are three major themes woven into the tapestry of our Holy Day liturgy, each of which brings home an important lesson about life. I think that we can apply these themes to the astronauts' flight to the moon and show how our tradition will help us live better and more beautiful lives during the lunar age.

These three themes are found in the Musaf service that follows the reading of the Torah, and they are the three most important ideas that distinguish the Rosh Hashana and Yom Kippur prayers. This morning I shall deal with the first of these, which is called "Malchuyot," or God's Kingship. We reaffirm our deep faith during these ten Days of Awe that we have but one King in the Universe, the King of Kings, the Holy One Blessed be He, Ruler and Sovereign of all creatures. In the Musaf Amidah we say,

> Our God and God of our fathers,
> Establish Your glorious rule over all the world,
> Establish Your glorious majesty over all the earth,
> Let all who inhabit the world behold the grandeur
>   of Your might,
> Let every creature declare the God of Israel King,
> And His dominion extends over all creation.

The ancient rabbis who created this inspired service held this idea to be supreme in the outlook of a religious human being. In the days when the image of the king conjured up the power of life and death, the ability to bring prosperity or tax groups into poverty, to rule benevolently and kindly with human rights, or wield the harsh whip of repression upon the backs of the populace, the image of the king was that power which made life happy or unbearable, which granted freedom or committed men into chains.

They knew that even though the king of Babylonia, or Persia, or Greece, or Rome had temporal control over their lives, it was the true Sovereign of the Universe, the King of all the other kings, who alone held rule over the minds and hearts and spirits of man. His Law and His Rule were ultimately sovereign above the petty whims and ephemeral commands of mortal rulers. For such a religiously committed human being, there could only be one loyalty—one allegiance to a Ruler in Heaven who controlled the destiny of all nations and all peoples. The highest tribute always had to be paid to God and His law.

This exalted ideal still holds significance for men who send their emissaries into space and walking on distant frontiers. *We still need—and need desperately—to know that man, despite all of his brilliant achievements—is still* MAN. We still must beware of the biblical warning not to forget our Creator and, in the pride of our great accomplishments, declare: "My strength and the might of my hand hath gotten me this wealth and this power. But thou shalt remember the Lord thy God, for it is He that giveth thee strength to get power." (Deut. 8:17)

We still need to beware of the dangers of inflation—not inflation of the dollar, but inflation of the human spirit in saying, "*I* am King," "*I* rule the earth and the heavens, the moon and the stars," "*My* rocket ships and my knowledge of space technology make me sovereign over all living creatures." This is a danger that is present today in proportions far greater than it could have been when Greece and Rome held sway over the world, and when the simple rabbis of Palestine set down the prayers that you and I recite on this sacred holiday. It is the danger that *human pride* will bring in its wake a neglect and even a rejection of the values which religions have attempted to teach man for millennia.

If we try to translate into modern language the thoughts of our ancestors when they said that God is Melech, God is King and Sovereign of all existence, we are saying that there is a ruling spirit in this universe that brings orderliness, that brings harmony and unity, that infuses life with significance, that breathes into the spirit of man his awareness of himself, his innate ability to think, and create, and achieve the seemingly unachievable. That is what it means in the twentieth century to declare that God is King. It means to acknowledge that a Spirit greater than ourselves gives moral purpose and direction to the deepest strivings of mortal creatures. It means that life is sacred, that man is a partner of God in creation, that the mind of man is given him for good and not for evil. These are the things that this ancient idea should convey to us who are of scientific bent when we picture God in the *metaphor of royalty* which comes to us from a society long gone and an age long dead.

Ever since the Soviets launched their Sputnik over a decade ago, American educators and national leaders have been in a race to show that the United States has greater scientific technological and military capabilities than any other power in the world. We have emphasized the pursuit of science in our school curricula to the detriment of the humanities. We have made of science an all-consuming god while relegating more spiritual pursuits to a lower rung on the ladder of national priorities.

Parents have emphasized a sound scientific education for their children while glossing over the importance of literature, art, music, religious studies, and the humanities. While the god of science and technology has reigned supreme, we have forgotten about that aspect of man which is what makes him really human: the cultivation of his ethical and moral values, the refinement of his conscience, the maturation of his emotions, the education of his heart as well as his mind.

A modern rabbi has recently written: "We seem to know so much and to understand so little. We know how to go to the moon and to the planets, but we don't really know where we are going. We know how to transplant a heart, but we don't know how to transform it. The deafening noise about us has silenced 'the still small voice' within, but this silence has brought an emptiness within, which has made life dark. It is at this point of darkness that the . . . prayers of [Rosh Hashana] assume great relevance."

The late Harvard psychologist, Gordon Allport, wrote in his book *The Individual and His Religion*, "A man's religion is the audacious bid he makes to bind himself to creation and to the creator. It is his ultimate attempt to enlarge and to contemplate his own personality by finding the supreme context in which he rightly belongs."

It seems as though the context of American life for the past decade has been the search for more and more power, more and more affluence, more and more luxuries, more and more destructive weapons, and less and less perfection of man's spirit, less and less reading of worthwhile books, less and less religious education, less and less prayer and less and less concern for our fellow man.

When Neil Armstrong stepped on the moon, the philosopher and novelist Arthur Koestler was asked his opinion of this great achievement. He replied as follows: "Coincident with cosmic euphoria, the world is in the grip of cosmic anxiety. Both derive from the same source: the awareness of unprecedented power operating in an unprecedented spiritual vacuum."

Now that we have achieved unprecedented power and glory by landing our astronauts on the surface of the moon, we have to begin pushing back the frontier of this unprecedented spiritual vacuum that Koestler is talking about, or else *all our science and technology will have been for naught, and will one day destroy us all.*

We cannot put our faith and trust in computers and expect to bind ourselves to creation and to the creator, as Allport suggested is the function of religion. We cannot find the supreme context in which we rightly belong by putting our faith in cybernetics.

The authors of the Psalms knew long ago that no one can ever really hide his true motivations and his selfish greed for more and more power from God the King: "Where shall I go from Thy spirit?" says Psalm 139. "Or where shall I flee from Thy presence? If I ascend to heaven, *thou art there.* If I make my bed at the bottom of the sea, *thou art there!*"

The prophet Obadiah reminds us of our need to remain humble even in the face of the greatest success: "Though thou makest thy nest as high as the eagle, and though thou set it among the stars, I will bring thee down from there."

In the biblical story of man's attempt at traveling into the heavens, the epic of the Tower of Babel, the builders say to one another, "Come, let us build a tower whose top reaches to heaven, and let us make a name for ourselves." The rabbis of the Talmud add the end of the sentence: "We will then set up an idol on the top of the tower, and in its hand we will place a sword, and we will make war against God—and all that He stands for." (Gen. R. 38:6, Sanhedrin 109A.)

The superpowers in the 1960s have been warring against the things that God stands for. By stockpiling more and more nuclear bombs and building better and faster bombers and missiles, they are warring against the very purpose of God's creation.

For the past two years the latest fad in scientific realms has been experimentation in heart transplants. Soon almost every vital organ of the body will be able to be replaced or transplanted. Norman Cousins wrote recently about a transplant operation that is far simpler and *more* life-giving than those performed in Capetown and Houston. In fact, you and I can be the surgeons in this transplant.

In his words:

> Phenomenal though these [medical] advances may be, they still fall short of an already existing non-medical technique for increasing longevity. A simple system now makes possible an incredible enlargement of human life. This system goes by the name of a book. Through it, one can live hundreds of lifetimes in one. What is more, he may enjoy fabulous options. He can live in any age of his choosing. He can take possession of any experience. He can live inside the mind of any man who has recorded an interesting thought, any man who has opened up new sluices of knowledge, any man who has engaged in depths of feeling or awareness beyond the scope of most mortals. This is what good books are all about. (*Saturday Review*, July 5, 1969.)

Some people in this world, and I among them, are of the opinion that it may be *more* important to discover the techniques for transplanting the feelings of one human heart to that of another, than the actual heart itself. Having learned how to transplant a live human heart from one person to another, we now have to learn how to transplant the love and compassion that glows in one heart to grow and take nourishment in another heart. We now have to develop better techniques and procedures for transplanting the sensitivity of one person's conscience into that of another.

It seems as though in our country dramatic areas of discovery in space technology, medical science, and military proficiency are outshadowing and dwarfing the important areas of character development, personal intellectual and spiritual growth, and humanization of mankind.

A story is told of a Greek painter who had created what he thought to be his masterpiece, a representation of a farmer holding a cluster of grapes. To test the genuineness of his conception, he carried the painting into a vineyard and set it up among the shrubbery. The artist and some friends hid themselves to watch. Soon they beheld that the birds flocked to the painting and began to peck at the painted grapes. His friends applauded when they saw that even the birds were deceived. The artist, however, took the painting and angrily slashed the canvas to shreds. When his friends questioned his wild behavior, he said, 'If the painting were really lifelike, the birds would not have pecked at the grapes, because they would have been afraid of the farmer. The grapes are perfect, but the man is a failure.' All the things around us today are well designed, but man is a failure. (Saul Teplitz, *Life Is for Living*.)

I would like to contrast for you statements by two young people in our country named Brian. Nine-year-old Brian Lang's eloquent poem about the spiritual nature of life was quoted in *The New York Times* on September 4, 1969:[1]

Ideas are a piece of clay that
Keeps developing bigger and bigger
Until it finally shapes itself into a sculpture
Which is one specific idea.
Life is an idea—an idea never to forget—
It keeps developing forever.

Unfortunately, by the time little Brian graduates college, he will probably be expressing something more like what

1. Copyright © 1969 by The New York Times Company. Reprinted by permission.

another Brian wrote—Brian McGuire, who graduated first in his class at Berkeley in 1968. The words of this young man are an example of the kind of dehumanization taking place in our universities that is the cause of so much of the unrest on the campuses throughout the United States. Just after his graduation, Mr. McGuire wrote: "My four years of university education, instead of helping me to become a man, have nearly turned me into an unfeeling, unthinking zombie, totally removed from the world outside my own specialized field. . . . I was letting the system dominate me and demolish me as an individual."

One of the sad lessons we are learning from our Vietnam debacle is that our nation will have more influence in the international arena by the power of our moral example rather than by the power of our arms (Cf. Arthur Schlesinger, *Crisis of Confidence*, p. 191). De Gaulle learned this years ago. He told President Kennedy in 1961 that the French could only exert influence in Southeast Asia *after* they had withdrawn their military presence. We too will have to learn this lesson. In doing so we must disabuse ourselves of the notion that American power and American might and American wealth can be the messiah and savior of the entire world, and solve all problems through more power, more might, and more money.

John F. Kennedy came to understand well the dangers of overestimating the importance of military might and space technology and other manifestations of the electronic age. He once said:

> When power leads man toward arrogance, poetry reminds him of his limitations. When power narrows the area of man's concern, poetry reminds him of the richness and diversity of existence. When power corrupts, poetry cleanses. . . . The men who create power make an indispensable contribution to the nation's greatness, but the men who question power make a contribution just as indispensable . . . for they determine whether we use power or power uses us.

In closing I would like to leave you with the words of another statesman who also had a great insight that came to him from witnessing the spectacular space achievements of our age: "We have learned to fly through the air like birds," he said. "We can swim under the sea like fish. What we have to learn now is how to walk on earth like men."

5

Sweeping Down the Walls of Oppression

YESTERDAY MORNING WE SPOKE OF THE FIRST ASPECT OF GOD which characterizes the Musaf Amidah of the Rosh Hashana service, namely, the Malchuyot—that God is King. We explained how in modern terms this means allotting a significant portion of our concern, our time, and our effort in the godly, or spiritual pursuits of life and being aware of the dangers inherent in a powerful, computerized, affluent society where pride in technology—characterized by the recent moon walk—leads man to dethrone God and neglect his own necessary spiritual development.

The second, and equally important section of the High Holy Day liturgy is known as Zichronot—the remembrance prayers. As in the Malchuyot, ten biblical verses are quoted to emphasize and illustrate the aspect of God's nature which show him this time as a remembering God. He remembers His covenant with Israel at Mt. Sinai, he remembers all our

Preached on the second morning of Rosh Hashana, September, 1969 (5730).

50

deeds and actions, even those we mortals tend to overlook, and he registers these into the book of eternal remembrance.
In this section of the prayers we say:

> Thou rememberest the deeds of all the inhabitants of the world, and Thou art mindful of Thy creatures from the beginning of time. All secrets, all hidden things, have always been known unto Thee. With Thee there is no forgetfulness, there is no concealment from Thine eyes. Thou rememberest each deed, and no creature is hidden from Thee. All things lie exposed before Thee, O Lord our God. . . .

In this brief but important passage lies a message to America that she ignores only at her own deepest peril. While the first sin we have committed in connection with the moon shot was being inflated with our own power and achievement, on this second morning of Rosh Hashana we must consider the sin of forgetting and ignoring the major problems of society today while achieving that power.

We may forget, but God remembers. There is no forgetting before His throne of glory. There is no concealment from His eyes.

While staring up at the moon, we may have forgotten the starving children in Appalachia, but God remembers!

While watching our spacemen orbit the planet and sail through the heavens, we may have suppressed our memories of the hunger in Biafra, but no creature is hidden from Him.

While pouring our money into blasting man out of this planet to the other side of the moon, we have desperately neglected the needs of the man on the other side of the street and on the other side of town. But there is no concealment before the throne of God's honor!

This is what our ancestors meant when they included this second section in the Musaf Amidah. They wanted to let posterity know that in this small world we inhabit, this global village of ours, we cannot pretend to close our eyes to human misery, even as we enjoy all the benefits that modernity can bring us.

When we recite the Zichronot service this morning, we

should awaken ourselves to the realization that built into the world is a moral law that does not permit the overlooking of festering sores like hunger, poverty, crime and disease. These come back to haunt us at every turn if we try to direct our consciousness to more dramatic and more spectacular goals such as landing a man on the moon.

When the rabbis said that God remembers, we in the twentieth century may interpret that to mean, in our own terms, that our real responsibilities as members of society will confront us in one way or another, even if we try to sweep them under the rug. This spirit of divine remembering may take the guise of the pangs of our own conscience; it may take the form of the vociferous protests of the oppressed classes in society; or it may take the form of the decay of our community that comes from forgetting and neglecting and from apathy.

Our nation spent twenty-four billion dollars on a program to send a man to the moon. That same amount of money could have fed, housed, and educated every poor American for the rest of their lives. It has been calculated that the cumulative cost of the trip to the moon was ten million dollars per minute. At this rate, about ten minutes of moon travel time would have solved the problem of hunger in Biafra for an entire year!

A visitor in Biafra (Norman Cousins, *Saturday Review,* August 2, 1969, p. 16) this past July, while the moon shot was in course, tells of a visit to a refugee camp, and of a discussion with a hungry old man who asked, "Is it true, that Americans will soon be walking on the moon?" Yes, was the answer. "Tell me," he continued, "will they also be able to send us some food? For more than a month there has been no food. Can you explain why they have stopped flying in the food?"

The visitor had no answer. There is no answer. The truth is that we have forgotten that old man in Biafra, even as we have forgotten the Indians in their American reservations, the grape pickers in California, the slum dwellers on Chicago's West Side, in Boston's Roxbury District, in North Philadelphia, and in every large city across our nation.

According to United Nations figures more than half the

people alive today are malnourished and therefore vulnerable to disease. Death from starvation comes to three million people every year.

While we were busy remembering the moon flight, the Secretary General of the UN had his memory set elsewhere. He made a special report, which was forgotten before it was even issued: "I continue to be struck," wrote U Thant, "by the magnitude of the stake and the relatively limited sacrifice, in financial terms, which would be needed to improve the life of the developing countries; only a slight reduction in expenditures on armaments would suffice to make available the external resources required for solving at least some of the gravest economic and social problems of today's world."

Arthur Schlesinger has written recently that American politicians remember only those in America who are their constituents and who have the power of the vote. But there must be someone to remember those without voting power! There must be some group, or some institution, or even some individual who will remember even when it is not profitable to remember. Someone, somewhere, must remember the untouchables of American society—the black Americans, the Mexican Americans, the Puerto Ricans, the migrant laborers in the Mississippi Delta, the poor whites in the poverty pockets.

Here is the role of the Jew who reads and takes seriously the words of this day's prayers. Ultimately these people will be remembered because God does not forget anyone or any deed. There is no concealment before the throne of His honor. There is no creature, no matter how poor, how hungry, and how lowly in caste, who is forgotten by Him. We as God's partners in building the better world must share in this enterprise. There is no more important function for religious groups and religious people in today's world. If we fail in caring for those who have no one else to care for them, then all our moon shots, and all our technology, and all our scientific advancements are for nought! They will only proceed to destroy us all from off the face of the earth, because we have no compassion, we have no heart, we have no remembrance for our brothers.

There was one politician who wished to draw these excluded groups into our national life, but he became the victim of the violence in society he tried to wipe out in caring for the disenfranchised elements in our country. Robert Kennedy has been described by a modern historian as follows: "When [he] went into Harlem or Watts, when he visited a share-cropper's cabin or an Indian reservation, these were *his* children with bloated bellies, *his* parents wasting away in dreary old age, *his* miserable hovel, *his* wretched scraps for dinner. He saw it all, with personal intensity, from the inside; he was part of it. It was because those he came among felt this that they gave him so unreservedly their confidence and their love." (Schlesinger, *Crisis of Confidence*, pp. 283–84.)

One of Senator Robert Kennedy's predecessors, an ancient lawmaker in Athens named Solon, was once asked: "How can we have justice in Athens?" He answered: "Justice can be had in Athens whenever those who have not suffered injustice are as outraged as those who have."

Is there any scientist living today who would dare declare that we haven't the capability to eliminate hunger and poverty and disease at least in our own country? Is it because we don't know how to do it, or is it because of our mixed-up priorities, our moral weakness, that forces us to forget, instead of remembering the dregs of our society whom only God remembers?

Is it possible to say that we don't have the money or the know-how in a society that spends one hundred billion dollars a year, and with technology that can calibrate to the thousandth of an inch the cutting edge of a mechanical tool, and can send men in rocket ships to set foot on the moon?

The Reverend Jesse Jackson, associate of the late Martin Luther King, wrote recently: "How can this nation swell and stagger with technological pride when it has a spiritual will so crippled, when it is so weak, so wicked, so blinded and misdirected in its priorities? While we can send men to the moon or deadly missiles to Moscow, we can't get food-stuffs across town to starving folks in the teeming ghettos."

The Commissioner of Education of the State of Massachusetts recently described an experience he had in visiting an underprivileged ghetto somewhere near Boston. "I found two young blacks," he wrote, "with I.Q.'s somewhere in the stratosphere beyond our measuring point, who had been locked out of school for four long years. While we go on searching for a cure for cancer and to find a mechanical heart, these black youngsters had not even been given Salk vaccine." (*The Jewish Advocate,* August 7, 1969.)

These two black youngsters represent millions more of white and black children and adults who have been locked out of society by the repression of our collective memory.

Today we are suffering from the most severe racial crisis in our recent history. We owe it to the accumulated injustice and neglect, the forgetting, if you will, of the majority of Americans of their duties and responsibilities. We are paying for this forgetfulness in the rise of black demagogues and extremists who threaten to burn our cities and destroy our society; who demand huge reparations for the forgetting of our churches and synagogues and who will haunt us in one way or another until every injustice is erased from America.

There is a corollary to the prayer that tells us that God remembers. It is that He brings judgment upon all His creatures for the things we forgot even as He remembers. As we watch our cities explode in violence and crime and disease, as we witness our atmosphere become polluted and our air unbreathable, as we see our water and natural resources wasted and contaminated, we are seeing the visitations of judgment upon our forgetfulness. We cannot live in a technological, computerized, industrial society and only sit back and wallow in the ease and comfort these advances bring us. We cannot rest easy in our living rooms and watch the great achievements of our scientists and forget about the smoldering cauldron of discontent and injustice and deterioration in our own back yards.

You have probably heard the story of Dr. Russell Conwell, founder of Temple University, and his famous lecture entitled "Acres of Diamonds." Conwell traveled throughout America telling about an old man who owned a large farm and was quite happy until a friend told him about the high value of diamonds. The old man's lust for wealth was

aroused; he sold his farm and went to discover a diamond
mine. After many discouragements he threw himself into
the sea and drowned.

The man who bought the farm from the old man one day
saw a flash of light and discovered the world's richest diamond mine—the Golconda—on his new farm. The largest
diamonds on earth originate from that mine. It is important
to seek out the rich new knowledge of the other planets, but
let us not neglect the diamonds we have right here on this
planet, in our own back yard, so to speak.

We spend billions of our national dollars on trying to find
out if life exists on other planets, when the real question
is whether we can assure the future of human life right here
on this planet. Our arms race escalates, our funds are spent
on bombs and missiles when they should be spent on domestic
crises. Our Senate recently committed itself to an expendi-
ture of eight hundred million dollars on an ABM system
that many feel will be useless anyway, only for the remote
possibility of defending ourselves in case of an all-out nuclear attack on the United States. And while we spend these
dollars on nuclear weapons, we must live not with the possibility of attack, but the certainty of attack on our national
life by the poverty and hunger that will consume our society
just as surely as a foreign attack.

The New York Times had this to say in a recent editorial:

. . . this new knowledge forces man back again to contemplation
of his own planet where innumerable life forms have carved out
ecological niches for themselves under the most varied possible
conditions in the sea, on the land and in the air. Why is this
third planet of a minor sun so rich a garden of life and why are
its nearest heavenly neighbors such seemingly arid deserts?
And when men ask that question in humility, they must realize
more than ever their obligation to treasure and to keep alive
this healthy garden of life. More than ever before, it now must
be understood by all how criminal a misstep it would be to turn
this earth into another space desert, one made lifeless by nuclear explosions and their radioactivity or by the murderous
poisons with which an over-affluent civilization is fouling its
lonely nest in the neighborhood of the star.

It was only this past month revealed that a military officer in California assigned three mentally unbalanced soldiers to guard a nuclear arms depot overnight. This only emphasizes the great area of risk that a minor slip-up by some official in the lower echelons of bureaucracy can touch off a holocaust that would bring to an end civilized life on this planet where life seems to be so unique in our universe.

Rosh Hashana comes, then, to help us remember our true and full responsibilities, even as God is He who never forgets, and before Whom nothing can ever be concealed.

Each of us has an important role to play in pushing back the forces of destruction of our society, our nation, our community, our own family, and bringing a happier, healthier, freer atmosphere in which all peoples and all nations can live. And we must never underestimate the importance of the role of each individual in this continual battle of remembering.

I close with an eloquent and moving plea of Robert F. Kennedy, warning us against the danger of a sense of futility in facing our problems:

> We must dispense with the belief [wrote Kennedy] that there is nothing one man or one woman can do against the enormous array of the world's ills—against the misery and ignorance, injustice and violence. . . . Few will have the greatness to bend history itself, but each of us can work to change a small portion of events, and in the total of all those acts will be written the history of this generation. . . . Each time a man stands up for an ideal, or acts to improve the lot of others, or strikes out against injustice, he sends forth a ripple of hope, and crossing each other from a million different centers of energy and daring those ripples build a current that can sweep down the mightiest wall of oppression.

6

Bitter Herbs or LSD?

THERE IS A STRIKING LEGEND IN THE MIDRASH THAT TELLS of an experience Moses had at age three, while still a babe in the palace of Pharaoh. Pharaoh was having dinner with his queen, his daughter, and several others. Pharaoh's daughter had baby Moses on her lap. Moses reached for the crown on the king's head and placed it on his own. The princes who were sitting there were horrified. The pagan prophet Balaam, who was also sitting at the king's table, told the king that the child was a Hebrew, and that he wanted to make sport of the king. Balaam suggested that Pharaoh call in his wise men and decide whether to slay the Hebrew infant.

Among the wise man was the angel Gabriel, disguised. Gabriel suggested that there be placed before the child an onyx stone and a coal of fire. If he stretches out his hand and grasps the stone, then it will be known that the child took the crown with wisdom, intentionally—with malice aforethought, and he should be put to death. If, however, he stretches out his hand and takes the coal of fire, then it will

Delivered Pesach morning, March 30, 1972.

be known that he did it unconsciously, and that he should live.

The king liked the idea, and when they placed the stone and the coal before the child, Moses was about to take the onyx stone when the angel Gabrial guided his hand away from it and placed it upon the live coal, burning the child's hand. Moses then lifted up the coal and touched it to his mouth, and burned part of his lips and part of his tongue. For the rest of his life, Moses became slow of speech and of a slow tongue.[1]

This legend came to mind as I contemplated the theme of this sermon: "Bitter herbs or LSD?" The choice between eating bitter herbs and participating in the way of life of which Passover is a foremost symbol, and the drug culture, is a choice not dissimilar to the choice Moses had to make. On the one hand, the glitter, the appeal, the excitement of a precious stone can be very tempting. It could have produced instantaneous wealth and riches and luxury. But only for a short time. For soon after, there would have been death. The parallel is obvious.

An article in our local paper just the other day told the story of the beautiful seventeen-year-old girl, Eileen Sullivan, who had finished high school with top grades, had a wonderful future before her, until she came into the drug scene. Last December she began to keep a diary. In it she wrote: "Drugs are hell. I hate drugs. They all put drugs before health, food and money. It's a terrible way to die. It's not the dying that worries me, it's before—when I can't get the money to buy drugs. What worries me are the wrinkles on my face and the infection in my veins. I'm very sad when I think what I have done with my life. I feel like dying. I've had all the good things. I marred all the chances and betrayed all the trust. Why did I ever start? Drugs are evil. They cause mental illness, aging skin, baldness and rotting teeth. I can no longer behave naturally."

On February 17, 1971, at 10 P.M., she left a party where she had been dropping acid and taking barbiturates, walked to the top of a multistory car park, and plunged thirty feet to her death on the concrete.

[1] Louis Ginzberg, *Legends of the Bible*, pp. 293–94.

Here we have one example, which could be multiplied in the thousands, of one who chose the onyx stone instead of the hot coals, the bitter herbs. And as surely as Pharaoh's servants would have put the Hebrew baby to death, so did choosing the glitter of fast, easy excitement bring death to a young and beautiful girl just beginning to drink from the cup of life.

What would have been her other choice? To risk being socially ostracized, to resist peer-group pressure, to deny oneself instant gratification and immediate pleasure, for the sake of a long, slow, hard path of achieving meaning and pleasure through traditionally established methods. To take the hard way, the *bitter* way, the slow way, but one which ultimately yields more permanent and happy results. The burning of Moses' hand and tongue were experiences that helped make him the seasoned leader he was to become. The rough experiences of watching his kinsmen in bitter slavery helped to shape for him a character that was sensitive, experienced, and mature; one that didn't look for any easy outs in life.

As we eat the bitter herbs, last night and again tonight, we feel the pain, the agony, the suffering of those in the world who have not achieved total freedom. As we identify with them in our eating of the bitter herbs, we help ourselves to see life for what it really is. In the words of Montaigne, "Virtue will have naught to do with ease. It seeks a rough and thorny path." Any conception of life that portrays living with only ease, pleasure, and excitement is a weak-kneed retreat from reality. Any conception of life that fails to take into account the bitterness that is experienced by all of us at some time or another is merely a storybook conception and one that can lead only to frustration, cynicism, and demoralization.

I think that describing the option of drugs or no drugs as the choice between LSD and bitter herbs is an apt one, for the symbol of bitter herbs carries many layers of significance within it. I have already described to you one of them. That life is bitter, difficult, and filled with suffering and with problems—especially on the teenage and college-age level. To jump into a quick escape by dropping acid or shooting heroin is a naïve and harmful way to experience the world.

But bitter herbs also symbolize something else. They symbolize identification with the downtrodden, the poor, the enslaved, the oppressed, the hungry, the needy. The overwhelming evidence indicates that those who need drugs are those who have no meaningful alternatives to a happy and exciting life. This thought was expressed by a non-Jew, Tom Zompanis, a ten-year veteran of heroin use and now a staff member of Gaudenzia House, a drug rehabilitation center in Philadelphia, where the seventy residents, mostly non-Jews, celebrated Passover together: "I'm not Jewish, but last year, when we had Passover, I learned a lot . . . I just can't imagine a good religious family that conducts a seder the way it should be done, having their children get caught up in drugs."[2]

The bitter herb, then, symbolizes a tradition of sympathy with the enslaved; it represents an ancient and rich cultural and religious heritage of ritual, pageantry, song, prayer, custom and ceremony, ideals and values. We must create these counterweights of attractive alternatives, to help provide other choices, in order to avoid the glitter and drama of the fast, easy way of private thrill through drugs.

A pamphlet published by the B'nai B'rith Youth Organization not long ago is called "Drugs Are Not the Problem." In it the author explains his point as follows: "We really don't think that the use of drugs in itself is the real problem. We're more concerned about what are the hangups, what are the problems that cause teenagers to experiment with drugs as a way of solving some of the problems or hangups. . . ." Drug abuse is, for each individual, a specific personal response to today's rapidly changing cultural and social climate. The drug problem, it advises, cannot be solved "as long as we focus primarily on drug abuse itself rather than on the whole syndrome of social and psychological problems that besets our own and so many other teenagers today. Parents need to know their youngsters even more than they

[2] B. Robert Anderson, "Drugs and Jewish Youth," *Hadassah Magazine*, March, 1972.

need to know the symptoms of drug abuse." Along with the anti-drug campaign that must be waged, it is even more important to greatly increase involvement of youth in vital programs for social betterment that is the long-term basis for a "counter-fad." Anti-poverty drives, the struggle for racial justice—and especially the new campaign for a cleaner environment, are regarded as promising alternatives to teenage drug-oriented culture.[3]

Young people today are going through an identity crisis. They are asking themselves, "Who am I?" and "What am I?" and "What is my life all about?" Implied in these questions are others, such as "What must I live up to? What are my obligations? To what must I commit myself?"[4] This is where Jewish teaching and Jewish observance comes in. When I say that the alternative to drug culture is bitter herbs, I don't mean literally and solely the *maror* on our seder table. I mean all the rituals of the seder, all the values of our Jewish festivals, all the ideals in our cultural heritage, and all the traditions of our 4,000-year-old ethical civilization. In the last analysis, this is the best answer to the drug scene, for it provides a preventive measure, a strength of purpose and meaning in one's life, without which one becomes susceptible to the lures and enticements of drugs.

Every human being searches in some way for his own identity and for some meaning and purpose in his life. Each of us tries to establish some aims, some goals, some understanding of our relationship with our neighbors, and our relationship to life's larger purposes. Whenever a person fails to achieve a conception of the universe that gives dignity and purpose and sense to his own existence, he exhibits what Paul Tillich has described as "the anxiety of meaninglessness," the "anxiety about the loss of an ultimate concern, of a meaning which gives meanings to all meanings."[5]

Let me quote to you some statements by young people who became addicts: A seventeen-year-old addict from a Wash-

[3] "Drugs Are Not the Problem," BBYO, August, 1969, by Seymour S. Cohen.
[4] John W. Gardner, *Self-Renewal*, New York: Harper, 1963, p. 103.
[5] Paul Tillich, *The Courage to Be*, p. 47.

ington, D.C. suburb, says: "I just wasn't doing anything. Life was kind of meaningless, aimless, every day was just there. I wasn't actively involved in anything, and I wasn't really enjoying anything. The way I see it, the people who are into drugs, nothing holds their interest and there's no real meaning for them, so this is what they go to."

This is the opposite of the kind of person described by the late pioneering psychologist Abraham Maslow of Brandeis University, who described the type of individual who, in my opinion, would be least likely to enter the drug scene. He calls such people "self-actualizing people." "Self-actualizing people are . . . involved in a cause outside their own skin. . . . They are devoted, working at something which is very precious to them—some calling or vocation in the old, priestly sense . . . which they love, so that the work-joy dichotomy in them disappears. . . . All, in one way or another, devote their lives to the search for what I have called the 'being values,' the ultimate values which . . . cannot be reduced to anything more ultimate . . . including the truth and beauty and goodness of the ancients."[6]

According to Maslow, most youth are searching for so-called "peak experiences." Drugs offer this through their ability to grant instant transcendence. One high school girl compared her experience of marijuana with a sensitivity group: "Sensitivity is not only as good as marijuana because you can experience fulfillment of emotions, but it is far better. It is not against the law and it has a more lasting effect . . . when it is over and you 'come down' from your sensitivity experience, you have the feeling with you for a long time, whereas with marijuana, when you 'come down' it is depressing."[7] If we substitute the word "Judaism" for "sensitivity group" in the above quotation, we have in one sentence the message of this sermon. "Judaism is not only as good as marijuana because you can experience fulfillment of emotions, but it is far better. It is not against the law and it has

[6] Quoted in Howard J. Clinebell, Jr., *The People Dynamic:* Changing Self and Society Through Growth Groups, New York: Harper & Row, 1972, p. 87.
[7] *Ibid.*, p. 88.

a more lasting effect . . . when it is over and you 'come down' from your Judaism experience, you have the feeling with you for a long time, whereas with marijuana, when you 'come down' it is depressing."

In today's world, of course, there are no guarantees in the fight against drug abuse. But we can be sure that those who held a meaningful Passover seder in their households, a seder that stressed close family ties, the warmth and beauty of tradition, the meaningfulness of faith, the values of empathizing with the oppressed, the recognition that life is often bitter and arduous, and the respect for the past as well as a commitment to the present and the future, such a family will have a far better chance of raising into adulthood young people who find inner strength and purpose and will be able to resist the enticing world of drug culture. Such a family will be well on the road towards the kind of life that Judaism requires of all of us.

7

Commandments for Our Day

SHAVOUT IS THE FESTIVAL OF THE TORAH, AND THOSE WHO are confirmed this morning are reconfirming their acceptance of the Torah as their heritage, their way of life. They are now free to be Jews, and free from the fads of immorality and aimlessness and lawlessness that pervade our modern world.

Part of that great Book which our people received at Sinai includes the Ten Commandments, which we read this morning in the Torah. These ten admonitions about personal conduct have become the bedrock of human existence in Western society for over two millennia. They still have great significance for our day, because we cannot really say that we observe and fulfill them perfectly. We really don't keep the Sabbath the way we should, nor worship God, nor honor our parents, nor avoid coveting, nor keep many other Commandments as well.

But for our day we must add to the ancient list given to Moses. Those Ten Commandments and the many others given

Delivered Shavuot morning, May 30, 1971; published in *Best Jewish Sermons, 5731–5732.*

in the Torah were sufficient for an ancient, agrarian people not yet settled in its own homeland.

I would add three commandments which I would like our young people to take away with them for the 1970s, as they confirm their faith and commitment to their people, and their tradition.

The first Commandment grows from the fact that our people has faced the threat of physical extinction in this century. One out of every three Jews in the world was put to death by a madman and a mad society just a generation ago. Subsequent to that horrible tragedy, that unspeakable Holocaust, the Arab peoples have attempted to finish Hitler's work in three wars which again threatened the lives of the remnants of European Jewry. Today, the Soviets are conspiring to destroy another three million of our people by wiping out any trace of Jewish identity from their communal living patterns. Other threats of assimilation and anti-Semitism face us around the world. All of these factors, all of this death, destruction, assimilation, and intermarriage, have joined together to create a new post-biblical commandment for world Jewry: THOU SHALT SURVIVE!!![1]

Thou shalt remain a Jew!! Thou shalt not grant Hitler a posthumous victory and let others complete his work for him.

This means doing whatever we can to assure the continuation of the Jewish people in the world. We know from sad experience over the past thirty years that our survival depends upon our own resources, our own efforts, and our own will to achieve the impossible.

Of course this includes giving to UJA, and helping to bring to the world's attention the spiritual genocide taking place in the U.S.S.R. That goes without saying. But it means more than that. It means remaining a Jew, even when being a Jew causes problems and sacrifices. It remains giving up some other benefits and pleasures in order to remain a part of the Jewish community. It means following the advice of the ancient sage Hillel, *Al tifrosh min ha-tzibbur,* do not separate yourself from the community. It means refraining from intermarriage, for every intermarriage is another nail in the

[1] I am grateful to Rabbi Eugene Borowitz for this thought.

coffin of Israel. It means living as a Jew, behaving as a Jew, thinking as a Jew, and helping to keep the faith and traditions of our people, the cement which has always unified and preserved us.

A young student at Brandeis University was quoted recently in *The New York Times,* Apr. 25, 1971, and I think he reflects the thinking of many young intellectuals in the Jewish academic community today. "Now we young Jews will look only to ourselves and to our own people. I, myself, am beyond the call of any American radical movement. In the final analysis, our destiny is simply that of Israel and of the Jewish people."

Yes, thou shalt survive!

The second commandment I would suggest for American Jewry, and for our confirmands this morning, grows out of our minority status in America, and elsewhere in the Diaspora. There was a time when some of our parents and grandparents tried to hide their Jewishness for various reasons, or change their names, or in some other way conceal their Jewish origins.

Back in the 1940s when being a Jew was in some people's minds more of a liability than an asset, one proud young Jew named Harry Golden would make a habit of beginning any of his public statements with the phrase, "As a Jew, my opinion on this subject is the following." People were amazed that anyone would openly declare that his Jewishness dictated his views, and that he felt his background to be an asset rather than a liability.

We still suffer from that kind of self-hating psychology of Uncle Tom Jews who fill our Jewish communities. I sense it intuitively every time someone begins his conversation with me by saying, "Rabbi, I'm not a very good Jew, but . . ." The issue of *Time* Magazine dated tomorrow tells the story of a young thirty-year-old folk singer who is now considering changing his name back from Bob Dylan, his stage name, to Robert Allen Zimmerman, his given name. Asked why he had chosen the name Bob Dylan, he explained that it was out of admiration for the poet Dylan Thomas, at a time when

"I had a lot to run away from. Now," says the young folk-singing superstar, "I've got a lot to return to." His friends explain, says the article, that he is now returning to Judaism, reading Jewish books about his faith, his history, about the Jewish resistance in the Warsaw ghetto, and even took a secret trip to Israel last year. (*Time*, May 31, 1971.)

A colleague and I recently exchanged stories about our experiences in the military chaplaincy. When he entered the infamous camp at Nordhausen, he met there a young Jew who had spent most of his life in the terror of Nazism, in a concentration camp. When he saw an American Jewish chaplain, wearing the Star of David on his lapel, the boy looked at it, and recognized the same symbol he had come to know as a badge of shame. "Do you wear that because you *have* to," asked the young Jew, "or because you are happy and proud to?"

That is the very question each confirmand and each American Jew must ask himself, "Am I a Jew because I was born a Jew, because society compels me to be one, or because being a Jew is the most wonderful and beautiful thing to be in the world?"

And so, our second commandment for the 1970s must be, "Thou shalt be a Proud Jew!" A Jew with dignity and self-respect and knowledge and commitment!

If the first commandment is to assure the survival of the Jewish people, and the second command is to be a proud Jew, then the third commandment is to be an *active* Jew!

We have enough Jews in this world who sit back and let everybody else worry about Jewish survival, about Jewish ethics, about Jewish institutions and communities. What we need today are Jews who will get out of the rut of being marginal, peripheral members of the Jewish community and become *radical* Jews, Jews who are so committed to Jewish values that this concern becomes the focal point of their life. For long enough now in American Jewry we have had leaders whose Jewishness is limited to gourmet cooking and ethnic chauvinism. We need Jews who care about the world, *because* they are Jews!

We need young Jews who will search into their heritage and find what is meaningful to them. It's not enough to say that we are skeptics and reject the kind of mindless acceptance of tradition that was good enough for our parents and grandparents. We need Jews who are willing to work hard at searching for *new* answers and *new* patterns of Jewish commitment and Jewish living, and do not just rely on an easy rejection of the old.

When we relate to world problems, and personal problems, we must do so as Jews, as active, knowledgeable Jews. Elie Wiesel made a plea for Jews to help save the world through being Jews, that bears repetition.

> . . . Remember: the Jew influences his environment only if he does not assimilate. Others will benefit from his experience to the degree that it is and remains unique. Only by assuming his Jewishness can he attain universality. The Jew who repudiates himself, claiming to do so for the sake of humanity, will inevitably repudiate humanity too. A lie cannot be a stepping-stone to truth; it can only be an obstacle. . . . By working for his own people a Jew does not renounce his loyalty to mankind. On the contrary, he makes his most valuable contribution. . . . By struggling on behalf of Russian, Arab, or Polish Jews, I fight for human rights everywhere. By calling for peace in the Middle East, I take a stand against every aggression, every war. By protesting the fanatical exhortations to 'holy wars' against my people, I protest against the stifling of freedom in Prague. By striving to keep alive the memory of the holocaust, I denounce the massacres in Biafra and the nuclear menace. Only by drawing on his unique experience can the Jew help others. A Jew fulfills his role as man only from inside his Jewishness.

Today's Torah lesson defines the role of Jews in society: To be a kingdom of priests and a holy people. I firmly believe that the world needs the Jewish people and the Jewish tradition if it is to find salvation from all the threats that imperil our lives. For almost a century we Jews have asked America to let us be Jews, to let us have our share in shaping America and the world. Today, we must DEMAND the right to be Jews, to be proud, loyal, and *active* Jews. And being an active Jew today means caring for justice throughout America, for justice in Southeast Asia, for equality in the South and North, in the schools and factories, for human decency on every front, *because* we are Jews.

Only those who are actively Jewish can make the most unique contribution to saving our world, a contribution that stems from our historical experience of persecution and discrimination, from our rich literature of spiritual and ethical wisdom.

When I was in Israel two months ago I saw the ruins of the Roman amphitheaters, where gladiators once fought to entertain large audiences. The Talmudic rabbis looked with disdain upon anyone going to witness such barbaric sports. But the Talmud records the opinion of one dissenting scholar who said that a Jew may go to the arena and *shout* "Thumbs up," and by doing so help to save a gladiator. According to Rabbi Nathan, the Jew is commanded to hear the voice of God in the anguished cry of a defeated gladiator, and respond by shouting. Today, "all the world is an arena. Gladiators are locked in mortal combat." (Rabbi A. Karp.) God is calling the Jewish people and saying to each of us, "Go forth and shout the word that saves." This is the third Commandment for our day. Be an active Jew!! Go and shout at the top of your lungs that we must stop hating and killing, and start saving and loving. That is my charge to each of you:

Thou shalt survive as a people!
Thou shalt be a proud, self-respecting Jew!
Thou shalt be an active, concerned, loving Jew!

Amen.

May you each in your own way be granted the ability to live not only by the Biblical commandments, but by these three for our day as well! May it be Thy will!

8

How Shall We Remember Them?

In Remembrance of the Six Million

THERE ARE TWO CHOIRS IN THE SANCTUARY THIS EVENING.
One will sing an oratorio in tribute to the Six Million.
The other is an invisible choir that we can see only in our
mind's eye. The task of you, the audience, is to keep alive
the vision of the Six Million members of the invisible choir
who speak to us tonight through our hearts even as the vision
of the living choir is captured by our eyes and ears. The poet
George Eliot spoke of "the choir invisible of those immortal
dead who live again in minds made better by their presence;
. . . whose music is the gladness of the world."

Our task for tonight and for always is to see that our
minds and our lives are made better by the presence of the
six million in our memory, so that the music of their lives,
the voices of their poets and teachers and singers, can continue through us to make undying music in the world.

Delivered Monday night, January 29, 1973, at Temple Beth El,
Rochester, New York, as introduction to the oratorio "Yizkor," by
Samuel Rosenbaum and Sholom Secunda. The oratorio was sung by
Richard Tucker, taped by ABC for national television, and shown
on April 29, 1973, Yom HaShoah, Holocaust Day.

An argument is recorded in the Talmud. Two sages, Akiba and Ben Petura, disagreed about the following hypothetical predicament. Two men have become lost in the desert and have just enough water for *one* of them to reach civilization. Ben Petura, the logician, claims that both should share the water in the flask, even it means that both will die. Akiba, the mystic, sees the case differently. *Chayekha kodmin*, he says. Your own life always takes precedence over the life of another. The man with the flask of water should save it for himself, and in that way at least one of the two will live. Elie Wiesel has given a novel interpretation to this Talmudic passage. Akiba, he says, realized that when the one man walked out of the desert, he was obligated to live for two men. He now had to live not only his own life, but the life of the friend he left behind. In this way, both lives would carry on.

There are six million Jews in America. Six million Jews died in Europe thirty years ago. You and I must live, each of us, for two people, so that both can go on, and so that they will not have been forgotten. We are living not only for ourselves, but for them as well. Each person in this sanctuary must live two lives. He must see the invisible choir of six million in his mind's eye, playing the music of Judaism and of life and of humanity in our ears and in our hearts.

We must each select someone of the six million for whom our life is a surrogate and emulate his life style, cherish his values, carry out his visions, consummate his desires. As we listen to the "Yizkor" tonight we can select from its words the one whose life we shall perpetuate.

> The mothers
> Who faithfully kindled
> The Sabbath lights. . . .
> The porters
> The drivers
> The beggars
> The peddlers
> The merchants. . . .
>
> And those giants

Who carried with honor
The precious residue
Of a thousand generations
Of painstaking study and
Exquisite talent.
The doctors
The teachers
The scholars
The musicians
The artists and architects.

And the craftsmen—
The golden-fingered
Jewish tailors
The watchmakers
The shoemakers
The printers and bakers
The mass
Who labored in sweat
And swore together
To free all mankind.

One of the great Spanish Jewish poets of the Middle Ages, Solomon ibn Gabirol, of the eleventh century, was said to have been killed by a jealous Arab poet, and was buried beneath a tree. Legend has it that the tree soon began to yield an unusual harvest of luscious fruit. Let our Yizkor this evening, and every Yizkor, and every day's remembrance, feed the roots of our tree of life. Let its fruits of wisdom and goodness and truth and purity be the richer because of the nourishment of our slain brothers and sisters.

When the world observed the 100th anniversary of the death of Charles Dickens, the *New York Times* editorialized in these words: "The genius of Dickens survives in a gallery of characters who dwelled not in palaces or on battlefields but in the streets and prisons and counting-houses of Victorian London. Children and adults will recognize themselves and their acquaintances forever in Oliver Twist, David Copperfield, Scrooge, Dombey." (June 9, 1970)

We too recognize in ourselves, and in our children, the Rachels, the Leahs, the Soras, the Chaims, the Yehudas, the

Shlomos, who no longer walk this earth. They will be remembered not in palaces or on battlefields, but in the home, the school, the synagogue, the academies, the Bet Hamidrash. Beth El Congregation in Rochester must stand now not only for itself, but for all the Beth Els, the Houses of God, in Plonsky, and Lvov, and Minsk, and Podolsk, and Vilna, and Slonim, and Stolin, and Kobrin and Karlin, and Kotsk, and Berditschev, and Volozhin, and Anipol, and Ludmir, and all the other large and small towns of Eastern Europe where Jews dwelt for centuries and studied and prayed and carried out the will of God. And as we pray and study, and sing and laugh, we shall be doing so not only for ourselves, but for the Jews who are members of the invisible choir, in the life that we live for them.

How shall we remember them? Through weeping, or through singing? Through crying, or through dancing? It is good to weep and to be sad. But it is far better to sing and to dance and to laugh. We bring not as much glory to our dead when we weep as when we sing and when we laugh. It is no great honor to them to make their memories a burden upon us, a bond, a shackle, to stunt our lives. These invisible six million do not want to live on in our sorrows, our sighs and our grief, but rather in our joys and in our smiles, in our dances and in our songs.

We remember them best when we chant in joy the words of God's Torah; when we celebrate the Passover in family love and harmony; when we gather around the Hanukkah Menorah and joyously chant the blessings in unison. When we live lives that resemble most the kind of lives which they lived.

Their lives were deeply wrapped up in studying and in living Torah. And if we would emulate their lives and cherish their values, we must do so through the life of Torah.

What kept them alive in the blackness of the ghetto was the supremely joyous delights of Torah study. Every ghetto in Europe, even under the rule of the madmen, had its own school system, from kindergarten until death. There were rabbinical seminaries, where students of all ages sat and studied. Books of commentaries and legal opinions were written and edited. Rabbis were asked questions on matters of Jewish Law. "Is abortion permitted if all pregnant women are decreed to die?" "Must a man divorce his wife if one day she returned with a tattoo on her arm reading, 'Prostitute for Hitler's soldiers'?" "What must be done with a Torah Scroll used to wrap fish and vegetables in the market?" Even in grave moments like these, questions of Jewish law were taken with utmost seriousness. Never was their religious life abandoned.

On the eve of the destruction of the ghetto in Bialystock, the community had a celebration in honor of the event of the 1,000th book taken out of the ghetto library. Children with nothing to eat, and nothing to wear, sat in the ghetto streets hungry and frozen, reading books. In Theresienstadt there was a children's operetta, where the teachers had to constantly train little understudies because after each performance another batch of children was led off to the death camps.

In many of the ghettos, there were cultural performances, drama, music, underground newspapers, archives, even a secret printing press for the production of books. There were artists, sculptors, actors, musicians, and poets. There were scientists who conducted bacteriological research within the confines of the ghetto walls.

A Christian scholar who visited Warsaw over 50 years ago wrote the following: "Once I noticed a great many coaches on a parking-place but with no drivers in sight. In my own country I would have known where to look for them. A young Jewish boy showed me the way: in a courtyard, on the second floor, was the *shtibl* of the Jewish drivers. It consisted of two rooms: one filled with Talmud-volumes, the other a room for prayer. All the drivers were engaged in fervent study and religious discussion. . . . It was then that I found out that all professions, the bakers, the butchers, the shoemakers, have their own *shtibl* in the Jewish district; and every free moment which can be taken off from their work is given to the study of the Torah. And when they get together in intimate groups, one urges the other: 'Sog mir a shtickl Torah— Tell me a little Torah.'"

A book that was saved from the burned libraries of Europe bears the inscription, "The Chevra Shas of the Wood-Choppers of Berditshev," "The Society of Wood-Choppers for the Study of Mishnah in Berditshev." It was this centuries-old tradition of joy and love of learning that was brought to an end for six million Jews in the gas chambers and firing squads of Eastern Europe thirty years ago.

It is this which we are bidden remember on this evening of "Yizkor." The late Abraham Joshua Heschel, poet laureate of East European Jewry, described the meaning of Yizkor in these words: "There is a slow and silent stream, a stream not of oblivion but of memory, from which we must constantly drink before entering the realm of faith. To believe is to remember. The substance of our very being is memory, our way of living is retaining the reminders, articulating memory."*

This year especially, we must *remember*. For it is now thirty years since the great uprising in the Warsaw Ghetto. And it is 25 years since the establishment of the State of Israel. These twin events help place this day in proper perspective. To Warsaw, we look back. To Jerusalem, we look forward. There is no present tense in the Hebrew language, only past and future. As we look back to Warsaw, we must also look forward to Jerusalem. Just as the man who marched out of the desert, brought the past with him as he walked into the future, so do we, American Jews, march from Warsaw to Jerusalem, carrying a freight of spiritual treasures never to be left behind, but never so burdening to prevent us from marching forward in joy and song. The American Jew must ever see himself as a pilgrim traveling on that same road, from Warsaw to Jerusalem; looking back to Europe but also looking up to the hills of Judea, to the mountains whence cometh our Help. It is that looking up to the mountains which gives meaning to the past road below and behind us.

Emil Fackenheim led a pilgrimage of survivors of the Holocaust that stopped first in Bergen-Belsen and then con-

---

* From Abraham Joshua Heschel, *Israel: An Echo of Eternity* (New York: Farrar, Straus and Giroux, 1969), p. 60.

tinued onward to Jerusalem. After climbing the hills of Judea, they reached the Holy City, and the Kotel, the Wall. There they were met by an old man with a bag of cookies and a bottle of liquor who greeted one of them: "My friend, I have a simcha, a celebration! Share it with me!" After having partaken of food and drink, he returned some days later to be met by the same old man with the same greeting. He asked, "What sort of celebration can last so long? Surely not a wedding, nor a Bar Mitzvah!" The old man replied: "I am a survivor of Auschwitz. Also, I am a Kohen, a priest, and, as you know, a priest may bless the people everywhere in the world only a few times during the year. But in Jerusalem, every single day. And since I must be at work at 8 a.m., I come here every single morning to observe my duty and my privilege. This is my simcha. It will last as long as I live." All sorts of men come to the Wall. The old man did not inquire whether they were devout or not devout, whether they were Jews, Christians, or Muslims. To everyone who came he said: "Share my simcha! And may it last as long as life itself."

In the words of the Oratorio we shall now hear:

Remember!
It was their last, hopeless hope.
Remember!

"Remember my yahrzeit!"
"Remember my name!" . . . .

It is time for Yizkor
Remember!

Remember the holy, the pure, and the innocent slaughtered.
They and we
Are bound
Forever.
They are our pain
They are our hope.

May their agony
Find an echo

In our hearts.
May their deeds
Be reflected
In our Lives.

May we be worthy
To remember!

It is time for Yizkor. Remember! Listen! And listen, too, with loving attention, to "the choir invisible of those immortal dead who live again in minds made better by their presence; . . . whose music is the gladness of the world."

9
Judaism and Demonstration Cities

THE PROBLEM OF THE "SHAME OF THE CITIES" DID NOT BEGIN in our day, nor did it spring up in the nineteenth century with the appearance of social and government reform.

The problem of the corruption and disgrace of the cities goes all the way back to the time of Noah. "Now the earth was corrupt in God's sight, and the earth was filled with violence. And God saw the earth, and behold, it was corrupt; for all flesh had corrupted its way upon the earth. And God said to Noah, 'I have decided to make an end of all flesh, for the earth is filled with lawlessness because of them. Behold, I will destroy them with the earth.' " (Genesis 6:11–13.)

From Noah's time until now we have been faced with crime and corruption, lawlessness and injustice, violence and turbulence in the cities and in the world. Centuries after Noah, we find in the Book of Job (24:12), "From out of the

Delivered Friday night, October 14, 1966 (Parshat Noah). Published in *United Synagogue Review*, January, 1967.

populous city men groan, and the soul of the wounded cries for help."

Today, our government is attempting to rectify many of these injustices and inequities, and to heal some of the festering sores that cover our sprawling metropolitan centers. Attempts are being made to revamp and rehaul our cities, to make them peaceful, productive, and beautiful.

Jewish Tradition and the Cities. What advice and counsel do our sages have to offer regarding the ideal configuration of a city?

In a remarkable passage in the Talmud, the rabbis tell us that a Talmud hacham, a pious, observant and learned Jew, should move into a community only if it fulfills the following ten requirements (Sanhedrin 17b): (1) that it possess an effective system of courts and law-enforcement agencies; (2) that it have an adequate network of charity funds, operated with care, concern, and honesty; (3) that it have a synagogue; (4) a public bath house; (5) a privy; (6) a physician; (7) a skilled person; (8) a scribe; (9) a butcher; and (10) a teacher for the youth.

If we examine these ten requirements, I think we will have a useful blueprint for creating the kind of demonstration city that is talked about so much of late.

1. First, we must have a community that respects law and order. A respectable community must have the realization that only through the orderly processes of the Congress and the courts can progress be made. Not through "black power" or "white power," but the power of *law*, respect for lawful and community-backed measures of social improvement.

The demonstration city our ancestors envisaged was one in which all the elements of the community strive for the total integration of all its parts, for the ultimate welfare of every citizen. An alert and public-minded citizen of such a community will recognize that he must fulfill the biblical injunction to "love thy neighbor as thyself." Only through observance of this cardinal ethical rule can true peace and harmony be achieved. He must be hospitable to the stranger as well as to the native, the different as well as the like, the black as well as the white. When someone with a different religious background or different-colored skin moves into the area, he must remember the words of Leviticus (19:33, 34): "If a stranger sojourn with you in your land, you shall not wrong him. . . . He shall be as one of your citizens; you shall love him as yourself, for you were strangers in the land of Egypt; I the Lord am your God."

To achieve such a community of harmonious relations, it takes the diligent efforts of all types of people: scholars, politicians, educators, clergy, etc. Rabbi Akiba once urged his son: "My son, do not dwell in the heights of the city and study your books." (Pesahim 112a.) No ivory-tower moralists can help solve the problem unless they roll up their sleeves, come out of their libraries and studies, and dig their hands into the soil of social ferment.

2. The second requirement is that a city have a "Kuppah," or Community Fund for the poor, the sick, the aged, the orphan and widow, the needy traveler. We have such funds today, both for secular and Jewish causes, and we are proud to say that the record of Jewish giving to causes locally, nationally, and overseas continues to show the influence of our tradition of love and compassion for mankind. Of course, we must never rest on our laurels, but continue to increase and expand the scope of philanthropic activities in our cities and towns throughout the land.

3. The third need for a vibrant and effective community is a synagogue. No Jew should even consider moving into an area where his religious needs cannot be fulfilled, where he cannot pray in a minyan. A community must provide a minyan not only for Sabbaths and holidays, but for the daily prayers as well—for those who want to hear the Torah read, who must recite mourner's kaddish, and for whom prayer is an important community function in their lives.

Elsewhere in the Talmud (Shabbat 11a) we are given further instructions as to what the synagogue should be like. It should be the tallest building in the city. Rather than take this directive literally (I don't think the rabbis anticipated skyscrapers and high-rise apartment dwellings), I think we can interpret this to mean that the synagogue must be a place of stature, of grace and loveliness, and that it must be the center of community attention. All other community activities must bow before the religious needs of the citizenry.

4. The public bath house in ancient times served more than a sanitary function. It was the community center for physical games and leisurely conversation. It would correspond in our times to centers of recreation and physical activities, including sports and social events. We must support the Y's and community-center movement if our cities are to be useful and enjoyable for our citizens.

Judaism has always counted the needs of the body as important as the requirements of mind and soul. We have never denigrated the good health, strength, and beauty of the human body.

5. Closely allied with the preceding is the necessity of proper sanitation. The prophet Zephaniah said (3:1–2):

> Woe to her that is filthy and polluted,
> to the oppressing city!
> She listens to no voice,
> She accepts no correction.
> She does not trust in the Lord,
> She does not draw near to her God.

I remember reading somewhere recently the statement that in Judaism cleanliness is not next to godliness, it is *part* of godliness. The pollution of our air, our water, our rivers and streams all affect our daily lives, and continue to cause concern to active citizens.

Rabbi Richard Hirsch, in this excellent book *Judaism and Cities in Crisis*, points out that housing codes are not something new for traditional Jews. In Maimonides' famous Code of Law (Mishne Torah) the medieval sage includes the following requirement for a landlord (Hilchot Sechirut, chapter 6): "He who leases a house to another is bound to supply doors, keep the windows in repair, reinforce the ceiling, provide props for the broken beam, as well as to make a bolt and lock and similar things which are produced by the craftsman and are essential to the habitability of houses. . . ."

The Torah requires (Deuteronomy 22:8) that a house have a parapet on the roof, to protect the life and limb of anyone using the house.

6. The next essential element is medical care. Again, as Jews we have contributed more than our share by creating Jewish hospitals which are outstanding in the country, and by scientific contributions of Jewish physicians who proportionately far outnumber their gentile colleagues in America. We must continue to support measures put forth by Congress and the President to provide medical care for the poor, the elderly, and the incapacitated.

The *rofe,* or physician, in ancient days was also the one who performed ritual circumcision. He fulfilled, of course, all of the requirements of a mohel, as an observant and learned Jew. Thus, we include in this sixth category a traditional mohel to preserve the mitzvah of *bris milah.* There is no doubt that community-licensed mohalim are as qualified medically as a physician in the performance of this operation. We need only remind ourselves that Queen Elizabeth had the crown prince circumcised by the mohel of London.

7. The seventh category in our passage is that of *uman,* the man of special skill and talent. Today the *uman* can mean for us the artist—he whom God has endowed with extraordinary talent in the field of music, dance, drama, art, writing, etc. We must further their creativity, support their endeavors, and laud their achievements. Jews are the people of the Book, and, if we are to believe the recent *Time* essay, the cultural heroes of America today. We have had our share of artists and patrons of the arts, and we should continue to do so, so that our cities will have the dimension of beauty and grace that our rabbis apparently deemed so important that they included it as a basic requirement of an enlightened city.

8. We need, next, the services of a scribe. In Jewish life this individual has played a dual role. He provided the necessary ritual objects for the observance of religious law—the scroll of the Torah, the parchments of the mezuzah and tefilin, and Megillah scroll for Purim, and since printing had not yet come upon the scene we must include all of the sacred books.

For us, this means that our community today must have a place where we can acquire Jewish books and religious objects—mezuzot, tefilin, calendars, wine, menorahs for Hanukkah, matzoh for Pesach, lulav and etrog for Sukkot, etc. We must have a source for buying copies of the Bible, the siddur, and other important classic and modern Jewish books. In short, we must have a local Hebrew book store.

In addition, we should have an active Jewish library, for distribution of books, journals, newspapers, and reference material.

But the *lavlar*, or scribe, provided another service in ancient times. He was the one who attended to preparing the documents in legal ceremonies. He wrote the *Ketuba* for a wedding, a *get* for a divorce, and notarized, if you will, other legal transactions of economic and religious nature. Today the rabbi fills many of these functions. He solemnizes marriages, and oversees other ritual ceremonies such as divorce, circumcision, baby-naming, funerals, unveilings, building dedications, and a host of other formal ceremonies. As the religious functionary in the community, his services are indispensable for a Jewish-minded citizenry. The rabbi's position should be one of respect and dignity, and the community should reserve for him the respect of our tradition for the rav, the religious teacher and leader of the community.

9. The *tabbach* in Talmudic times was the meat dresser, the butcher, and the cook. Today as well as then, without the services of the kosher butcher, Jewish life could not go on. If we have any respect for the dietary laws, we have to do our share to support the kosher facilities in the community. If one chooses not to keep kosher outside the home, let him at least keep it in the home, the center of Jewish religious life. Let him make sure that his wedding or bar mitzvah party, and all public functions are held within the confines of kashruth. Whether it be a synagogue function, a B'nai B'rith dinner, a Hadassah luncheon, community center banquet, or a privately catered anniversary celebration, let it be in the spirit of Judaism.

10. Last, but perhaps most important of all, a community worth its name must have a teacher for the young. Our an-

cestors were particularly diligent to assure the continuation of our tradition and the preservation of our heritage by insisting on intensive Jewish education for our children.

This applies as well to adult education. "May a man always seek out and live in a city whose House of Learning is nearby." (Shabbat 10b.) The Yeshiva or Bet Midrash was the place of learning for adults. The children's school was called Bet Rabban—the master's house. Any city that did not provide the youth with such a master and teacher was doomed to destruction (Shabbat 119b).

A City with God's Spirit. All in all, our ancestors felt it the obligation of every Jew to make sure that his community was one filled with the fear of God and the love of man. One whose values were spiritual ones, whose actions were just and honest, and whose respect for law was profound. One whose concern for all the elements and needs of the public were taken into consideration.

In short, they demanded a city filled with the spirit of the Lord.

> Unless the Lord builds the house,
> Those that build it labor in vain.
> Unless the Lord watches over the city,
> the watchman stays awake in vain. (Psalm 127:1.)

10

Judaism, the Swallow, and Fair Housing

THE HEBREW WORD "D'ROR" IS NOT USED FREQUENTLY IN THE
Bible. It appears only seven times, the Concordance informs
us. Furthermore, in the seven appearances of the word *d'ror*
it seems to have two completely different meanings. In most
cases it is translated as "liberty" or "freedom."

It is in that sense that it appears in this morning's Sidrah:
Ukratem d'ror ba-aretz lekhol yoshveha—"Proclaim Liberty
throughout the Land unto all the Inhabitants Thereof." This
verse is well known to every American school child as the
verse which is etched on the Liberty Bell in Philadelphia's
Independence Hall, cradle of American freedom.

In only two verses in the entire twenty-four books of
Scripture do we find the word *d'ror* in its other meaning. Its
secondary meaning is usually given as "swallow," the bird
that roams freely about the heavens with the freedom of
the skies.

Delivered Saturday morning, May 20, 1967 (Sidrah: *Behar*).
Published in *Best Jewish Sermons of 5727–5728*.

In fact, this is exactly how the Bible pictures the swallow. For example, Proverbs 26:2—"Like a fluttering bird or a swooping swallow, a causeless curse does not alight." The swallow is here used in a simile that compares a harshly spoken word to a freely flying fowl. They are alike in that they never come to rest; both the causeless curse and the sweeping swallow are forever in flight, flapping around the heavens.

The other place that the word *d'ror* means swallow is in Psalms 84:4. In this verse we get a clue to the one place in the universe that the poor ever-soaring swallow can come to rest. "Even the sparrow finds a home and the swallow a nest for herself, where she may lay her young, at thy altars, O Lord of hosts, my King and my God."

In God's own house, at the altar, in the Temple, the bird that cannot find a home anywhere in the world can find sanctuary and rest.

I would be the last one to question the translation of both ancient and modern scholars who declare that in the last two verses quoted the word *d'ror* denotes a swallow. But it is true that the Hebrew language and the Hebrew Bible have an organic quality which binds together words of common roots, and makes it possible for certain words to have several meanings. In fact, Professor Robert Gordis has shown brilliantly that in many cases the Hebrew authors specifically chose their words because they had two different meanings, and could be translated both ways in the same context. He gives many examples of this in his new commentary on the Book of Job.

According to Rabbi Gordis, this very subtle literary device, used frequently in Arabic poetry, is known as *talhin*. "In *talhin*," he writes (*The Book of God and Man*, p. 167) "the effect derives not from the sound but from the meaning. The poet uses a word which has two distinct denotations, one primary to the context and the other secondary but also appropriate. His choice of the particular word, rather than a synonym, is dictated by the desire to bring both meanings simultaneously to the consciousness of the reader, who derives a delicate aesthetic pleasure from the instantaneous recognition of both meanings."

Whether or not Dr. Gordis would accept the present example of *d'ror* as a valid one is immaterial. If it is not valid from the point of view of biblical scholarship, it is certainly valid within the midrashic frame of thought of Jewish tradition.

What I would like to suggest is that the two verses from Proverbs and Psalms just quoted we translate the Hebrew *d'ror* not as swallow, as is customary, but as "liberty," its more frequent English rendering. This will lead us to a deep insight about the concept of freedom.

The first verse, from Proverbs, then becomes:

> Like a fluttering bird or restless liberty,
> A causeless curse does not alight.

What this verse now says is that freedom is something that is very "flighty." Liberty is a notion which strains to find a home, a place to rest, to alight. No one wants to give sanctuary to this homeless bird of liberty. No one wants to nurture and care for liberty and to espouse her cause. When the liberty bird knocks at our door, we are usually not home. When the idea of freedom and justice for all mankind seeks a place to grow and develop, it is forced to constantly fly through the blue skies without a patch of ground upon which to descend.

But the other verse gives us the clue to a partial solution for the elusive and intangible concept of freedom.

With our new, secondary translation, we read:

> Even the sparrow finds a home and freedom a nest for herself,
> where she may lay her young,
> at thy altars, O Lord of hosts,
> My King and my God.

The one place in the world where freedom finds a home is apparently in the house of God—at the divine altars. The sole spot in this planet where freedom can be brought down to earth, and find a welcome nest to feed, nourish and sustain her, is within the confines of God's house. The place where mother freedom can lay her young, and care for her burgeoning offspring of justice and equality, is under God's sheltering roof.

We should take special note of the fact that the word "altars" in the verse in Psalms is in the plural. This gives us a hint that not only the altar in the Temple in Jerusalem is meant, but all altars anywhere in the world. All churches and synagogues throughout this great nation and throughout the world have the special responsibility of embodying the idea of freedom within the confines of their hallowed walls.

Any great idea is powerless unless it finds people to espouse it, praise it, and implement it; unless it finds an institution to put that idea into practice, to see it blossom forth into full bloom as its influence reaches out into the homes and shops and factories of all communities.

The house of God must be the institution that puts the idea of freedom into practice for all people, but especially for the American Negro. It is our task as a community in Israel, which exists by virtue of our ancient covenant with God, to do everything in our power to see that civil rights are not just an empty phrase, an unembodied ideal, but a living reality for all Americans, an idea implemented and fostered by the religious community of our country. No greater responsibility faces us in this decade than the fulfillment of the verse in today's Sidrah for the black American, "Proclaim Liberty (d'ror) throughout the Land unto all the Inhabitants Thereof." It is our special and undeniable responsibility to see that we are the ones who open our doors and our hearts to the elusive swallow of freedom. Otherwise she might fly in the sky forever, never coming down to earth.

The same Psalm that praises God's house as being the home of the swallow, praises it for being the home of the priests. In ancient times, priests dwelled within the Temple precincts. The Jewish people are all priests, says the Torah— a kingdom of priests. We must dwell together with freedom, and freedom must live with us. And both of us must live together with God and His will. We must so live our lives that it becomes the mark of the Jew and the mark of the synagogues that they stand in the forefront of the battle for civil rights.

The very verse which praises God's house for being a sanctuary for the swallow is followed by this verse:

> Blessed are they who dwell in the house,
> ever singing thy praise.

Blessed is freedom when it finds rest in the house of God, and blessed are they who dwell together with her, God's own people.

We have defined the Hebrew word *d'ror* as being related to the idea of flowing freely, and have seen that it has two separate translations, both "liberty" and "swallow."

However, the rabbis of the midrash saw in this word *d'ror* an entirely different Hebrew root. In commenting on the verse in our Sidrah (Leviticus 25:10), Rashi quotes Rabbi Judah in the Talmud (Rosh Hashana 9b). *"Mahu leshon d'ror?"* he saks. "What is the etymology of the word *"d'ror?"* And he proceeds to answer his own question. *"K'medayer bay dayra."*—"A free man is one who can dwell at an inn."

In so defining the term *d'ror*, Rabbi Judah connects it with the Hebrew root *dur*—to dwell, to reside. To his way of thinking there is nothing more basic and fundamental to the way of life of a free man than to reside in the place that he chooses. Whoever can stop at any inn, says Rabbi Judah, and be welcomed hospitably, is truly a free man.

This is the freedom which the people of the churches and synagogues must fight for. The freedom to dwell where one wishes. The freedom to stay at any public accommodation, but even more importantly, to buy a home wherever one desires to live.

Wherever a man refuses to sell his "castle" to another because of the color of his skin, he is refusing admission into God's house to the swallow of freedom. He is declaring that both man and freedom cannot abide together in God's own house. He is denying that man the freedom to be human. For to be human is to be free, and to be free, at least according to Rabbi Judah in the Talmud, is to dwell wherever one chooses. *D'ror* and *dur* are two inextricably interwoven concepts. In fact, they are synonymous. To be free *is* to live in the home one chooses unmolested and unafraid.

Rabbi Judah goes one step further in his definition of freedom. To him, the free man is the one *she-dar bekhol makom she-hu rotze ve-ayno bireshut acherim*—"The free man is the one who may dwell in any place he chooses, and is not subject to the control of others." Not subject to the control of restrictive convenants, prejudiced landowners, discriminating real estate brokers, nor shortsighted legislators, but free to live anywhere at all, and not be subject to the control of people who themselves have no right to dwell in God's house.

If God himself invites the swallow of freedom and liberty to abide together with him in His house, can we human beings do less?

We would surely not be fulfilling Hillel's maxim, "If I am not for myself, who is for me?" if we were to limit the application of Rabbi Judah's definition of freedom only to the American Negro. For we Jews also suffer from the hostility of those who would deny their neighbors the right to dwell where they choose.

First our brethren in the Soviet Union, who languish under the yoke of a modern pharaoh. They too would like to have the right to choose to live wherever they please, and not be under the control of others. Many, if not most of them, would prefer to emigrate from Russia and live in the State of Israel. Others would prefer to join relatives in Europe or America. By denying them the basic right of choosing their place of domicile, the Soviet Union is denying them their most fundamental freedom. The Soviet Union is hostile to the existence of houses of God, and therefore the swallow of freedom has nary a place to alight, nary a home to feed and grow. We, then, must be the ones who fight the cause of our Jewish brothers in Russia. We must take up their cause as ours. Until they can live freely, we should not breathe freely. For freedom to live is really as fundamental as freedom to breathe.

Secondly, the independent and sovereign State of Israel is being denied its right to exist by hostile Arab neighbors. In their way of thinking, Israel has no right to live, and therefore no right to be. The proud and noble inhabitants of the Jewish state insist on their right, with Rabbi Judah, to live in their ancient homeland, without being under the control of others.

Our people, like the biblical swallow, has flown the length and breadth of the world seeking a place to alight. No one has wanted us for two millennia. Finally, through our own efforts, we have fairly purchased land, settled it, and built a homeland. Through the untiring efforts of philanthropists and pioneer workers, we have earned the right to live in that land and be recognized as having possession to it. But Israel's neighbors refuse to recognize that right, and by doing so, are denying the Jewish people the most fundamental right a nation can have—the right to dwell in peace with its neighbor, subject to its own sovereign authority.

For the American Negro, for the Soviet Jew, and for the nation of Israel, we pray for freedom and for life. We affirm our solidarity with them, and pledge our best efforts to invite freedom and liberty and justice to dwell together in the House of God with all mankind. Amen.

11
Equality NOW!

WHAT IS THE MOST IMPORTANT PROBLEM FACING AMERICA
today? Three years ago the answer would have been civil
rights. Today, the answer most of us give is Vietnam. For
the past three years our nation has been involved in a futile
effort at escalation, defying both the will of the nation and
many of its Congressional leaders. This week we also learned
that the Secretary of Defense has his own serious doubts
about the escalation of the bombing war.

Judaism has an old and wonderful method of making
peace, and perhaps it would have validity in this instance.
At the end of the Amidah we take three steps back, and we
say, *Ose shalom bimromav*—May He who makes peace in the
heavenly bodies grant peace to us here on earth. A Hasidic
rabbi once said that the reason for taking three steps back
during the prayer for peace is that peace is often achieved
by stepping back, by giving in, by descending, if you will,
instead of ascending—or, may I add, by de-escalating instead
of escalating. Reports from scores of visitors, like Harrison
Salisbury, tell us that although Hanoi would never make a

Delivered Yom Kippur Morning, October 14, 1967.

firm promise, a bombing pause would be the first step toward negotiations. McNamara's testimony to the Senate's Preparedness Investigation Subcommittee has confirmed that the value of the bombing has been negligible. While it was intended to bring the enemy to the negotiation table, it in effect has done the opposite. President Johnson's stature would rise to what it was in the 1964 election were he to declare an immediate unconditional halt to the bombing. This courageous step would be in the tradition of Khrushchev, who, when he backed down, or stepped back, in the Cuban missile crisis, gained the world's thanks and respect together. It may be precisely now that the advice of a Hasadic rabbi about the stepping back at the end of the Amidah would bring relief and peace to the world.

While the conflict in Vietnam was being escalated, another war was, unfortunately, de-escalated. In the same last three years the problem of equality for the black people of this nation has been taking second place on our national agenda.

Following in the tradition of the same Hasidic rabbi, I might point out that when beginning the Amidah—which is a series of important blessings, *berachot*—we take three steps forward. Here too, in the case of black equality, in order to achieve a series of important blessings, we must take three steps forward.

Three steps forward at this point in the history of the Negro's struggle for equality would make a significant escalation of the war against racism and discrimination, a war that all of us agree needs winning.

In the Catholic magazine *Commonweal*, a prominent thinker made the following frustrating observation in the September 29, 1967, issue: "The summer is over. The study commissions have been appointed. Congress remains conservative, and the Administration remains war-preoccupied. Neither the shouts of the rioters nor the empirical reasonings of the economists find an answering echo. The nation, leaderless, torpid, and distracted, shrinks nervously back within itself. . . ."

The paralysis of the 90th Congress is our failure as well as theirs. They are our democratically elected representatives, and if their voice was not loud enough, or their votes on the wrong column, then we too must bear the burden of guilt for remaining quiet and placid while it happened.

Thus, the first step forward for us must be to recognize the role of the individual in the racial crisis. We cannot blame the Congress alone, or the minority of rioters alone, or the Black Power psychopaths alone. It is Yom Kippur, and on this day we are concerned only with our own guilt, not that of others. Our Father, our King, we have sinned before thee—*Selach lanu, mechal lanu, kaper lanu*—Forgive us, pardon us, grant us atonement. This is the sin we committed before Thee—silence, inaction, apathy, turning our eyes away from the festering sore spreading disease in the body of our nation.

We who are Jews have a special responsibility in this area. We too have known oppression, and persecution, and racial hatred. Each year at Passover we say that we ourselves went out of Egypt. We do that so that we can feel and identify as closely as possible with enslaved peoples all over the world this very day. Our tradition is one of humaneness, of compassion, of uncompromising social justice. We are the Amoses, the Isaiahs, the Micahs of the world. Where is our calling to prophetic justice in 1967 when a nation that generates seven hundred billion dollars in goods and services each year harbors within itself a fifth of its population so poor and so mistreated that it must resort to massive violence and destruction to focus attention on their problems?

It is easy to find excuses, but none of them is adequate. Of course, we Jews pulled ourselves up by our bootstraps; why can't they? Did we ever stop to think that our poor and uneducated Jews on New York's East Side and elsewhere were carrying in their baggage a four-millennia-old heritage of respect for knowledge and for the good life? What heritage does the Negro carry in his baggage? Slavery, repression, illiteracy.

Others find it easy to point to Negro anti-Semitism, an ugly yet undeniable phenomenon in recent years. Such a person must also ask himself, Why am I helping the black person; why must I raise my voice in behalf of economic and social equality for the black man? Is it because we feel sorry for him, that we feel sympathy for him? If it were only that we could say "Alright, he is not grateful to the Jew, he hates us anyway, let's forget the whole thing." But that is not why we do whatever little we do. We do it because it is demanded of us—not by the Negroes, but by our conscience. In Hebrew we have a word for it—*tzedaka*. *Tzedaka,* as you know, means justice, not charity. We do it because it is right, not because it is appreciated or not appreciated. We do it to wipe out the evil in the world. We do it most of all to cleanse our own souls of the hatred, the prejudice, and the evil we as a nation continue to commit against the Negro minority.

A *New York Times* editorial some time ago said it better than anyone else; "The racists have a formidable ally—that is, the present and renewed *silence* of the religious community. Open housing and other provisions of pending bills offer incomparable challenge to the religiously committed today."

If all religionists have a responsibility, then Jews have a double responsibility. If Jews have a double responsibility, then Jews who come to synagogue and worship God and attempt to commit their most grievous sins on Yom Kippur have an additional burden of responsibility.

Dr. Harvey Cox, noted Harvard theologian, asserted recently that the most essential religious task of this decade is to grapple with the problems of the inner city and the persons caged within it. His definition of "sin" is to avoid our responsibilities in the field of social-mindedness. Particularly do we who reside in the suburbs have this religious obligation. For were it not for our moving out of the cities and leaving them to deteriorate, things might not be as bad today as they are.

A second step forward, one that is perhaps radical and that I know is highly unpopular, is a policy of reparations towards undoing the sins we have committed against the Negro. Jewish tradition demands that when we confess our sins we must also repair the damage we have done before we can be forgiven.

In terms of the war for better education, better jobs, better homes for the black man, we must pay reparations.

To me, and I know few people agree, that means giving the Negro more rights than the white man. It means paying him with opportunities in schools and jobs and homes when he has not even on the surface earned the right to such opportunities. This is our way of paying for the damage we caused to his people.

This is practiced today in Israel. Israel's somewhat comparable "racial" problem is the gaping breach between the European immigrants and the so-called Eastern, or Oriental, communities from North Africa, Iraq, Yemen, etc. To gain admission to high school, a European child needs to receive a grade of 80 on the entrance exam; for an Eastern child, a grade of 70 is sufficient. Is this discrimination? Yes. The kind that is necessary to repair the breach between the two communities. It is the only way that the sons of the ditch diggers will be able to gain the same opportunities that the children of the lawyers and doctors have.

A policy of reparations would go a long way towards bringing the blessings of America to the nation's black minority.

A third step forward in the fight for black economic and social equality is to win the war of communication. Because the black person cannot receive a good education, and cannot win equal employment with his white brother, he remains isolated in the ghettos, far apart from prosperous and affluent America. There is no communication between the black person and the white person.

There must be a dialogue between us, if any further cooperation is to take place. Confrontation of the frankest and hardest kind is the first rung on the ladder of understanding and mutual respect. We all know that we harbor many prejudices, even the most enlightened and sensitive among us. We look upon Negroes as common laborers or domestics.

One member of our congregation told me that one night while her young daughter was watching the TV, Lena Horne appeared to sing. "Mommy, whose maid is she?" asked the young girl. This is the image our children have of the black woman and by and large the one we transmit to them.

Confrontations like the Fair Housing Sabbath we had last

December, and the Tuesday night course on "What Color Is Power" which we are now sponsoring with six local churches, are the third essential step forward in this war on our home front. Unless we can hear the words of bitterness and frustration spoken from the mouth of a black person, we can never begin to know how he or she feels, what his or her problems are, or what we can do to solve them.

It is well known that there are two camps now in the civil rights movement. Those who have maintained a nonviolent posture despite being called "Uncle Tom" and "Fat Cat," and those who would tear up the nation's cities in protest over discrimination. If we want those who espouse nonviolence to win out, we must respond to their wants and their needs. We must hear their cries, and give them some victories. Otherwise their opponents will emerge victors, and all the world the losers.

Of all days of the year, let us not turn aside and point our finger behind our backs. Let us, for a change, in the spirit of the Day of Atonement, point the finger of guilt at ourselves and see what we have done or have not done to win this war for humanity.

An ancient midrash tells us that when God offered the Torah to the Israelites when they had left Egypt, he lifted up Mount Sinai above their heads, and said, "Either you accept the Torah or here will lie your graves." As Jews in 1968, we must either accept our responsibilities towards winning the war against poverty, hatred, racism, and discrimination, or here in this country lies the grave of Judaism and of America.

On this solemn day of the year let us pledge to continue our role as God's partners in bringing this world and this country closer to the realization of God's Kingdom on earth. Amen.

12
Jews and Blacks—Past, Present, Future

THE TASK ASSIGNED TO ME THIS EVENING IS TO EVALUATE the present state of black-Jewish relations. Although this date was fixed several months ago, it could not have been done with better timing, in light of the release a few days ago of the Report of the President's National Advisory Commission on Civil Disorders.

Landmark in Civil Rights Movement. To my mind this Report will be seen in coming months and years as one of the greatest landmarks in the history of the civil rights movement in America. Nothing expressed in it is anything different than what Martin Luther King and others have been saying for a long time. The difference is that this Report has about it the aura of an official government document, emanating from the highest echelons of American policy-making circles. Six of the eleven-member panel are members of the Congress or high state and city officials. Furthermore, most

---

Delivered at Adult Studies Institute, Har Zion Temple, Monday night, March 4, 1968. A revised form was published in the *Reconstructionist*, May 17, 1968.

of the panel are whites. What the blacks have been telling us for years is finally being given credence and total acceptance by distinguished, informed, and reliable whites.

The basic conclusion of their report is significant in evaluating the present status of Jewish-black relations. That conclusion is that the essential cause of today's racial crisis is not poverty or ignorance; nor is it communistic conspiracy or other outside influence; nor is it the militancy of Black Power hate-mongers. It is clear and simple *racism* on the part of the white community. And when we say white, we include, of course, the Jewish community, who are, by and large, as racist in attitude and action as the rest of white America.

If you disagree, ask yourself when was the last time you used the word "shvartza." Ask yourself when was the last time you took any concrete action whatsoever to alleviate the burden of exploited Negro masses in this country. Ask yourself how you would react if you even heard a rumor that a black family might buy the house next door. Ask yourself if you have ever complained about black anti-Semitism and at the same time never even considered how much Jewish anti-Negroism there is in the Jewish community. Ask yourself how often you have been part of the backlash movement that finds easy excuses for hiding our faces ostrich-like in the sand of our smug complacency and buried along with our noses our Jewish sense of decency and justice for all men.

Exploding the Myths in Black-Jewish Relations. The conclusion of the President's Commission, spoken in the most solemn and sober tones, is that "Our nation is moving toward two societies, one black, one white—separate and unequal." If ever anything threatened to destroy the democratic fiber of the American dream, it is the possibility that we could have apartheid here in the land created by a group of far-sighted men who sought equality, religious freedom, and a just society for all men. And yet, unless we radically reorient our thinking and our actions, this is precisely what might happen to us.

When we speak specifically about black-Jewish relations, there are several myths that must once and for all be exploded and rejected by every Jew, before this radical re-orientation can take place. Only by seeing these deeply entrenched myths for what they are can we Jews begin to rub the racism out of our own eyes and look upon the black man as our neighbor, our friend, our equal, and our fellow American.

I count five myths which pervade the thinking of the masses of the Jewish community today.

The first myth is that blacks are more anti-Semitic than white American Christians, and that black anti-Semitism is a major threat to black-Jewish relations since the inception of the Black Power movement in June, 1966.

This myth is one which was furthered, if not caused by, the kind of sensationalist press that thrust nobody dema-gogues like Rap Brown and Stokely Carmichael into national prominence.

This myth was given the lie by a scientific study sponsored by the Anti-Defamation League and published in a book only recently (*Protest and Prejudice: A Study of Belief in the Black Community*, by Gary T. Marx, Harper & Row, 1967). This study was done after the riots of the summer of 1964, but later, more limited surveys have shown that the basic results have not been altered even after the worsened riots of 1965 and 1966. (See "Protest and Prejudice: the Hard Facts," by Will Maslow, *Congress Bi-Weekly*, November 20, 1967, pp. 9–10.)

The findings of this ADL study show that blacks are *less*, and not *more* anti-Semitic than white Americans. That three-fourths of the black community either evince no anti-Semitism or very little. That 82 percent of the black respondents did not believe that Jewish merchants treated them unfairly; that there are more blacks who prefer to work for Jews than blacks who prefer to work for non-Jews. That 73 percent of those interviewed made no distinction between Jewish and non-Jewish storekeepers, and that of those who did distin-guish, at least a fourth saw Jews in a more favorable light than non-Jews.

Clearly, then, those who have moved out of the civil rights movement because of black anti-Semitism are merely finding excuses. There is no denying that there exists anti-Semitism among many Negroes. But it probably exists less among blacks than it does among Wasps. And while we hear more about it of late, it has not sunk deep roots into the vast majority of the black community, and there is no great cause for alarm. It is a false issue, a diversion from the real problem of white racism. It is an excuse behind which ignorant, prejudiced people can hide. It is a mask and a myth, and it must be exposed and exploded. The anti-Semitism that exists among rabid black racists such as the SNCC people and others of their extremist nature has been given too much attention by the press, and hence has created a needless fear among Jews. Let's relegate it once and for all to a back seat where it belongs. Cecil Moore no more represents the majority of blacks than Norman Rockwell did the whites of this country.

The "Bootstraps" Theory. The second myth has to do with what I like to call the "bootstraps" theory. That is, that we Jews in the early part of the twentieth century were poverty-stricken immigrants who pulled ourselves up by the bootstraps and brought ourselves out of our own dilemma. Why cannot the Negro do the same?

The implication is that the solution to the black problem in America today lies entirely in their own hands. Subconsciously, to be sure, there lies the stereotype of the lazy, unmotivated black who does not have the same qualities of initiative and responsibility that we Jews had two or three generations ago.

The parallel between the black of the 1960s and the Jew of the 1900s and 1910s is a false one, and a misleading one. In fact, the only parallel between the two groups is that both experienced poverty. The differences between them are far deeper and more significant than this one similarity. If there remained a shadow of a doubt in our minds about the differences, they were removed by the scalpel lowered on this myth in chapter nine of the Report of the President's Commission, called "Comparing the Immigrant and Negro Experience," (as summarized in *The New York Times* of March 1, 1968, page 21).

Michael Harrington, in his classic study on poverty, *The Other America,* has shown why so many poor Americans remain caught in the web of indigence, not being able to extricate themselves without outside help. Such poor elements suffer from four characteristic conditions which have been absent or nonexistent among Jews: (a) poor physical health; (b) poor mental and emotional health; (c) inadequate education; and (d) weak family ties.

Furthermore, our parents and grandparents were braced against whatever discrimination they faced with a 4,000-year-old history of a thriving religious culture and a history of intellectual pursuits. The only heritage the black man had was one of two centuries of slavery and a century of racism, deliberate disruption of family structure, and the denial of rights. We weren't in chains when we arrived here, and whatever handicaps we may have faced, our skin was white, and that makes all the difference in the world. As Robert Gordis has put it, "There is only one thing in the twentieth century cheaper than the blood of the Jew—it is the blood of the Negro." Their blood was even cheaper than ours, in the eyes of WASP America.

But perhaps most important of all, when our ancestors arrived in the cities of America, the industrial economy was hardly as sophisticated as it is today. Unencumbered by racial prejudices, they could take advantage of a maturing economy with a great need for unskilled labor. While the black today may want a job every bit as much as the immigrant Jew or Italian or Irishman, he simply cannot find one. Under these circumstances, it is hardly fair—it is even cruel —to suggest that such a person pull himself up by his bootstraps. He can't even afford to buy a pair of boots! There's the rub.

But as stated earlier, we have preserved and disseminated this myth, at least partially because it was an easy way to pat ourselves on the back and place the blame on the black community for their own lack of social mobility. Let us make no bones about it. If the black man cannot find a job today, it is more likely because racist white America refuses to let him get one. This is the conclusion of the President's Commission on Racial Disorders, and this is what the black leaders have been saying to us, those who have been listening, for a long time.

Black Power Is Negro Zionism. Having said that the black person cannot pull himself or herself up alone, I want now to say something that seemingly contradicts that view. That is, that the black person *does* have a great deal to do with his future, even though he or she must have the full-hearted, strong support of the white majority to do it. Just as we must do more for the blacks, so they must do more for themselves. Blacks need the feeling of group pride and group responsibility that our religious tradition has fostered in us these four millennia.

This brings me to the third myth. That is that the Black Power movement, per se, is evil, destructive, racist, and prone to violence. While the respected civil rights leaders like King, Young, Wilkins, and others had misgivings about the phrase "Black Power," they have all backed the mainstream trends of the movement as wholesome, positive, and useful for solving the black problem.

What I am saying, in short, is that Black Power can be viewed as Negro Zionism. Of course the analogy is not exact; that is, if we look upon Zionism in its narrowest definition as the movement for a Jewish state. But Zionism in its broader aspects means Jewish group unity, constructive use of Jewish economic and political power, giving full expression to Jewish ethnic pride, and Jewish national development.

If indeed there is a way for the black to pull himself up, then it is by the bootstraps of Black Power. We have always felt that being Jewish is "beautiful." Why not then foster slogans such as "Black is beautiful"? It is beautiful, because it's the color God gave them. The black must feel that it's beautiful to be black before he can achieve the self-respect that we have taken away from him through slavery, repression, and racist discrimination.

In this sense Black Power is nothing new, and we should not be afraid of it. It is only a resurgence of the advice given by Negro Abolitionist Frederick Douglass in 1848, who said that "It is evident that we can be improved and elevated only just so fast and far as we shall improve and elevate ourselves." For goodness sake, after all these years of demanding that the black man pull himself up by his bootstraps, when he finally does take our advice, why do we condemn him for it?

Black Power, in its best sense, in the way that most blacks understand it, in the way that those who see in it great potential for black self-understanding and growth have defined its implications, in this sense Black Power is black pride and black consciousness (cf. *Time* essay, December 1, 1967).

The violence in the streets over the past summers is not due to Black Power, it is due to white apathy. A few black extremists are guilty of this violence, and we don't condone it for a minute, but all of us are responsible for it. Having perpetuated a society that thrives on injustices in which the haves get more and the have-nots get less, and the gap between them gets wider and wider, we have incited the extremist elements in the black jails of the city ghetto to cry out for help in the only way open to them: physical violence.

Our tradition long ago recognized that far more than the perpetrators of violence, society at large is guilty for this outcry by the victims of injustice. "The sword comes into the world," says Pirke Avot (5:11) because of the delaying and perverting of justice."

Deuteronomic law requires (21:1–9) that if a dead body is found in the field, the elders of the nearest community must make the following declaration: "Our hands have not shed this blood." The rabbis (Sota 48b) ask the question: Is it conceivable that the elders of a city would be considered murderers? And they answer that the leaders of a community must make this oath to declare to the rest of the world that they were not remiss in providing food and housing and the full protection of the law for those passing through.

The rabbis of the Talmud saw that responsibility for a crime is a serious and complex matter. It is too easy to pin the blame on the person who commits the act itself, and yet ignore the role we played, which is much more crucial in the final analysis, in bringing about the conditions in which the violence erupted.

The members of the President's Commission were following this ancient rabbinic pattern when they laid the blame for the riots of last summer at the door of the white man, even though it was a minority of the black people who actually perpetrated the crime.

No Room for Jews. A corollary of the same third myth about the nature of Black Power is that there is no longer a place for the Jew in the scheme of civil rights activism. "With the coming on the scene of Black Nationalist extremists, who are so anti-Semitic and anti-Zionist, why should we Jews break our backs for them? Let's worry about ourselves?" so goes the argument.

I might add that some of our own Jewish scholars hold to this opinion. Rabbi Richard Rubenstein of the University of Pittsburgh Hillel Foundation is one of them. You may have heard very recently the statement by a Jewish spokesman that carrying a Torah on marches in Washington is a *Hillel Hashem.* I say that it was a *Kiddush Hashem*—not a desecration of the divine Name, but a sanctification of the divine Name. Wherever man battles for human rights and human dignity, the Torah should be in the forefront of that battle!

Much more balanced and sensible is the advice given in an analysis printed by the National Community Relations Advisory Council ("A Jewish View of the Crisis in Race Relations in America," July, 1967, pp. 18–19):

> Anti-Semitism breeds in ignorance, want, frustration and alienation; and the most effective counteractive approach to it is through the amelioration of those conditions. For the Jewish community to be deflected from its support and advocacy of equality for Negroes on the ground that Negroes are anti-Semitic would not only be self-defeating, exacerbating precisely what we mean to combat; but would be to repudiate a fundamental tenet of Jewish tradition—equal justice to all.

Reparations: Racism in Reverse? The fourth myth is that preferential treatment for the black is reverse racism. The so-called white liberal in America is in favor of giving the black everything coming to him, so he says, but he shouldn't be given more rights and more privileges than the white person, because that is racism in reverse.

I submit that this is a myth—one which we espouse because it masks our prejudice and creates a legitimate channel of obstructionism, and because it is an issue we would never raise if we considered the black truly our brother.

Rather than consider it as reverse racism, we should look upon preferential treatment as fair and due reparations for the bitterness of slavery and discrimination which white society inflicted upon the black man for three centuries.

There are many parallels for such treatment. If German payments to Jews individually and to Israel collectively is not an exact parallel, then surely our American G.I. Bill of Rights is a fair and useful analogy. This bill recognized the fact that while fighting for freedom abroad, young Americans were denied the educational and vocational opportunities they might have had. Our nation made this up to them by offering them an education at a cost lower than that available to those who did not serve in the military. Preferential treatment? Yes. Discrimination? Yes, of the best kind.

Let me offer an even more striking parallel. In Israel today educators are making giant strides forward in trying to integrate the majority Oriental communities, which are less educated and less affluent than the descendants of European Jews who are cultured professionals. To speed up this process of social integration—exactly the same as our ultimate goal in America—they offer free education to the Oriental Jews who hail from North Africa and Yemen, while the Ashkenazi Jews must pay tuition fees. Furthermore, the Sephardi Jew needs only a 70 in his entrance examination while an Ashkenazi Jew needs an 80 to gain admittance to the same secondary school.

Certainly this is preferential treatment. But Israel knows that this is the only way that the gap dividing the two groups can possibly be bridged in a reasonably short space of time.

As in many other areas, we American Jews should take a cue from our Israeli brothers. If we sincerely wish to integrate our society, we must do so even if it involves, on a temporary basis, a little extra help for the black than the white child or the white worker may receive. This is the kind of discrimination that redounds to the good of all concerned on a long-term basis.

Myths About Housing. The most destructive myth, in many

ways, is the myth—which is really a whole cluster of myths—dealing with the questions of fair housing and integrated neighborhoods.

This question is somewhat more involved, and has had more exposure than the others raised here. Let it suffice to say that it is simply not true that when blacks begin to buy homes in a new neighborhood that property values decline, that neighborhood standards deteriorate, that once a neighborhood is "broken" by one black purchaser, the whole area becomes a black ghetto.

These are all myths. Property values decline only when the majority of the residents in a community panic and sell their homes in a short period of time, creating a flooded market. Even then the value decline is temporary. There is no decline—on the contrary, there is an increase in property value, when a neighborhood integrates in a civilized, sensible, mature, and ordinary pattern. What happens to your homes, therefore, is up to you entirely, together with the other residents of the community.

There is no reason for a neighborhood to decline, nor is there reason for panic selling, just because people of different-colored skin begin to move in. More and more enlightened Jews are beginning to realize that closer contact with Christians and blacks provides a more diversified, enriching experience for their children. Our world is too small today to be concerned about isolating ourselves or our children in Jewish ghettos. We should welcome with open arms all Americans who want to reside in a community whose reputation can continue to be a proud and noble one for generations to come. This community can become in the years and decades to come, a showcase to all America of how Jews and blacks can live in harmony, brotherhood and peace.

The answer to this myth is the same as to the others. The deterioration of a neighborhood comes about not by the low standards of any black man, but by the racism and discrimination and intolerance of the white man—including the white Jew. If this community's Jews decide that it will stay a desirable and respectable neighborhood, then it will stay a desirable and respectable neighborhood, and nothing anybody of another color or another religion does can change that decision.

What of Tomorrow? What of the future? Have we already marched too far on the path of bigotry and hatred to turn back? The age-old Jewish doctrine of *Teshuva* tells us that it is never too late to turn back.

The future of America, as the future of black-Jewish relations, lies in the hands of the alert, informed members of the community. It is up to us whether we shall continue on the path towards two societies—separate and unequal, or whether man can finally demonstrate his essential humanity and live together as brothers in a world of peace and cooperation.

The matter was put succinctly by the editorial writer in *The New York Times,* March 3, 1968: "The commission's report is sure to mark a major turning point in the history of this nation. If Congress and the public respond affirmatively to its recommendations—as they should and must—the American people will move decisively toward that one nation of free men enjoying domestic tranquillity that the founders of this nation envisaged. If they turn away in anger, in false racial pride, and in selfish complacency, then Americans will move equally decisively to become two nations, divided by fear. Every citizen, by his actions and inactions in the days to come, will share in the making of that fateful choice."

As happens so often, our own Talmud anticipated the wisdom of the latest thinkers. The rabbis expressed essentially the same idea when they said: "Whoever is able to protest against the transgression of his city or indeed the misdeeds of all mankind, and fails to do so, becomes accountable for their sins." (Shabbat 54b.)

In another insightful passage, the Jerusalem Talmud advises: "The world exists by reason of three things: truth, justice and peace. The three are in reality one, for when justice is done, truth prevails and peace is established." (Jer. Taanit 4:2 on Avot 1:18.)

13
Martin Luther King—
Two Eulogies

1

A DEEP SENSE OF GLOOM SPREAD LIKE A THICK CLOUD OVER our nation last night as we were shocked by the tragic news of the brutal assassination of the Rev. Martin Luther King, Jr.

Our country has lost one of its greatest sons, certainly one of the most distinguished spiritual leaders our nation has ever known. As Jews we mourn a friend of our people, a sincere and true opponent of anti-Semitism, a staunch ally of the State of Israel, and a man whose spiritual qualities marked him as a modern-day prophet.

During the ceremony at which I was ordained as a rabbi, Dr. King received the honorary degree of Doctor of Divinity from the Jewish Theological Seminary. Just ten days ago, he spoke to the convention of the Rabbinical Assembly, and reaffirmed this abiding friendship with our people. He has

Delivered Friday night, April 5, 1968.

been particularly a close friend of Conservative Judaism, since one of his chief allies in the Jewish community had been Rabbi Abraham Joshua Heschel, professor at the Seminary. Dr. King has spoken out against the oppression of Soviet Jewry, and in favor of every cause dear to our people. Thus our loss is double—as Americans and as Jews.

It is the Sabbath, and we are forbidden to mourn. Rather than lament this tragic, senseless, and needless act of violence, let us see what we can learn from it, and what constructive actions can flow from it.

Primary in our minds should be the question, what was Martin Luther King trying to do for America? Secondly, how can we continue his work in a way that will lend honor to this saintly memory?

Martin Luther King was not a Negro leader. He was an American leader. He was our leader. He contributed as much to our lives as he did to the blacks. His message to us was the message of Judaism as well as of Christianity, as well as of the American dream. In that sense, his life and his work helped us to be better Jews.

What Dr. King wanted for America was justice—the same thing the biblical prophets wanted. He wanted America to live up to its highest ideals and to fulfill its best promise. He enunciated these ideals in the summer of 1963 in his famous address in the shadow of the Lincoln Memorial, during the massive march on Washington: "Even though we face the difficulties of today and tomorrow, I still have a dream. I have a dream that one day this nation will rise up and live out the true meaning of its creed: 'We hold these truths to be self-evident, that all men are created equal.'"

His dream was spelled out more clearly in the moving speech he delivered on December 10, 1964, when he became the third Negro in history to receive the Nobel Prize for Peace:

"I refuse to accept the idea that man is mere flotsam and jetsam in the river of life which surrounds him. I refuse to accept the view that mankind is so tragically bound to the starless midnight of racism and war that the bright daybreak of peace and brotherhood can never become a reality.

"I refuse to accept the cynical notion that nation after nation must spiral down a militaristic stairway into the hell of thermonuclear destruction. I believe that unarmed truth and unconditional love will have the final word in reality. This is why right, temporarily defeated, is stronger than evil triumphant."

Our task in the days ahead is to see to it that we do our share in continuing the sacred task assigned to America by this great spiritual dreamer—that man fulfill his divinely given potential, and that American society be a just one.

Today the black people are still trapped in their ghettos, in their abject poverty, and in their rut of despair, frustration and deprivation. White America has not seen fit to share its bounty with this minority of nineteen million Americans.

Only weeks ago we were informed by the Kerner Commission that the violence that took place in this country last summer was a result not of Communist conspiracy but of white racism and of the intolerable conditions in the urban ghettos.

The Riots Report told us that we are moving toward two societies, one white, one black, separate and unequal. We have a veritable war going on in our country. The end of this war can be brought about only through the removal of the conditions of poverty and discrimination, and of the physical suppression on the part of our governments and our police forces.

We are in a domestic war in which we, the whites, are the guilty, the aggressors. We must fight this war with love, compassion, and deeds of righteousness. The solution to the urban crisis, the civil rights problem, and the poverty web that surrounds the black man, in the words of the Kerner Report, "will require a commitment to national action—compassionate, massive and sustained, backed by the resources of the most powerful and the richest nation on this earth. From every American it will require new attitudes, new understanding, and above all, new will."

Martin Luther King was a casualty of this war between the races. His tragic death must show us how futile it is to continue the battle between white and black. Our share in ending this war will be to do something positive about ameliorating the lot of the impoverished, alienated blacks among us.

I am happy to report to you, if you have not heard already, two decisions taken by your Board of Directors sitting in session last evening, even as this act of violence against Dr. King was taking place.

First, our Temple will sponsor, along with several other churches and civic groups on the Main Line, a nonprofit housing corporation, which will help bring to this lily-white suburb families who want to get out of the ghetto but might not be able to afford to do so otherwise.

Second, we have approved a plan to permit a hundred young Girl Scouts from a poverty area in North Philadelphia, mostly black, to have a two-week day-camp program on our camp grounds from August 19 to 29.

These are small steps, but they are a beginning. We hope to do more in the near future. We ask that each and every member of our congregation accept these projects with enthusiasm and with maturity. We ask that our subconscious prejudices and senseless fears be superseded by our sense of decency and justice, and that our moral obligation be seen as primary in any issue of social justice that comes before this congregation.

The black militants have been strengthened, and the moderates have been weakened, by last night's assassination. If we want to prove to the black man that what happened last night was *not* approved, but on the contrary *condemned*, by white Americans, then we must demonstrate our feelings with *action*. We must balance this act of violence with acts of love and justice. Otherwise the black man will be reinforced in his view that white America refuses to accept him as an equal member of society.

One of the ironies of Dr. King's death is its occurrence one week before Passover. On this Festival of Freedom we remember all those people throughout the world who are denied full freedom and equality. In his own words, spoken just before his death, Dr. King said that he was not afraid to go to Memphis and face whatever was in store for him, because he had seen the Promised Land. Like Moses, he sensed that he would not ever himself be privileged to live to see the day when complete independence and security for his people was achieved. But heroically he continued to march towards that Promised Land, unafraid, with his high purpose pushing him forward.

We take comfort in the fact that we know there will be a Joshua to complete the job he did. Dr. King's cause was too strong and too important and too sacred to be stopped by the irrational act of one racist. And when that Day of Deliverance finally comes to the black man in America, all of us will remember the valiant role played by the black minister from Atlanta who gave his life for America.

2*

Jews of this community and all through America bow their head in grief at the loss of America's foremost spiritual leader.

Martin Luther King was an enemy of prejudice and discrimination against all minorities in America—Negroes, Jews, Indians, and others.

He fought anti-Semitism, as he fought racism. He spoke out against the suppression of the Jewish community in the Soviet Union, and for the right of the Jewish people in Israel to live at peace in their own state.

He was a friend and a staunch ally of every cause of justice and righteousness, and was therefore beloved of all America.

I am a better Jew because Martin Luther King lived; a better American and a better human being. I take comfort only in the words he uttered recently, when he reminded us that what is important is not the length of one's life, but the quality of one's life. Can anyone leave this service today and worry about how long he will live? Can anyone leave this service today and *not* be concerned about the quality of his life today and tomorrow?

I think that if Martin Luther King had been asked last

*Delivered at interfaith services, Sunday, April 7, 1968, at Villanova University and later the same day at Wayne Presbyterian Church.

Thursday morning if he would sacrifice his life on the condition that throughout America the following Sunday, Jews and Christians, white man and black man, would all gather in their churches and synagogues and pray together as one united country, for peace, for nonviolence, and for justice in our society—his answer would have been *yes*. In that sense his martyrdom can have a constructive purpose if each of us leaves here today committed to the notion that America will be a better place because he lived.

It is an ironic coincidence that the Reverend King lost his life in this holiday season. This coming Friday night, Jews will reread the Passover story in their homes, and they will acknowledge that the Moses of today was Dr. Martin Luther King. Although he may not have reached the Promised Land, some Joshua somewhere will bring his people to shores of freedom and equality.

The title of Dr. King's last book is *Where Do We Go from Here—Chaos or Community?* Today we have community and fellowship. We must all vow to see that the answer to Martin Luther King's question is "Community," and not "Chaos."

King is dead. Long live King!

14

Bobby Kennedy and the Skull of Uncle Sam

THE WORLD IS A DARKER PLACE TODAY THAN IT WAS A WEEK ago. The smiling face of America has become a frown. The bright optimism of our youth is obscured by disillusionment and grief. The excitement of the coming presidential election has now turned to a period of mourning as the nation prepares for yet another national funeral.

Our newspapers and television sets bring us nothing but more and more details of a bloody national tragedy—the second in two months. We relive the nightmare of November, 1963, as we watch a Kennedy widow and orphaned children grieve over their fallen husband and father. Another shattering blow strikes our hearts as we watch bereaved parents whose third son died by violence. America and the world mourn a valiant son, a talented leader, a devoted citizen, an undaunted warrior for the principles and ideals of our country.

Many somber and frightening questions enter our minds.

Delivered Friday night, June 7, 1968.

When will it all end? How many times will we have to raise our hopes, create an idol, pin our dreams on a youthful, courageous leader and see him cut off in his prime? When will the violence in the world finally put an end to the grief and unbearable horror and shock of the good people of all nations of the world? Where will it strike next? Who will be the next victim of the capricious mistress of hate, prejudice, and blind vengeance?

Perhaps the most important question which we must face up to at such a tragic hour in our national history, is this: Who is truly responsible for the death of Senator Robert F. Kennedy? Who killed our young, charismatic, dynamic spokesman for social justice and human dignity?

The answer is not a simple one. Many people helped kill him. Many forces, many passions, many twisted, narrow minds contributed to his undoing.

First of all, we must say that Robert Kennedy died because he was caught in the cross-fire of the Six Day War. He died because he took a side in the conflict between Arab and Jew, between Communist and Zionist. One of the battlefields on which he can be numbered as a casualty is the battlefield of the war against the Jew and against the Jewish state.

Only a coward stands on the sidelines when a fierce battle for human rights is taking place. Robert Kennedy was anything but a coward.

A little over a month ago (April 29, 1968) he made the following statement about the Middle-East situation:

> . . . those who again would embroil the Middle-East in war must not be encouraged. If Israel's most antagonistic neighbors are rearmed by others who would stir further hatred in that troubled part of the world, then Israel should have equivalent military strength. A balance of forces is necessary to dissuade those who promote armed aggression. To that end, the United States should stand ready to sell Israel jet aircraft and the other arms she needs effectively to defend herself from attack, and thereby lower its probability.

And so we must say that one of the things that killed Robert Kennedy is hatred of one Semitic people for another, the hatred of brothers.

The ancient sage Hillel made a wise observation once as he was gazing upon a skull floating on the surface of the water (Pirke Avot 2:7). He stared down and said to the skull, "Because you drowned others, they have drowned you. And, at the last, they that drowned you shall themselves be drowned."

What Hillel was saying was that there is an inevitable chain of responsibility that redounds always to its origin. One act of insanity begets another. Violence, and the passive acquiescence in witnessing violence, breeds another act of violence. When one drowns another person, that person is in turn drowned.

Hindsight cannot prevent past mistakes, but it may prevent future ones. One wonders what would have happened if the United States had met its commitments to Israel last June swiftly and without equivocation. Would there have been a War of Six Days had our government called Nasser's bluff and sent its ships through the Straits of Tiran June 4? If they had, there might not have been a war. And had there not been a war, Robert Kennedy might be alive today. Had the United States not been "neutral in word, thought and deed," but stood up quickly for justice and equity, then it might not have lost one of its best leaders.

Because you drowned someone else, you in turn will be drowned.

Today's world is too small to think that we can stand idly by and watch evil be perpetrated in a far distant corner of the world. Especially when the issues of right and wrong are as clear as they were last May, 1967, in the Arab-Israel crisis.

If we stand idly by the blood of our neighbor, we not only violate a sacred command of the Torah (Leviticus 19:16), but we must ultimately pay a price for our apathy and our selfishness.

Second of all, Robert Kennedy was caught in the crossfire of the violent spirit of this decade. It is not impossible that future historians will look back upon the decade of the 1960s as "the violent decade." We started with the violent destruction of the Republic of Vietnam, and we continue with the violent destruction of our cities, and we end with the violent death of our nation's outstanding leaders. One good drowning deserves another.

We teach our youth to destroy cities and villages in a small Southeast Asian nation, and they come home and destroy their own cities. We teach people that power talks loudest, that bombs and guns determine causes, that strength is more important than quiet negotiation, that military attacks speak louder than diplomatic offensives, and they learn their lessons well.

I am not opposed to defending a small beleaguered nation from outside attack. I was never opposed to our sending troops to South Vietnam. But I do oppose that type of militaristic thinking that says the way to protect South Vietnam is by destroying it. I think more people in this country oppose the way the Vietnam war is being conducted than they do the fact that we took sides in the war and gave of our effort and means to further a peaceful outcome.

The historian Arthur Schlesinger said two days ago that this nation has become "a violent people with a violent history, and the instinct for violence has seeped into the bloodstream of our national life." He concluded that "we are today the most frightening people on this planet." Certainly, we are living in the most frightening decade of this century. And it may just be because we tried to frighten other peoples with our power that we are now beginning to suffer from fear of ourselves and from a debilitating sense of fright and gloom.

The third force that killed Robert Kennedy is a national lethargy that culminates in a do-nothing Congress. A healthy, dynamic and progressive nation must think creatively and act courageously. Its legislators and political spokesmen must forge a program of legal action that leads the country forward, not backward.

Our nation and our Congress helped kill Senator Kennedy by avoiding its social responsibilities. It should have passed laws that would bring a speedy end to poverty, discrimination, ignorance and disease. It should have provided better education and mental health facilities. It should not have cut back funds for the War on Poverty. And perhaps most important in this instance, it should have passed an adequate gun-control bill.

Apparently the pressure of the National Rifle Association, and other gun lobbyists, and sporting goods stores, was deemed more important than the lives of Medgar Evers and President John F. Kennedy, and Martin Luther King, and now Senator Robert F. Kennedy.

Yes, all of these forces are responsible for, and helped to bring about, the death of Senator Kennedy.

Arab hatred for Israel, Communist hatred for Jews, American violence abroad and at home, Congressional and national apathy—all of these are a part of it. But you and I are also a part. We live in this violent decade, and as long as we go about our daily business without doing something positive to stop the violence, and the hatred, and the apathy, and the smug complacency, then we too have a share. Because we watched others drown, we too must drown in our tears for Robert Kennedy.

Today God is asking us to accept the responsibility for all our brothers, Americans and others. We must not answer, with Cain, "Are we our brothers' keepers?" Because if we do, then God will say to us what He said then: "The voice of your brother's blood is crying to Me from the ground."

The one hope for our country and our world for the 1970s is that the world will finally accept the idea of world law. If the United Nations becomes an organization with power and respect and the ability to act in emergencies; if it becomes a court of justice instead of an arena for power politics; then there will be peace in the Middle East, and in Asia, and in Europe and in the cities of America. And then, hopefully, we will not have to watch our leaders be sacrificed on the altar of violence.

Are we some primitive tribe of pagan warriors who must sacrifice one of its leaders each time the god of violence demands to be placated, before a just law can be accepted by our politicians?

What does it take for us to have respect for social justice more than for political pressures? What does it take for the nations of the world to accept the rule of world law and avoid daily conflicts across borders of nations all over the globe?

Rabbi Hanina says (Pirke Avot 3:2) "Pray for the welfare of the government, of those who have the power to rule, because were it not for respect for law, each man would swallow his brother alive."

Until the idea of world law is recognized, we will continue to devour our brothers, our neighbors, and our leaders.

When the rule of law and justice is recognized in the world, then conflicts between Arabs and Israel, between Communists and America, between East and West will finally cease. And if that happens, violence at home will have a chance to end, and we might be able to live in a world of tranquility and serenity and peace.

Meanwhile, until such a concept is accepted, we will have to be prepared to lose more talented, dedicated, vigorous, and youthful leaders like Robert Kennedy. We pray that his sacred memory will spur us on that much faster to achieve peace at home and abroad.

Yehi zikhro baruch!

May his memory be for a blessing!

15

When Consensus Is Blasphemy

DANGEROUS AND ILL-FOREBODING WINDS HAVE BEEN BLOWING across our nation of late, buffeting the very fabric of our corporate and individual American life. Threats to the sanctity of man and to the dignity of individuals are looming large on the horizon of religious, governmental, and political arenas. They must be halted by carefully defining their danger, and dismantling their power of locomotion.

Some of these are old and persistent, some relatively recent. I refer to the polluted atmosphere in our cities and towns which is threatening to stifle and smother the right of each individual to his own opinion and to express that opinion openly.

We don't have, to be sure, heresy trials or public lynching parties, as in the Middle Ages. But the more sophisticated and subtle heirs of these primitive vestiges of yesterday are nonetheless fraught with the greatest danger to American life.

Let me furnish several examples of this ugly phenomenon, beginning with the oldest. While I am a religionist and

---

Delivered Rosh Hashana night, October 4, 1967.

deeply committed to the religious life, it must be said that religion, being a conserving force in life, can be called the first sinner in the area of stifling individual opinion. Much to the credit of Judaism, its own record is remarkably free of this moral, intellectual, and religious iniquity. It is its daughter religion, Christianity, a religion for which all of us must have the highest respect generally, which bears the greatest burden of guilt for crushing free thought. Among many proud pages in Christian history, this is a shameful one.

Much to our deepest regret, in large segments of Christianity this desire for uniformity of thought and opinion still persists. It is a staple of the Catholic doctrinal diet, although less and less so. It remains a cardinal principle in many Christian circles that the only path to God is through Jesus and the church. We certainly have no right to dissuade any Christian from espousing his own faith, including his belief in Jesus and the authority of the Church. What we do and must resent and be on guard against is the claim that by being Jews we stubbornly forfeit our right to final salvation, in whosoever's definition of salvation we live. Christianity by and large still accepts the premise that either Jesus is for everybody or he is for nobody.

Christianity in both its Protestant and Roman Catholic forms still falls prey to that moral self-righteousness that denies a place in God's sun to non-Christians. The whole whirl of ecumenical activity since Pope John XXIII convened the Second Vatican Council some six years ago has been an effort to bring together the two separated branches of Christianity. Judaism as a whole has been largely ignored in the effort to achieve religious brotherhood. The attempt has been to diminish the number and form of the differences between the various faiths, rather than to accept them as they are. Not open-minded acceptance is the goal, but compromise and moving together—give and take, for the ultimate goal, perhaps never achievable altogether, of total reunion. This type of ecumenism finds no room in its narrowly defined quarters for the total outsider—the one who failed to acknowledge the first coming of the "Messiah."

Christianity is guilty of other breaches of the right to

freedom of expression and thought. It has in its Episcopalian form attempted to defrock and demote one of its great intellectual spirits, Bishop James A. Pike of the Archdiocese of California, and has forced him into partial retreat. In its Roman Catholic manifestation, it has successfully limited the right of its clerics to preach civil rights, to take part in social action programs, and to otherwise fulfill the dictates of their conscience.

Despite the fact that Judaism has never had its own heresy trials or mind-shutting activities, some of its secular Jewish leaders have been guilty of late of the same sin in a different sphere. Some months ago the Jewish world was shocked to learn that the talented and dedicated editor of Britain's Zionist journal, *The Jewish Observer and Middle East Review*, Mr. Jon Kimche, was banished from office for telling the truth about unemployment in Israel. We are not speaking of military security of nationals in the State of Israel, but the right of an intellectual to print the news and its interpretation as he sees fit. After pressure was brought to bear upon the British Zionist Federation by the authorities in the Israeli government, Mr. Kimche was forced to muzzle his forthright voice. It was not prudent to have the world know the truth about some of Israel's current economic problems. It might harm the UJA image of a healthy young nation where all people found employment and a livable wage. So a brave and honorable intellectual was sacrificed on the altar of political power struggles and diplomatic manipulation.

In a larger sense, this is the same type of sin as stifling freedom of speech in religion—except that it is in politics. Kimche committed political heresy, and was lynched for it.

Also within recent months we were treated to the news that that octopus-like arm of our government, the C.I.A., was paying the salary of some of the organizations and associations whose responsibility is to independently work out their own scheme of ideas and ideologies. Most people agree that these groups were, thank goodness, not adversely affected in this case by their newly gained status of being "bought" by the C.I.A. But that is only a case of a bomb whose fortune it was not to explode. The danger, though often unknown and never actualized, still existed. Our concern can be no less to prevent another such episode whose capability for destruction might be more than potential.

By far the act of muzzling potentially most fraught with danger for the people of this country is the demand made by the present administration for what it euphemistically refers to as "consensus."

To the purveyors of the idea of uniformity of thought, anyone who walks his own political or ideological path in the United States is willfully turning his back on the needs of political health and military security of our nation. They are giving aid and comfort to the enemy.

According to our distinguished Secretary of State, those who dissent publicly from the national foreign policy are helping to prolong the war they decry. The implications are obvious—dissent means national heresy. It is seditious and dangerous, and spells disloyalty to our President, and is not the mark of an enlightened citizen.

After the military hero of our Vietnam effort expressed his views before the Congress earlier this year, Senator Fulbright, whose opinion I do not always respect, said wisely that after Westmoreland's speech it is doubtful whether anyone "will have the courage to say anything else about the war." (*Time*, May 12, 1967, p. 23.)

We begin to ask ourselves how far are we really from those Communist bloc countries whose reputation stands on brainwashing and thought-control techniques. Were it not for the safeguards of our system of law, who knows but that the next step might be to subject our own citizens to the kind of state heresy trials that regularly take place behind the Iron Curtain. Even the intellectuals in the Soviet satellites are beginning to recognize the heavy burden of what they call "the chains of October"—the big-brotherly censorship exercised by the Communist nations on their writers and thinkers, since the October revolution of 1917. The half-century celebration we now witness should present the starkest evidence of the dangers inherent in a system where dissent is coupled with disloyalty and the omnipresent monster of consensus eats away at the vital juices of national life.

The Message of Judaism. In the midst of this atmosphere of intellectual pollution, the Holy Days come to us to blow fresh winds of clarity and vision and the prophetic call to freedom from the shackles of "ecumenism" and heresy and consensus into our spiritual lives.

Rosh Hashana speaks to us with a most important message as we enter the year 5728. The theme of these ten Days of Awe is that there is one King in the world—the Lord our God. And that loyalty to Him is supreme and exclusive. It must not be sacrificed to lesser loyalties of national states or parochial churches or any political forces. God's kingship signals a return to the life of fulfillment for the mind and spirit of His divinely made creatures. It tells us that the greatest blasphemy against the King of Kings is to deny the individuality of each human being and his inalienable right to the fullest possible expression of his God-given uniqueness.

For the Jew there is only one ultimate loyalty—to God Himself, and to the divine spark implanted within man, his own conscience. No rules or laws of churchmen or state loom as large within the scheme of things as this ultimate loyalty. This is clearly what is meant by the phrase we repeat again and again during this season, that God alone is King.

For the Jew the mind is God's greatest gift. It is what distinguishes us from the animal kingdom. There is consensus in the animal world. There, there exists no blasphemy, no heresy, no dissent. But God created us for other purposes.

Says the Talmud, "Just as no two human beings look alike, so no two of them think alike." This is a statement uttered by rabbis who lived in an age when dogmatism reigned and when history had not yet known of the First Amendment and its far-reaching effect on human conduct. It preceded American freedom by over a millennium, and furthermore it encouraged a people to be in every way human beings who fulfilled God's highest dreams for man.

As a people whose ancient tradition demands the completely unfettered play of the human mind, we Jews have the responsibility to call to task those who violate God's uncompromising mandate for human freedom.

When we celebrate God's kingship, we pay homage to our

Creator who made us each as a unique creation. Only He could create the infinite variety of people and nations that populate this universe, yet never duplicate His divine pattern.

Our ancestors were the first to see this pattern in God's creation, and the first to declare its glory. Variety of opinion and divergence of interpretation—dissent if you like, are not concepts to be tolerated in our tradition. They are required! Life is not full or complete without them. Whoever thinks he can require consensus in thought or opinion, or in the expression thereof, thinks he can make man over in his own image instead of in God's, that he can improve on creation, and write his own Torah. He challenges God's very authority as Supreme Being. Such a person is the blasphemer and the heretic, not those whose minds he would lock up and shape as with clay for his own purposes.

Has Jewish teaching always been consistent with the doctrine that man's mind can be loyal only to God and one's own conscience? Yes, it has. Whoever wants to find examples of so-called blasphemy and heresy and dissent can find it scattered throughout the warp and woof of the sacred Scriptures. No book or books is more filled with a respect for difference of opinion. The Bible is the product of the muses of the most contrasting figures who ever marched across the stage of history. Pietist and heretic, sage and poet, priest and prophet, rationalist and mystic are all given their due respect. No other literature could abide an Abraham who dared challenge God's judgments, or a Job who questioned the very justice of the universe. No other writing could show more sympathy to pagan sailors than to a Hebrew prophet—one Jonah the son of Amittai. No other Scripture could praise so highly and warmly a Moabitess named Ruth, whose non-Jewish background did not prevent her from becoming the ancestor of King David.

The remarkable open-mindedness of the biblical tradition made it impossible for later Jewish tradition to be any less tolerant and worldly or to require any the less a multiplicity of opinions and views. Not a page of the Talmud is devoid of controversy and argument. Yet we are told that both sides of the question have legitimacy, and that "Both these and these are the words of the living God." Historians point out that the most creative periods of Jewish history were those during which a host of sects proliferated throughout the Jewish world. There was no need for ecumenism to make all the schools of thought into one official catechismal mold. When Maimonides defied tradition by formulating thirteen principles of the faith, his theological formulation was treated as a single effort added to the mass of opinions and views expressed by the hundreds of thinkers who preceded him and followed his own contribution. When the same medieval thinker declared those who believe in anthropomorphisms to be heretical, he was roundly chided by a senior contemporary for denying another man the right to his own thoughts and definitions. No condemnation or censure of any type is to be offered to any of God's creatures who sincerely offers the best product of his own mind.

I dare anyone to offer me the Jewish view of any number of significant theological concepts important in Jewish thought: Messiah, resurrection, revelation, the Divinity, life after death, etc. There is no Jewish view of these concepts—there are Jewish views, a host of them, any one of which may be selected as valid and legitimate for any Jew to espouse as his own. Professor Heschel has written a seven-hundred-page book trying to summarize all the Jewish opinions about the definition of Divine Revelation.

For Judaism, freedom of thought extends even to the precincts of organized religion. We never missionized because we have always been willing to accept any man's path to God, if it were sincere and humane. Christianity and Islam in the eyes of Judaism are both legitimate vehicles to bring man closer to God.

"I call Heaven and earth to witness," says the midrash, "that whether one be gentile or Jew, man or woman, slave or free man, the divine spirit rests on each in accordance with his *deeds!* (Yalkut Shimoni on Judges, Sec. 42.)

Not in accordance with his ideas, his thoughts, his political or religious loyalties, nor in accordance with his views on foreign policy—but in accordance with the ethical standards he lives by and acts by. Not in accordance with his acceptance of this Messiah or that Messiah, not in accordance with what party line he follows, and not in accordance with his church affiliation or social standing, but in accordance with his deeds alone.

By recognizing the sovereignty of God, we affirm the sovereignty of each individual creature of God to the dictates of his own conscience, and commit ourselves to the judgment of God alone. No court of human opinion can force us to deny God's Kingship by accepting a view or a position that is not rationally palatable to us.

By demanding a rigorous adherence to the laws of free expression, we become better Jews and better Americans. Our Founding Fathers captured the Jewish view of things when they wrote that all men are endowed by their Creator with certain inalienable rights. One of these inalienable rights is to live a life of intellectual freedom. Noam Chomsky pointed out that it is the responsibility of intellectuals to demand the truth. He was expressing a view held by his American and Jewish traditions, one that must ultimately prevail in this country if we are to be true to ourselves and our dual heritage. Theodore Sorenson wrote that "The greater danger to this country over the long run lies not in debate or dissent but in placing any topic, policy, man or institution beyond the realm of criticism." (*Saturday Review*, April 2, 1966, p. 26.)

Freedom of thought and freedom of the mind is one of the contributions of Judaism to the world that is eternally relevant, but particularly so in our time. It is merely a part of a huge treasure of wisdom and philosophy and ideas that has untold potential for improving the quality of our personal and corporate lives both as Jews and as Americans. When we let our tradition be exposed by studying it and learning from it, we do a great service to this nation, as well as to ourselves. As the heirs of a millennia-old tradition, it is our right and solemn duty to share our precious mine of wisdom with those around us. We can only do that if we ourselves earn the right of possession of this treasury. We can earn that right only by seeking to find out what the tradition has to offer us. When we do that, and when we take our Jewish heritage with the seriousness it demands and deserves of us, there is no limit to the possible qualitative results.

Let this year be one in which all God's children are students of the Torah, and help to bring His kingdom on earth closer to reality. Amen.

16

On Not Surrendering One's Conscience to the State

TWO WEEKS AGO I INVITED TO THIS PULPIT A YOUNG JEWISH professor from Haverford College, who had three days before turned in his draft card. Since that time I have heard that some people intentionally stayed away that night.

Although I cannot be sure, I would venture to say that there were two general reasons for this intentional absenteeism. One was a form of personal protest to the individual. People of this opinion may have felt that by not coming they were protesting the action of draft-card burning. The other possible reason that occurred to me, and that was expressed to me through third parties, was that those who stayed away were not only protesting the action of the professor but his presence in the sacred precincts of the synagogue and its pulpit.

Regarding the first motivation, I must grant the right of any individual to come or not to attend services, as he sees

Delivered Friday night, Hol Ha-Moed Pesach, April 19, 1968. Excerpts were published in *Conservative Judaism*, Vol. 22, No. 4, Summer, 1968.

fit. Staying away is the legitimate exercise of one's rights in a synagogue with which he freely associates. On the second count I feel that those who would divorce religion and the synagogue from current political and social issues have a parochial view of things, and are unaware of Judaism's unique approach of wedding everything religious with everything in the individual and corporate lives of its adherents. There is not and can be no bifurcation in Judaism between religion and life, religion and the world, religion and society, religion and nationalism.

On this same count, it is wise to point out that our tradition, beginning with the biblical prophets, demands that religious leaders exercise the right of free speech, and use their platform to have others exercise that same right. Freedom of the pulpit, in that sense, is very similar to academic freedom. Such a policy demands that as long as a rabbi is the elected spiritual leader of a congregation in Israel he shall be free to espouse any doctrine, advocate any program, and promote any view that he feels is morally sound and ethically supportable. His only censor is his own interpretation of the will of God.

When a rabbi invites a guest to his pulpit, it does not necessarily mean that the rabbi agrees with everything the guest may say. It does mean that the rabbi feels that such an outside speaker has something valuable to add to the store of information and the arena of ideas in his congregation. The right to have a guest occupy the pulpit, or speak after services, is a corollary of the right to speak freely himself, to express his own convictions on current issues.

But the real question at hand, it seems to me, is not one of freedom of the pulpit, or the association of religion and politics—although these are very significant issues in their own right. The essential question is: "What should be our attitude towards those who resist the draft?" The view of those who purposely stayed away two weeks ago seems to be that such people should not have our sympathy nor our respect. Perhaps some might even say they are disloyal or unpatriotic.

This is the view that I most seriously challenge at this time.

I think it was a mistake for people to shun a speaker who holds views contrary to those of our government, even though it is their right to do so. I think it is a mistake to look upon draft resisters as people whose patriotism is to be called into question, or whose moral fiber is weak, or whose bravery is to be challenged.

To the contrary. These are people who have earnest convictions on an issue that most Americans have not taken the time or effort to delve into as deeply as they should. These are people who find it repugnant to remain quiet at a time they feel demands vigorous protest and active opposition.

We are not debating the issues of the war. Whether we are doves or hawks, we must defend the right of every individual to follow the dictates of his conscience. The point is that however *we* feel, draft resisters feel convinced that this nation is involved in a war that is both immoral and illegal. In the conflict between their nation and their conscience (or their God), they choose their conscience.

Some among us would freely permit protest of the war in legal fashion, but object to the step over the line of legality which changes their status from protesters to resisters.

If one truly opposes a major military action of his government on moral grounds, how shall he act? Shall he say, with Stephen Decatur, "My country, right or wrong"? Shall he participate, in whatever small or large way, in the implementation of such policies and actions which he considers to be immoral? Shall he let himself be drafted, and fight against people he knows in his heart are not his enemies nor those of his state?

Just how far should a person go in following the mandates of his government? Where is the line that we draw which says, "Here and no farther"? Is it when we are told to build gas chambers? Or is it also when we are told to commit untold quantities of our national resources and manpower in a conflict that we see as one which is leading our nation on an immoral path? What would be our verdict if we had judged the Eichmann case? Eichmann claimed that his first and only loyalty and duty was to his government. Should all young Americans follow Eichmann's example? It does not matter that the crimes may be thought to be quantitatively or qualitatively different. Our military establishment is killing thousands of Vietnamese and losing thousands of our own soldiers. If a person feels that this is being carried out without adequate justification, how should he act?

The Solicitor General of the United States made a statement three days ago which was radical in its implications. He clearly differentiated between one's legal rights and his moral rights. Civil disobedience is clearly not a legal right, and anyone who commits acts of civil disobedience must be punished by the law. Draft resisters are all men who are prepared to face the consequences of their acts, even if it means facing incarceration. Dr. Spock even stated publicly that he thought the government had a duty to prosecute him for his action.

But Mr. Griswold, the chief legal officer of the United States government, declared unequivocally on Tuesday that one has the moral right to commit acts of civil disobedience. In doing so he acknowledges the fact that the law may not always coincide with the moral dictates and ethical conscience of each citizen. Naturally, a sovereign state cannot permit its citizens to violate the law with impunity.

What we are concerned about is not the government's attitude, which by nature must carry out the demands of the law. What we are concerned about are our own attitudes. How should we view such purveyors of civil disobediance? Are we automatons and bureaucrats who automatically condemn all violations of the law? Or should our concern be with the moral aspect of the problem, not with the legal one? Certainly, it seems to me, that as Jews and as members of a synagogue, whatever our views on any specific political issue may be, we must vigorously support the moral right of each individual to follow the dictates of his conscience, even when they diverge from the statutes of our nation.

Not only should we support his right to dissent, but it is the further duty of the synagogue to give such a man an opportunity to express and debate his views publicly, and to hear him out. This is particularly true when his moral convictions are based on Jewish tradition, as was the case with the Haverford professor.

Some American Jews are afraid to have their co-religionists speak out on the Vietnam issue and participate in the draft resistance movement, lest all American Jews become implicated. By the same token, some members of our congregation may have the feeling that when the rabbi, or someone speaking from his pulpit, advocates policies that are contrary to those of the United States government, all of the congregation will be implicated and will in some way suffer for this association.

Here, too, I must disagree. No rabbi, and no clergyman, speaks for anyone but himself and his tradition. If no clergyman could make any statement publicly unless it was approved by the majority of his constituents, we would be in a sorry state of affairs.

Furthermore, I think it high time that American Jews begin to take a stand on issues without being afraid of what the gentiles will say. Where is our self-respect? After twenty centuries of being dissenters in a world of gentiles, shall we now, in America, of all places, deny our historical position of speaking our minds freely and without fear? Of living according to rules and norms that others may consider strange or different? A Jew who is a proud Jew will not be ashamed when his rabbi expresses an opinion that may not be popular in the community at large. And he will not be embarrassed or defensive.

Tonight is the Festival of Pesach, and the eternal message of this holiday rings out with greater clarity and force than it ever has. Freedom is something that cannot be achieved by sitting by. To the contrary, it must be fought for constantly, and judiciously preserved by its adherents. The Hagaddah tells us that "this year we are slaves," and offers the hope that next year we will be free men. Perhaps one of the ways we in America are slaves is that we have been enchained by government propaganda, and bound up by purveyors of superpatriotism. We will be truly free men only when we follow the dictates of conscience even before those of the authorities.

To Jews, who have lived in every country of the world for over twenty centuries, there has only been one supreme loyalty: to the King of Kings, never to flesh and blood. The prophets would never have tolerated the superpatriotism that says that the government's way is the only way.

In his recent book, Senator Edward Kennedy wrote, "I, for one, do not accept the belief that a man owes nothing to his country. But I also reject the notion that we should run roughshod over the conscience of our citizens. . . ."

That about sums it up. We must never impugn the loyalty of any of our citizens who find their obligations to God conflicting with their obligations to the state. We must recognize always that there is a loyalty even higher than that of the state—call it God, call it conscience, whatever you will—but never let us lose that highest loyalty, because it is that which ultimately makes us human.

17

What Can a Congregation Expect from Its Rabbi?

THIS SACRED HOUR OF KOL NIDRE IS A TIME TO EXAMINE THE quality of our relationships. A time to heal, to mend, to cement friendships and associations.

The best kind of friendship is one built upon a foundation of mutual understanding, of sincerity, and yet of honesty and candor. Only if two people understand one another can they be true friends. A sound relationship is one in which the two parties have explored with one another their goals, their philosophies, their purposes in life.

It is therefore appropriate at this time, when our relationship, that of this congregation with its new rabbi, is new and fresh, that I share with you my views on what a rabbi should be. In short, I would like to present before you what I believe to be the role and the qualifications of rabbinic leadership. Briefly, I shall try to answer the following question which is probably prominent in your minds at this hour

Delivered Kol Nidre night, September 17, 1972, at Temple Beth El, Rochester, New York. Co-author of this sermon is my colleague and friend Rabbi Marshall Maltzman.

when many are curious to know more about "their new rabbi." That question is: "What Can a Congregation Expect from Its Rabbi?"

This is not an easy question to answer, because many people, even rabbis themselves, disagree on the matter. All I can do is to render my own, very subjective, point of view.

Some of the contradictions involved in defining the role and responsibilities of the rabbi are delineated by the late Rabbi Morris Adler, one of the giants of the American rabbinate until his tragic assassination in 1966. Rabbi Adler wrote:

> Jewish tradition defines the rabbi as a layman, yet to his parishioners he is a clergyman and pastor, and he has not yet grown comfortably into the new role that has been thrust upon him. A teacher of tradition, he is now in the service of an institution; an interpreter of a history, he has in fact become the executive of an agency. By calling and temperament a student, he has been turned into an official, a steward, a member of a staff. Interested in ideas and disciplined to study in privacy, the logic of surrounding circumstances has led him to serve as an apostle of affability and conviviality. . . . He is a frequent guest at testimonial dinners, receptions, and the multiple bizarre festivities that clog the calendar of American Jewish life, and yet in the brief moments when he is not "socializing" he finds himself agonizing over the question, "What am I doing here?" (*May I Have a Word with You*, p. 232.)

If Morris Adler, a leading luminary in the American rabbinate, can describe the frustrations and paradoxes of his role in this way, how must lesser men feel who try to accomplish a task that is becoming increasingly more complex and difficult as time passes? In a study reported not long ago in *The New York Times* Sunday news section, February 22, 1970, some five hundred Protestant ministers were interviewed, half of whom had left the ministry, but all of whom shared common attitudes. Three basic reasons were outlined for their common sense of frustration. First, inadequate seminary training. I don't know of a seminary in the world, Jewish or Christian, that can adequately prepare its students to meet all of the various roles and problems they will meet in the active ministry. Second, a widespread resentment at the pervasive lack of support and understanding from parishioners. Third, pastors see themselves as agents of change, while they find congregations suspicious of anything new—from liturgy to social action.

I feel compelled to say at the outset that while I have at times felt frustrated and disillusioned, I have never succumbed to cynicism or demoralization. Some years ago, after I had completed my tour of duty as a military chaplain, I was interviewed by a congregational board, one of whose members asked me, "Aren't you too young to be our rabbi?" Whereupon another veteran member of the board spoke up: "I'm afraid that with us he'll age very quickly." Well, I have aged very quickly during my years in the rabbinate, but thank God I have not soured. I am happy to say without reservation that to me serving as a rabbi remains a challenging, meaningful, and fulfilling calling. I am grateful to Almighty God for permitting me to serve Him and help Him shepherd the flock of Israel.

I do think, however, that it is often possible to avoid some of the frustrations usually attendant upon the rabbinic calling, by sharing with the congregation my views of what a rabbi should be.

I have found no more cogent description of the role of the rabbi than the one given a century ago by a pioneer American rabbi, Isaac Leeser, the first rabbi to introduce an English sermon into an American synagogue. He was a man of independent spirit who went so far as to resign from his illustrious pulpit after more than twenty years of service because he refused to submit to the demands of a dictatorial board of trustees.

Isaac Leeser said that there are three prerequisites for an effective rabbinic calling. These are: scholarship, an uncompromising honesty of purpose, and a spirit of fearlessness.

The primary role of the rabbi is to study Judaism and to interpret and transmit the contents of his studies to his congregation. He does this from the pulpit, in the classroom, in personal counseling, on the telephone, in the office and at home, in his writings, and in every community forum in which he is called upon to serve. Without knowledge there can be no piety, no religiosity, no Jewish people, no Judaism. Without completely familiarizing himself with the classic sources of Jewish law and lore, the rabbi cannot be an effective teacher, preacher, pastor, counselor, or educator. Without knowing how Jewish scholars met religious and moral problems in past ages, he cannot begin to solve the manifold complex issues that face us today.

The function of the rabbi as teacher and interpreter of Judaism is not acquired easily or quickly. It involves years of study and preparation, in pre-seminary, seminary, and post-seminary study. In Wellington, England, which is famous for its grass tennis courts, the greenkeeper was once asked the secret of such fine courts. He replied: "It's all very simple. First we plow very carefully; turn the ground with our hands; then we sow the seed and tend it for five hundred years. Then you have a fine tennis court." So is it with the rabbinate. It involves a long-term, constant saturation with a knowledge of the past and the present so that this knowledge can inspire people to set aside the false values of human life and adopt more genuine ones. Blessed is the congregation which encourages its rabbi to continue his studies in order to be better prepared and equipped to serve.

A sympathetic congregation is one that understands the rabbi's need to have time to pursue his own studies and reading. Just as a businessman cannot continue to write checks without making deposits in the bank, and just as a carpenter must constantly sharpen his tools, so the rabbi cannot teach and preach without replenishing his supply of knowledge and information regarding both Judaism and the world.

While I have always in the past, and hope to in the future, do my very best to serve my congregation as pastor and counselor, administrator and organizer, I shall never be able to be all things to all men. There may be a patient in the hospital who will inadvertently be missed on my weekly rounds; there will be a parent with a problem who will feel that I should have given him or her more attention; there will be an invocation or a benediction that I will not have time to deliver; there will be a committee meeting and a sisterhood luncheon that I cannot attend from time to time. I would hope that those who make demands upon my time, and proper and just demands, will be sympathetic if I cannot always be in all places at all times. If I am derelict on occasion, it will be because I believe in living a Jewish life myself before I dare attempt to ask others to do so. And to live a full Jewish life means to study Torah and try to live up to its demands.

The story is told about the saint, Levi Yitzhak of Berdichev, that Satan appeared before the heavenly throne before Reb Levi was about to be born. "If such a soul is created," argued Satan, "then it will have such an influence upon people for good that I shall no longer be able to tempt them to sin and will have no role to play in the world." "Don't worry," Satan was appeased, "Levi Yitzhak will be a rabbi, but he will be so busy with committees and meetings that there will be no opportunity for him to hamper your work."

And so, if your rabbi, dear friends, is unavailable on occasion when you feel that you need his time, just remember that he is busy trying to hamper the work of Satan.

I have already quoted to you the words of one great American rabbi, Morris Adler. Now let me read to you an excerpt from a synagogue bulletin in which another distinguished figure in the American rabbinate, Edward Sandrow, reflects on his thirty-five years in the rabbinate.

> The truth is, the average layman does not have any conception of what a week's activities are in the life of a modern rabbi. The rabbi does not mind. His only worry, which gnaws at him is, do these activities in the long run effect a positive change and an improvement in Jewish religious life? He searches for an answer to this question while large segments of the laity, busy with their own activities, . . . must say to themselves, "What does that rabbi do anyway?" Nothing much except attend meetings mornings, afternoons, and evenings for various kinds of organizations, not to speak of the synagogue's own affiliates and departments. Nothing much except teach on four or five occasions a week, preparing such teaching material

during all hours of the night. Nothing much except help plan programs for our synagogue organizations—the school, the youth, the men and women. Nothing except officiate at funerals and weddings, sometimes at several such occasions a week. Nothing except meet with people who come to the study often without appointment, people who just walk in, for advice and for help—people who phone at all hours from early morning until late at night. Nothing except cooperate and work with local and national Jewish agencies—Seminary, Federation, United Fund, UJA, Hebrew University, Rabbinical Assembly . . . Inter-faith groups, B'nai B'rith, etc., etc. who ask the rabbi to assume engagements, to speak on their behalf, to attend meetings of boards and committees since they form the foundation of community life. Nothing except conduct services, prepare sermons which to most rabbis must show some literary merit and scholarship. . . . In his spare time, the rabbi has nothing to do but make a few calls on the sick and aged, and even a few moments for social expression at the synagogue or in homes of people. And more and more! So, where is the time for creative scholarship which his laymen should urge him to do? Where is there time for personal life with the rabbi's own family? Were is the time for throwing himself into social causes which stir all Americans? Laymen say, "this rabbi is not outspoken enough." Others say, "he is too radical." So, there you are.

So there you are. You can see that fulfilling Isaac Leeser's first requirement for the rabbinate, of being a scholar and teacher, is not easy in the midst of the busy and exacting ministry the rabbi must fulfill. But nevertheless he must make it the most important item on his daily agenda and give it his top priority.

Leeser's second prerequisite for an effective rabbinate is that the rabbi must possess an uncompromising honesty of purpose.

The congregations I have been associated with during my lifetime, as student, as teacher, and as rabbi, have been made up of men and women who realize that the rabbi cannot agree with everyone at all times. Benjamin Franklin said that "To serve the public faithfully and at the same time to please it entirely is impossible."

As long as what a rabbi says is carefully thought out, and based on solid fact and reasoned opinion, a congregation should not object to the full expression of his views—even when, or especially when, they disagree with their views. It must be remembered that the rabbi does not speak *for* his congregation, but *to* his congregation, and therefore *his* views need not necessarily reflect *their* views. The rabbi represents Judaism and Jewish tradition when he speaks his mind, not the members of his board or his congregation. The rabbi who is a man of honesty and integrity must make it clear to his congregation that he demands total freedom of the pulpit, even as a professor in a classroom demands academic freedom.

In the words of Martin Luther King, Jr., the clergyman is "not merely a thermometer that records the ideas and principles of popular opinion; [he is] a thermostat that transforms the mores of society."

If and when a rabbi chooses to express his views publicly, beyond the walls of the congregation, in the newspaper, in a public forum, or even in a public demonstration, it should be understood and *accepted* that he speaks not for his congregation, but for his own conscience which does not permit him to remain silent in the face of evil, injustice, or oppression. The rabbi is responsible only to God, to the Torah, and to his own conscience in such cases, and not to those whom he serves as teacher, guide, and leader. In moral and religious issues, he is to be the *leader* of the congregation, not the follower.

The story is told of a synagogue committee which came to the seminary seeking a rabbi and the chairman said: "We want a rabbi to suit our congregation—not too much to the left and not too much to the right, just mediocre." I believe that this congregation is a great congregation, not a mediocre congregation—and therefore I hope to be a rabbi of integrity and honesty, and not "just mediocre."

But even beyond the spoken word, the rabbi must reflect his integrity and honesty in his actions. It has been said that the greatest eloquence of a preacher is in the sermon of his soul. The rabbi's most lasting heritage is in the impress of his character upon the lives of his people. The congregation may neglect his exhortation; but it will treasure his example. When the community may have forgotten what he has said, it will remember what he has been.

Leeser's third prerequisite is "fearlessness." A fearless rabbi need not be a brash and arrogant person, and he must not disregard the opinion and advice of those working with him. But in the last analysis he must arrive at his own conclusions, maintain his own set of standards, and adhere fastly to them. The rabbi who has the quality of fearlessness will not be a "status quo" rabbi who is afraid to rock the boat, who is a "yes" man to those in the congregation who wield the power and who sustain the budget. Rabbi Israel Levinthal wrote, back in 1936, "Leaders are not true leaders when they simply follow the masses, when they are ever ready to approve all the whims and fancies which the people may express. There must be authority that speaks for truth, for justice, for righteousness, and for all that is noblest and purest in life." (*A New World Is Born*, p. 259.)

In a society where gold rules all, the rabbi must lead the people to obey the Golden Rule. In a society where prayer, the Sabbath, kashrut, holidays, and study of Torah are ignored, the rabbi must persuade and cajole and upbraid his flock until they see the beauty and majesty of Jewish tradition. In a community where wealth is spent at country clubs and vacations and fancy cars and homes, the rabbi must teach that wealth must be regarded as a trust, to be shared in noble causes, not hoarded. In a society where success can seduce men into ruthlessness and selfishness, the rabbi must demand honesty and integrity in the business world as well as at home. In a world where ethics are ignored and morality spurned, the rabbi must demand that Jewish values play a central role in one's daily life.

If I shall be able to inspire you to build upon the foundations that have already been laid; if I can motivate you to perpetuate high standards in your personal and community lives; if I can make the message of Judaism vital and meaningful; if I can be a rabbi who leads you as an authentic interpreter of Jewish tradition, as a man of honesty and integrity, and as a fearless leader of this congregation, then my highest hopes for you and for me will have seen their fulfillment.

But more than anything else, in these challenging and exciting days and years of growth that lie ahead of our congregation, I want your abiding friendship.

Like the poet, let me say:

> Let us stand together everywhere
> Whether there be joy or grief to share.
> I, *alone*, am like a bow unstrung;
> Like a hearth unlit, a fruitless tree.
> I shall be with you until life's song is sung
> And you, too, my friends, do not abandon me.

18

What Can a Rabbi Expect from His Congregation?

LAST EVENING I SPOKE ON THE SUBJECT "WHAT CAN A Congregation Expect from Its Rabbi?" That sermon was only the first installment of a two-part message. This morning's part can be called "What Can a Rabbi Expect from His Congregation?" I hope that I will be able to live up to the image of the rabbi which I painted for you last night, and I also hope that you as a congregation will be able to live up to the image of the synagogue that I shall describe this morning.

Walt Whitman once said that in order to have great poets, there have to be great audiences. Without a waiting audience, without a responsive and eager reader and listener, the poet will hardly be motivated to call upon the best within his creative Muse. The same can be said of a rabbi. Without a great congregation, there can be no great rabbi. I can deliver the best sermon in the world, and can suggest the best programs ever devised, and give my "all" to the life of this congregation, but without people who are willing to take these

Delivered Yom Kippur morning, September 18, 1972.

sermons seriously, without people prepared to accept new ideas and implement them, without people who are anxious and eager for direction, my own enthusiasm and energy and creativity will soon dry up and become exhausted for lack of stimulation. In short, if you want me to be the kind of rabbi this congregation deserves, you have to be the kind of congregation which is bold enough, concerned enough, resourceful enough and devoted enough to put into practice the ideas and suggestions of its rabbi.

The Torah tells us: "And the people believed in God and in Moses His servant. Then sang Moses . . ." Ask the Hasidim: How could Moses sing? Did he not stutter? And they answered: He could sing because his people now had faith in him. Thus, he had faith in himself. When there is mutual trust, respect and faith, we can both sing a great song, rabbi and congregation, to God.

What are some of the things which make a congregation great, which in a rabbi's estimation raises it above the level of a fraternity, a canasta club, a lodge, a social group, or a country club?

A rabbi expects from his congregation, first of all, that its vision be broad and its perspective be wide. As someone put it, the world is our parish. There was a time when Jewish congregations were related in an organic way to the entire Jewish community and through them to the Jewish people as a whole. Unfortunately, today congregations are for the most part totally "autonomous, self-determining groups of individuals associating for social and economic rather than for spiritual and cultural reasons." (Alan Miller.) A rabbi expects that his congregation will see itself integrally and organically related to the Jewish people as a whole, and not just to its own members. He will expect his members, and the congregation collectively, to support all Jewish cultural, spiritual, and philanthropic activities, regardless of doctrinal differences. For our overall concern must be with the Jewish people and its survival on the highest possible level of creativity, and not just with a segment of the Jewish people. Our own survival is inextricably intertwined with the lot of our fellow Jews in Chicago, in Los Angeles, in Buenos Aires, in

Jerusalem, in Leningrad, in Paris, and in Casablanca. "The wider the circles of committed and responsible life with which the congregation has contact, the richer and the more meaningful will its own life be." (Alan Miller, "The Ideal Congregation.")

Some of the implications of this broad view of congregational responsibility include the fact we should work together with other synagogues, Reform, Conservative, and Orthodox, towards achieving our mutual goals. They are to be viewed not as our competitors but as our partners! We must extend our hand in support and aid to Hadassah, ORT, B'nai B'rith, the ZOA, UJA, JNF, and any and every worthwhile Jewish effort that seeks to enhance the quality of Jewish life in America. To paraphrase the Latin poet, "I am a Jew and I count nothing Jewish alien to me." Our view should be outward, towards the whole congregation of Israel, *Bet Yisrael ba-asher hu sham*. According to Jewish Law, a synagogue must be constructed with windows, so that the worshippers do not become immured in their own four ells and cut off from contact with the living, breathing world of day-to-day life. A congregation must constantly see itself as part of a much larger whole, and not as the totality of Jewish existence.

I am one of those who believes that no one should be privileged to join a synagogue unless and until he contributes to the United Jewish Appeal. In today's world, with Jewish financial needs in Israel, Europe, America, and elsewhere being what they are, a contribution to one's local Federation and to the UJA should be considered the purchase price of our ticket of admission to the Jewish people. If one does not feel the responsibility, and share the burden of his fellow Jews around the world, he does not, in my humble opinion, deserve the privilege of membership in a congregation of praying Jews. When a UJA solicitor beckons at our door or our telephone, we should not treat him as we do a bill collector, and ward him off as long as possible, and get away with as little as possible. On the contrary, we should be grateful to such a person for doing a job we would have to do were it not for him. We should treat him as one not only who serves our People and our cause, but as one who enables us to perform one of the greatest mitzvot that there is: Tzedaka. Our response to him should be one of gratitude and appreciation, rather than one of annoyance and irritation.

I am also one of those who refuses to sit by when Jews in another part of the world are being persecuted, oppressed, denied their full religious or human rights, or treated in a way unbecoming to a child of God. I will not permit myself to repeat the mistakes of the generation of the thirties and forties who, for whatever reason, did not respond to the call of their people as they might have.

I will not sit idly by when the Soviets attempt to dehumanize my Russian brothers by placing a ransom on their heads, and by selling them like slaves, and exporting them like another item in their list of consumer goods. That is why we are calling upon each of you to wire our President tonight after the Fast, using the suggested texts in the slip inserted by our USYers into the Machzor. Surely this is not too much to ask of each of us to support the international effort now being staged to have this vulgar, inhuman, and unconscionable head tax removed.

The Ethics of the Fathers informs us: "If I am not for myself, who will be for me? But if I am for myself alone, what am I?" We discussed the second part of that statement already. Now to the first clause. While it is true that we must share our burden of the responsibilities of world Jewry, we must not forget the home front. How ironic it would be if we were to be so preoccupied in saving Jews from Russia and Israel that we neglected to save a Jew in Brooklyn, or Philadelphia, or Rochester, or of Temple Beth El! How ironic it would be if in all the hyperactivity we seem to muster for Zionism, and for political, economic, and social freedom for our fellow Jews all over the world, we were to neglect the spiritual and educational needs of our own Jewish community! While all the activities of the Jewish community are fundamental for our survival, in the last analysis it is the synagogue which is the heart of the Jewish body. It is the House of Prayer and the House of Study which demand our highest priorities and our supreme devotion.

Not long ago, Prime Minister Golda Meir told a delegation

of American Jews that "the dangers of assimilation and intermarriage are as serious as the existence and security of Israel itself." "Are you certain," she asked, "that your children and grandchildren will remain Jews?" Her proposed solutions included an intensive dose of Jewish life in America, *now*, with Hebrew education and love of Israel as its central features.

It is my firm belief that while we must feel ourselves bound firmly together with all Jews in this country, it is the Conservative movement which is uniquely qualified to meet the needs and serve the interests of the average American Jew. With a young and dynamic new Chancellor at the helm of the Jewish Theological Seminary, Rabbi Gerson D. Cohen, our movement has a future which has the potential to build a great and vital force on the foundations already laid, and raise us to a new level of achievement for American Judaism. To release the full potential of this new surge of progress in Conservative Judaism, it will be necessary to support even more generously the central institution that gives spiritual nourishment and cultural edification to the far corners of our people in the communities large and small throughout the world.

To accept the challenge of Golda Meir, in assuring ourselves that our grandchildren will remain Jewish, we must accept upon ourselves an ever greater level of commitment to the fundamental purposes for which the synagogue was created: study and prayer. Living our lives as peripheral Jews, with the synagogue and its major activities down in the middle of a long list of priorities, will not assure us that our children will remain Jews. Finding a million excuses why we don't attend this, and why we don't observe that, and why we don't become more involved and more committed, may delude ourselves, but not our children.

The list of excuses is legion: the sanctuary is too lavish; the other worshippers are too materialistic; my presence is only a blade of grass in a large field—mostly unnoticed; it's run by a small clique, etc., etc., etc. This challenge, and an answer, were put into a poem by Muriel C. Margolis that expresses in a forceful way the answer to such complaints.

Tell me a "Tale of my Temple"—
Was it not in ancient times that the need began?
What demands are there now for this structure?
Is God not everywhere with Man?
I view our imposing edifice, but I am not impressed—
Be it "Contemporary," "Modern," "Gothic" or
    in alabaster dress
This building I enter so awesomely,
Is there more than my eyes can see?
How can this House of Sacred Torah
Become a home-like shelter for me?
I am not noticed within these walls,
My emotions remain well hidden.
For how can I summon the courage, to speak of
    them, unbidden?
I tread the halls, I fill my seats,
But I feel no sense of belonging.
Must I come at my "time of despair,"
Lonely, pleading for ease of my longing?

Tell me a "Tale of my Temple"—I ask but I know
    full well
No one else can compose this missive
For the Tale is mine to tell!
I've come to this point in my searching,
Yet how near can my answer be?
Why does it then elude and not reach out to me?
Is it I who must do the reaching, to at last
    become a "part?"
Is it herein the "Arms of the Temple"
God has placed its "working heart"?
Will I know then its tangible strength
When at last I lend it mine?
Torah, and the Fellowship of Man—
This is my Temple's design!
I'll tell you a Tale of My Temple,
Of what so many have already known,
When their arms uphold the Temple,
The Temple becomes their home.

This then, is the formula of success which this rabbi expects of his congregation: to have a twin commitment to the
Jewish community all over the world, as well as to our own

synagogue and its most important functions of prayer and study. To do the things which have been the ultimate purpose and function of devoted Jews from Abraham until our own time. And not to wait until you are pushed or dragged, but to come forward and take part on your own, and to find your own level, but always to increase it and deepen it. Only when our arms are extended to uphold the Temple will it truly become our home.

There is one more thing that a rabbi expects of his congregation. Assuming that the congregation will keep an eye to the outside world, and that at the same time its members are devoted, concerned, committed, and active in the programs of prayer, study, and good deeds in their own congregation, it is still necessary to add this: that a congregation be prepared to accept new ideas in a graceful way. While revering the past, it must be concerned too about the future. Change is a law of life, and religion is not immune to this law. A religious tradition that fails to keep pace with the times will not stay alive very long.

When changes are introduced, not everyone will agree with them. On no single issue can there be unanimity in a congregation this size. Sometimes we will be pleased with changes, sometimes we will not. At all times we must be tolerant, patient, polite, and respectful to our fellow congregants, our leaders, and ourselves. We can disagree without being disagreeable. We can walk shoulder to shoulder without seeing eye to eye on every subject. We must learn how to accept differences of opinion, and without minimizing our convictions or relinquishing our beliefs, realize that often in the life of a group of intelligent and thoughtful people there will be positions, stands, ideas, and even programs and procedures which we cannot accept for ourselves but must be content to permit for those who desire them.

James B. Conant, former president of Harvard University, kept on his desk a little model of a turtle under which was the inscription: "Consider the turtle. He makes progress only when he sticks his neck out." No turtle ever moves forward when he is enclosed within his shell.

Applying this same advice to human behavior, psychologist Carl Rogers recently wrote: "Unless the government, schools, churches, industry, and the family can react with great alacrity to the necessity of change, we are indeed a doomed culture. What we need in fact is not changed institutions but a *changingness* built into institutional life: an instrument for continued renewal of organizational form and institutional structure and policies."

If a congregation is to remain creative and dynamic, it must encourage an atmosphere of tolerance, freedom of expression, and room for experimentation. One of the most creative congregations I know is one in Chicago called Sollel (The Pathfinder). One of the rabbis of that congregation summed up the principles by which it has found success over the years. (Its humorous overtones should not mislead us into thinking that it is not basically very serious):

1. Since there is no such thing as a perfect anything in the synagogue, be it services, religious school, class or whatever, there can never be too many programs or things going on.
2. Every member of the congregation has the freedom and the responsibility to initiate virtually anything he deems worthwhile as long as he supplies the Excedrin.
3. It is better to have intense and even painful controversy than false and dishonest peace.
4. If there is not something important to argue about, people will argue about something stupid and turn to mongering scandal.
5. Creativity within an institution stands in inverse relation to the number of people and groups empowered to prohibit anything.
6. It is good for Jews to trust each other to determine for themselves (and sometimes even the congregation) what needs to be done. God help us if we cannot.
7. Real growth comes when people try to do what at first sounds to be idealistic, much too pious, and probably impossible.
8. People would rather go on doing what they've been

doing (even when the only dynamic is the closely kept secret that what they've been doing is ineffective, narcissistic and boring) rather than try the NEW thing.

9. You get what you pay for.
10. There is only one worthwhile goal for a synagogue and that is the service of God.

It is my hope during the coming months and years to propose ideas and programs which will enable all of the Beth El family to become more actively involved in the life of the congregation, in the Jewish community, and in practicing a living Judaism in their personal lives. It is my earnest hope that many of you will respond to these ideas as they are translated into reality. It will mean spending more time and more effort in working at our Judaism, but I think that it will be worth the time and effort expended. In the end we must fulfill the challenge of Golda Meir, and assure ourselves that the Judaism we received from our ancestors will be transmitted to our children and grandchildren.

At this sacred Yizkor hour, there is nothing more important for us to consider than this. That the trust which our parents bequeathed to us not be abused, squandered, or disdained. The best tribute and honor we pay our beloved dead is that their ideals and values are kept alive in the coming generations. In that way, all of us, rabbi and congregation, can achieve the immortality we want for our parents and our parents' parents. And in that way, too, the faith of our fathers will live in our children. There is no greater hope we can have than that.

To summarize, then, the two sermons of last evening and of today, I bring to you the statement of a famous nineteenth-century Protestant minister and one of the outstanding preachers of his day, Phillips Brooks. If we change the word minister to rabbi, his description of the relationship between congregation and its spiritual leader is an ideal one for our day:

> The whole of the relation, then, between the [rabbi] and the congregation is plain. They belong together. But neither can absorb or override the other. They must be filled with mutual respect. He is their leader, but his leadership is not one con-

stant strain, and never is forgetful of the higher guidance upon which they both rely. It is like the rope by which one ship draws another out into the sea. The rope is not always tight between them, and all the while the tide on which they float is carrying them both. So it is not mere leading and following. It is one of the very highest pictures of human companionship that can be seen on earth. . . . It has much of the intimacy of the family with something of the breadth and dignity that belongs to the state. It is too sacred to be thought of as a contract. It is a union which God joins together for purposes worthy of His care. (*Lectures on Preaching*, pp. 215–216.)

May our relationship in years to come find purposes worthy of God's care. Amen.

19

Aliyot for Women

THE ISSUE I SPEAK ABOUT TONIGHT HAS IMPORTANCE, I think, because it has been brought up by people who are affected by it. Very often a halachic question will be raised by the Rabbi or by the Ritual Committee, but I have the feeling that the issue of whether or not women should have aliyot is being originated throughout the country by women themselves. I think this is the case also in our congregation because the initial request for discussion in our Ritual Committee came from someone in whose family the issue was raised by a woman. I think this is the case in all drastic changes in laws and social customs. It is always the person who feels discriminated against, or who feels oppressed, that is the one who insists on making a change. There is a clamor by women for change and equal rights, and I am told that in some document women are officially classified as one of the oppressed minorities in America.

Looking at the Bible, we have a very good example of how the same thing happened in ancient times. Women who felt

Delivered Friday night, March 9, 1973. This lecture is printed as it was transcribed from the tape, with only minor editorial changes.

that their rights were being infringed upon made a request for a change. This is the law of inheritance. In the Book of Numbers a gentleman named Zelophchad had five daughters but no sons. According to prevalent custom, only sons could inherit property. The five daughters came to Moses and complained, "We are being discriminated against; we are an oppressed minority; women can't inherit property. Do something for us." Moses, the Torah tells us, pondered on this very serious problem, consulted God, and then he came up with an answer (Num. 27). The answer was: You are right. The daughters of Zelophchad are correct. The present custom does not deal with their problem and we have to change the law; we have to modify the present custom for you. Here again, change came after the insistence of the women themselves.

In today's situation we have the same thing. Last March (1972) when I was at the Rabbinical Assembly Convention, there was a group of women who called themselves Ezrat Nashim, an organization for Jewish women's rights. This organization is made up of traditional, Jewishly educated women, who are graduates of Teachers Institute, Yeshiva University, and other institutions of higher Jewish learning. They had a special table at which they were distributing literature to the rabbis. I want to read to you the statement they distributed. I think it will give us a feeling of the mood among American Jewish women:

The Jewish tradition regarding women, once far ahead of other cultures, has now fallen disgracefully behind in failing to come to terms with developments of the past century.

Accepting the age-old concept of role differentiation on the basis of sex, Judaism saw woman's role as that of wife, mother, and home-maker. Her ritual obligations were domestic and familial: *nerot, challah,* and *taharat ha-mishpachah.* Although the woman was extolled for her domestic achievements, and respected as the foundation of the Jewish family, she was never permitted an active role in the synagogue, court, or house of study. These limitations on the life-patterns open to women, appropriate or even progressive for the rabbinic and medieval periods, are entirely unacceptable to us today.

The social position and self-image of women have changed radically in recent years. It is now universally accepted that women are equal to men in intellectual capacity, leadership ability, and spiritual depth. The Conservative movement has tacitly acknowledged this fact by demanding that their female children be educated alongside the males—up to the level of rabbinical school. To educate women and deny them the opportunity to act from this knowledge is an affront to their intelligence, talents and integrity.

As products of Conservative congregations, religious schools, the Ramah Camps, LTF, USY, and the Seminary, we feel this tension acutely. We are deeply committed to Judaism, but cannot find adequate expression for our total needs and concerns in existing women's social and charitable organizations, such as Sisterhood, Hadassah, etc. Furthermore, the single woman—a new reality in Jewish life—is almost totally excluded from the organized Jewish community, which views women solely as daughters, wives, and mothers. The educational institutions of the Conservative movement have helped women recognize their intellectual, social and spiritual potential. If the movement then denies women opportunities to demonstrate these capacities as adults, it will force them to turn from the synagogue, and to find fulfillment elsewhere.

It is not enough to say that Judaism views women as separate but equal, nor to point to Judaism's past superiority over other cultures in its treatment of women. We've had enough of apologetics: enough of Bruria, Dvorah, and Esther; enough of "ayshet chayil" ("women of valor").

It is time that:
    women be granted membership in synagogues
    women be counted in the minyan
    women be allowed full participation in religious observances—aliyot, baalot keriah, shleechot tzibbur
    women be recognized as witnesses before Jewish law
    women be allowed to initiate divorce
    women be permitted and encouraged to attend Rabbinical and Cantorial schools, and to perform Rabbinical and Cantorial functions in synagogues
    women be encouraged to join decision-making bodies, and to

assume professional leadership roles, in synagogues and in
the general Jewish community
women be considered as bound to fulfill all *mitzvot* equally
with men

For three thousand years, one-half of the Jewish people have
been excluded from full participation in Jewish communal life.
We call for an end to the second-class status of women in Jewish
life.

I don't know how representative this is but at least it does
speak for a well-educated, committed segment of American
Jewry, which is important. Whether the organization has
large numbers or not is not important.

The Women's League convention last November also dealt
with this subject. I was not present but I understand it was
discussed quite feverishly and a poll was taken that was
reported in the latest issue of *Women's Outlook*. Of those
responding to this poll, 68 percent were under 50 years of
age; 25 percent were over 50 years of age. The vote was as
follows: 60 percent of the women voting said women should
have aliyot; 31 percent said they should not; 9 percent ab-
stained.

I quote from another very articulate young lady, whose
position is being quoted more and more frequently. I noticed
in today's issue of the *National Jewish Post and Opinion*
(March 9, 1973) a picture of and a whole speech by Rachel
Adler, who writes in the Summer 1971 issue of the magazine *Davka*:

The halachic scholars must examine our problem anew, right
now, with open minds and with empathy. They must make it
possible for women to claim their share in the Torah and begin
to do the things a Jew was created to do. If necessary we must
agitate until the scholars are willing to see us as Jewish souls
in distress rather than as tools with which men do mitzvot. If
they continue to turn a deaf ear to us, the most learned and
halachically committed among us must make halachic decisions
for the rest. . . . To paraphrase Hillel, in a place where there
are no menschen, we may have to generate our own menschlich-

keit. There is no time to waste. For too many centuries, the Jewish woman has been a golem, created by Jewish society. She cooked and bore and did her master's will, and when her tasks were done, the Divine Name was removed from her mouth. It is time for the golem to demand a soul.

A conference was held by the United Synagogue of America, the lay branch of Conservative Judaism, last October 8, 1972, in Tarrytown, New York. The proceedings of that conference were distributed nationally and one line, I think, is important: "A strong majority view was expressed in support of full participation of women in Aliyot, Torah reading, as well as other aspects of the synagogue service. . . ." This is something that other Conservative synagogues are dealing with. Some synagogues have been granting aliyot for women for over a decade—the Germantown Jewish Center in Philadelphia, Park Avenue Synagogue in New York. This year, Beth El Congregation in Springfield, Massachusetts, has just granted aliyot to its women; a prominent Chicago congregation is now discussing it and many, many others throughout the United States. It is not something that is a quiet matter; it is a very live and hot issue.

Does this mean that a congregation that opts for granting aliyot to its women is becoming a left-wing congregation? This is the objection I've heard over the past week after the announcement of this lecture was made. Are we all of a sudden turning into a Reform congregation, or a left-wing, Conservative congregation? I don't think it's a question of left wing or right wing. It is a question of going forward or backward, rather than of going left or right. We are a Conservative congregation, not an Orthodox congregation. Judaism as we understand it is a religion of change, of development, of adaptation to environment, to the best insights and wisdom of our own day. For a Conservative congregation to make a change in its liturgy does not mean that it is becoming left or right wing. It means it is traditionally orienting itself to the very same pattern which established Conservative Judaism and with which Judaism has been kept alive all through the centuries.

It was very interesting to read last November, in *Jewish Week* (Nov. 16, 1972), that Rabbi Emanuel Rackman, a very distinguished Orthodox Rabbi and assistant to the President of Yeshiva University, wrote an article about the position of women in Judaism in which he criticizes some Talmudic attitude towards the position of women:

> Perhaps there is one thing that Orthodox rabbis can and ought to do in the cause of truth and at the behest of Jewish women who are active in the Women's Liberation Movement and that is to concede that there are many statements in Talmudic literature without foundation in fact and demeaning and insulting to women.

This leading Orthodox rabbi recognizes that the need for a reorientation and reassessment of our attitude toward women must take place today.

Recently I received a copy of a position paper created by a number of young Conservative rabbis, whom I respect very greatly—among the cream of the most intelligent of the Conservative rabbinate. I want to read to you a couple of paragraphs from it:

> The contemporary Jewish woman is not bound by the routine of the household as were the women of previous generations. The development of new household devices has made the various chores of the home far less time-consuming. Extensive opportunities for Jewish and secular education have provided the Jewish woman with the option of entering the professional world. Moreover, even assuming that a woman is bound to the home while raising children, it must be conceded that this activity involves only 25 percent of her mature life, and for the remaining 75 percent of her years no such restrictions limit her activity. These are examples of the social and material changes affecting today's Jewish women which make the principle *mitzvot shehazman grama* obsolete.

The principle in Jewish law of *mitzvot shehazman grama* means that women are exempt from performing those positive commandments that have to be done at a certain time of the day because they are tied to their household responsibilities. Women are exempt from putting on tefillin, wearing a talit, saying the shaharit service because these things are tied to a specific time of the day. According to this statement this principle of *mitzvot shehazman grama* is now obsolete in modern society. Two more sentences from this same statement reveal:

> Given changes in women's activity resulting from social and material progress the principle *mitzvot shehazman grama* is obsolete and women should be held obligated for all mitzvot.

> Given the above, women can participate fully in Jewish public ritual, as cantor, Torah reader, or recipient of an aliyah. Having been vested with the responsibility of shmirat mitzvot the woman can serve as sheliach tzibbur, acting to free the congregation from its ritual obligations.

We thus have a picture of some of the feelings of different groups, rabbis, young women, other congregations. Of course, like all other ideas that are new and mark a radical departure from past custom, this will not happen overnight. It will have to take a great deal of getting used to. When the subject of mixed seating in Conservative congregations was first broached, it was a very controversial subject. Many people were opposed to it. In fact, some congregations even took their officers and leaders to court over whether or not they could be permitted to integrate men and women in the seating in the sanctuary. Now this is a rule in Conservative congregations and something natural that we accept without question. As a matter of fact, at the last Rabbinical Assembly convention, one rabbi, who is the chairman of the Rabbinical Assembly Law Committee, a very distinguished rabbi, made the suggestion that those congregations that do not accept the principle of mixed seating should be eliminated from the Conservative Movement. They are too Orthodox, they don't go along with Conservative procedure. Here, in a generation or so, we have come from the position of arguing over whether it is permissible to the suggestion of eliminating congregations that don't accept the new innovations. I am not suggesting that this will happen in a generation from now with congregations who do not permit women to have aliyot. But if past history is a guide, it certainly would be possible.

Let us look at the question of the *fairness* of the matter. We shall get into the halachic aspects of the question in a moment. On this question I bring to you the statement of Rabbi Moshe Tutnauer, who wrote in his synagogue bulletin, Congregation Beth El of Phoenix, Arizona, in April 1972, the following letter:

A couple has a baby—Thank God! Let's go to the synagogue and give our baby a name. The mother, who has carried the child, who has suffered the pains of childbirth, who, more often than not, is the first to hear it cry and the first to bring it comfort, that mother is required to sit in the congregation—her husband, and he alone, has the honor of "going up" to the Torah and of naming the baby. Why?

A young man and a young woman are about to be married. Both have studied at religious schools, both are committed to maintaining a Jewish home, both are looking forward to a meaningful, traditional marriage ceremony. The Shabbat before the wedding he is called to the Torah, she sits in the congregation. Why?

A brother and a sister, twins let's say, register for Hebrew School. They are both fine students—serious, bright, attentive. They both learn the skills necessary for meaningful participation in Jewish life. In Junior Congregation they are treated as equals. Then, the time of their Bar and Bat Mitzvah arrives. The boy participates Friday night and Saturday morning, the girl on Friday night. The boy reads from the Torah and the Haftorah, the girl only the Haftorah. An indignant father and mother write me an angry letter asking that we stop the hoax, stop giving our young girls in school the impression that they are equal. Why?

I think this is a valid challenge to the equity of the situation.

Let us get into the halacha itself which, of course, is crucial in any discussion of changing Jewish ritual patterns. There are two questions of halacha. First, is there a matter of ritual impurity? A woman menstruating, or not going to the mikveh since her last menstrual period, would touch the

Torah, or come in contact with the Torah, and therefore
defile it ritually, or make it impure ritually. Jewish law on
this subject is unequivocal and the statement in the Talmud
is as follows: "En Divra Torah mekablin tum'a" (Berakhot
22a, Baba Kama 82b). The scrolls of the Torah cannot in
any way become ritually defiled. They are too sanctified;
they are immune, completely, under any circumstances, from
any ritual impurity or defilement. There is absolutely no
question that halachically this does not enter into the subject.
It is a false issue which many people have in their minds
that did develop in the Middle Ages against every major
principle of Jewish law. You will find this in the Talmud, in
the medieval law code, the Shulchan Aruch, any authoritative
source you want to turn to: "En Divra Torah mekablin
tum'a." The scrolls of the Torah cannot in any way become
ritually defiled. A Torah can become unkosher if it is torn,
words are smudged, if there are mistakes. If it is not kosher,
it cannot be read in public. It has to be repaired. But this is
a totally different question.

That's one aspect of the halachic problem. The second
aspect is: Has it been done in the past? What do Jewish law
codes specifically say about the permissibility of women
coming up to have an aliyah to the Torah? Most authorities
agree, based on a specific passage in the Talmud, that some
time prior to the twelfth or thirteenth century Jewish women
did have aliyot in the synagogue. This is very little known
among the public at large—that Jewish women had aliyot,
that it was permissible according to Jewish law. I use the
word *was* because obviously it has not been for several centuries.

In 1955 the Rabbinical Assembly Law Committee, which
is composed of 25 leading scholars in the field of halacha,
Jewish law, took up the issue of aliyot for women. There
were two papers read, one by Rabbi Aaron Blumenthal and
the other by the late Rabbi Sanders Tofield. Both teshuvot
declared that according to Jewish law it is permissible for
women to have aliyot with certain qualifications, that it be
done gradually, and carefully, etc. Rabbi Blumenthal's statement has just been reprinted and is now available in our gift

shop in the form of a brief pamphlet. If you want to look into this question further, all the halachic sources and talmudic and medieval codes are quoted right there in this little 15 page pamphlet and I urge you to buy yourself a copy and read it.

The vote of the committee was 15 to 1 to accept both of these position papers. Since 1955, therefore, it has been the official policy of the Conservative movement that those congregations who wish to accept this option may do so. It does not mean that a congregation must accept this opinion, but it is a permissible option. The decision was based upon the following statement in the Talmud:

> Anyone may ascend for an aliyah for the seven honors; even a minor, even a woman, but the sages later said that a woman shall not read in public because of K'vod hatzibbur, the dignity of the congregation. (Megilla 23a)

This is when the custom of aliyot for women stopped and it has not been practiced for the past eight or more centuries.

A later authority, the Ran, who lived in Toledo, Spain, in the fourteenth century, said that women are permitted to have *some* of the aliyot but not *all* of them.

Rabbi Moses Isserles, known as the Rama, an outstanding authority on Jewish law, says, similarily, in the sixteenth century: "You may call women to the Torah. However, do not discriminate against the men. Do not give all the aliyot to the women." (O.H. 282:3)

What is the meaning of the expression, *kevod hatzibbur*, the honor and dignity of the community? Why did the rabbis suddenly reverse history and deny the privilege of an aliyah to women? The phrase, *kevod hatzibbur*, the honor and dignity of the community, is used in several other passages in the Talmud as follows: certain people are not permitted to have an aliyah because of *kevod hatzibbur*. A naked person cannot have an aliyah because of *kevod hatzibbur*; a person who is clad in rags (dungarees, shall we say) cannot have an aliyah because of *kevod hatzibbur*. The Torah reader cannot keep the congregation waiting while the Torah Scrolls are rolled. If two separate passages have to be read, one at the beginning and one at the end, the maftir section can be recited from memory, which is against general custom, because of *kevod hatzibbur,* the dignity and honor of the community. It is forbidden to read from a printed Pentateuch *mipne kevod hatzibbur,* because of the dignity of the congregation. What does that phrase mean, therefore, in the context of these passages? It means it affronts the sensibility, it is offensive, impolite, for a congregation to sit there while somebody nude has an aliyah, while somebody is rolling the Torah scroll for 20 minutes and the congregation has to sit and wait. Or reading from a printed Pentateuch rather than from a real Torah scroll—this is an offensive thing. Why was it, therefore, offensive for a woman to have an aliyah?

Rabbi Blumenthal has tried to come up with some logical explanation and it seems to him that the reason is that when a woman has an aliyah and makes the brachot and reads her own section, that would indicate to the community that there weren't enough knowledgeable men who could read the Torah in that community. (In Talmudic times a person who had an ailyah was the person who read his own Torah portion; there was no professional Torah reader.) That would be an insult. That would mean of the ten men who made up that minyan there weren't seven among them who could read the Torah and it would embarrass them. It is, therefore, not a halachic issue, but a matter of sensibility; a matter of taste, not law. Each generation, each community and each congregation must decide for itself what its own taste is, what its own *koved* demands. It is possible in many instances for an individual to defer his requirement of *koved.* Our whole notion of the status of Jewish women has drastically changed as Rabbi Rackman, the Orthodox rabbi I quoted, himself admits. Jewish law has a status for women that we would not recognize in many instances today and, therefore, why should we in this one? For example, women were included in Jewish law in the same category as minors and Canaanite slaves, when it came to certain things. The testimony of a woman is not accepted in a Jewish court (Shevuot 30a, RH 22a).

Pirke Avot said that a conversation with women is likely

to result in gossip and lewdness (Avot 1:5). In another passage women are classified as inadmissible witnesses along with gamblers and pigeon racers and other individuals of unsavory repute. (RH 22a) We know that the laws of marriage, divorce, and inheritance are unfair to women. Jewish law which clearly permits an aliyah was subverted because of the question of *kevod hatzibbur*, and I don't think it is a valid criterion for our own day.

If aliyot are halachically permissible, what about the question of our own tastes, our own psychological readiness for such a drastic step? That, too, has to be taken into consideration. Something that has not been done for centuries cannot be suddenly changed. Looking around the country we find that several congregations are proceeding in a very gradual and evolutionary fashion. Just as congregations experimented with mixed seating, they are now experimenting with women having aliyot. Various procedures are being followed and I would like to suggest, for our own congregation, that the following few steps be tried on a temporary, experimental basis to see how they work out.

1. A Bat Mitzvah. There is no reason why a young lady should not have the same ceremony that a young man has at the age 13.
2. The parents of a baby. Both parents had a share in the creation of the baby, both parents should have an aliyah together thanking God for that great blessing.
3. A bride and groom. Most of the weddings I have performed include both under the huppah, not just a groom. Therefore, it seems to me that in giving thanks to God for the privilege on the next day, the bride and the groom should have the opportunity to come up to the Torah and have an aliya.

Other congregations do it in the following way in order not to create a situation in which the women would take over the ritual of the synagogue and men would relinquish their responsibility. Men might think: "I don't have to come to shule, I don't have to be responsible for the synagogue; the women will handle it." We don't want that situation to occur. Thus the following procedure is suggested in some congregations: that after the Kohen and Levi aliyot, of the next six aliyot, no more than three be given to women. These are some of the ideas being tried.

In conclusion, I want to bring to you three brief quotations, which I think summarize the general subject of women's rights and the specific subject of aliyot for women. Abigail Adams, the wife of John Adams, one of the framers of the Declaration of Independence, wrote to her husband the following words:

> I long to hear that you have declared an independency. And, by the way, in the new code of laws which I suppose it will be necessary for you to make, I desire that you would remember the ladies and be more generous to them than your ancestors. Do not put such unlimited powers into the hands of the husbands. Remember, all men would be tyrants if they could. If particular care and attention is not paid to the ladies, we are determined to foment a rebellion, and will not hold ourselves bound by any laws in which we have no voice or representation.

In Rabbi Blumenthal's Teshuva, which was accepted by the Rabbinical Assembly, he concludes with the following example:

> The time has come for someone to reverse the direction in which the Halachah has been moving for centuries. In referring to the law which requires one to recline at the Seder table, the question arose whether a woman too, should recline. The answer was that only 'an important woman' was permitted to do so. The Maharil protests with a statement which we might set as the foundation stone of the activity of the Law Committee: *'Today all of our women are important.'*

And finally, a lovely little Midrash:

> Woman was not taken from man's head to be ruled by him, nor from his feet to be trampled upon by him, but from his side to walk beside him, under his arm to be protected by him, and from his heart to be loved by him.*

---

* From Saul Teplitz, *Life Is for Living* (New York: Jonathan David Publishers, 1969), p. 155.

Part II

THE SIX DAY WAR
AND AFTER

20

The Time Is Now!

I HAVE JUST RETURNED FROM A FIVE-DAY TRIP TO OUR
nation's capital, where I, together with five hundred other
rabbis of the Conservative movement, met with some of the
nation's leaders. We had a dialogue with Vice-President Hubert Humphrey, a conference with the entire Congressional
delegation from Pennsylvania, and a tête-à-tête with Senators Clark and Scott. We did almost nothing else at that
convention but discuss and pray for Israel. We were led in
special prayers by Rabbi Abraham Joshua Heschel, noted
American theologian, and we held a rally at the Shoreham
Hotel, jointly with the Jewish Community of Washington,
D.C., where over five thousand Jews gathered to hear Senator Eugene McCarthy and several distinguished national
leaders among the Christian clergy.

I return from Washington to report to you, as each of my
five hundred colleagues return to their respective communities to bring them back word. I left Washington on Thursday
in a mood of both deep depression and great confidence.

Delivered Sunday morning, June 4, 1967, hours before the outbreak
of the Six Day War.

I am depressed because the crisis is severe. Much more severe than Lyndon Johnson, or U Thant, or Charles De Gaulle or Alexei Kosygin, or any of the world's leaders seem to realize. Israel's existence has been extremely precarious for the last two decades, and yet none of the nations of the world seem to have felt the seriousness of their crises.

For twenty years the great powers have been dismissing the provocations on Israel's borders as a minor political diversion for the Arabs. Sniper shots at farmers in a valley, bombs set for tractor drivers, mines for military border patrols—all of these and more have been the constant harassment Israel has had to face from the day the nation was born, when seven Arab enemies converged on her borders trying to prevent her very birth.

Because the leading powers denied Israel the proper recognition in these endless, agonizing border clashes, she took matters into her own hand in 1956. For a short while France and Great Britain lent her a hand, but all three nations were forced to turn back by the long and mighty arm of America. At that time, our country made certain promises to Israel, which were conditions that Israel accepted as part of the agreement to withdraw to her own borders. One of those conditions was that she would have access to the Strait of Tiran and the Suez Canal.

Israel never saw access to the Suez Canal, and now she is being denied use of the Gulf of Aqaba. By rights, she should have no more faith in the second guarantee than she should in the first, which in ten years has proved a fraud at her expense.

All these years the State Department of our country has been saying that Egypt is not ready for a confrontation with Israel and would never attack. It has again dismissed Israel's claims of harassment and border incursions. Nasser's recent actions in the Gulf of Aqaba and in the Sinai Desert shattered all of the worn-out notions of our State Department in its Middle East evaluation.

Again, our government had the temerity to ask Israel to be patient and to sit out the fight, while the world's diplomats think they can change the mind of a mad dictator by joint declarations and moral pressure. We know and Israel knows full well that nothing will come of this verbal game-playing, but still Israel is showing great patience and restraint, as she sits and watches her rights being washed down the drain more and more as each day follows another. She is truly a saint—letting Egypt smack one cheek while the Western powers smack the other.

The Israelis are the last ones in the world who want war. Their entire country is smaller than the state of New Jersey. Their economy was in a state of recession long before this latest crisis. Now it has ground to a total halt. Their factories are empty, their fields lie fallow, their stores are closed, their tourists have fled, every available penny is being poured into total mobilization.

Milk is being delivered by children, buses do not run, streets are empty. No family has seen its father or brother or son in two weeks. Their oil supply is totally cut off, their exports have ceased, food stores are being depleted.

No, Israel does not want war. But if no one else will, she must protect herself. If, as in 1956, the world sits by and lets the Egyptian madman gobble up more and more power and transgress all of the moral and legal principles of the United Nations and of international law, then Israel must and will act on her own.

If she does, and if she is not helped by the United States because they are too busy in Vietnam, then even if Israel comes out on top, unbelievable destruction will have taken place. Her cities will be devastated, her farms scorched, her industries wiped out, and thousands of her youth will be dead or wounded. This is if she wins the war. If she loses, and we must face this possibility too, however remote it is, the result would be unthinkable.

In any case, her territory is so small, and weaponry in that part of the world so highly advanced, that no one will emerge from such a war as complete victor. All will be losers. We shudder to think how many dead in all Middle Eastern countries will be counted when the last gun is fired.

This is why I returned from Washington depressed. This is why all of us must be depressed these terrible days. This is why all of us must have Israel foremost in our minds and our hearts every minute of every day, until the Arab bomb is defused and the hands of the dictator are tied behind his back.

And yet, I also came back confident. Confident for several reasons. I am confident, because after having spoken to many important government leaders, I know that most of the leaders of our country stand squarely with us. Most of our leaders know that the decision America faces is a moral one and not merely a political one. Most of our leaders realize that America's moral fiber will be tested in the Middle East far more than it is in Southeast Asia. There the issues are foggy and unclear. Is it really aggression in Vietnam, or subversion? Is communism good or bad for the Vietnamese? Has America a role to play in Southeast Asia? Do we have it in our charge to bomb civilians in North Vietnam who themselves have never bombed anyone? I don't pretend to know the answers to these questions, and by and large I have left it up to Lyndon Johnson to settle the matter with his own conscience, without praising him *or* criticizing him for it.

But in today's crisis in Israel, the issues are clear and unequivocal. Israel did not demand the withdrawal of the UN troops. Israel did not mass its troops on its neighbor's borders, and Israel did not deny any shipping rights or any rights to its four contiguous neighbors. But Egypt did!

Egypt has choked Israel's throat, and as the days progress its grip is becoming tighter and tighter. One day soon Nasser will have overplayed his cards, and find his hands cut off with sudden force. We don't relish the day when that happens.

I am encouraged because I have heard our Vice-President and our Senators and our Congressman place the blame squarely where it belongs—in Nasser's lap. I am encouraged because I have heard many of our Christian and Negro brethren express in no uncertain terms that this issue is not a Jewish issue nor an Israeli issue, but a world issue. The issue is not only whether Israel will survive, although that is extremely important to us as it should be to all men of good will. The issue is how long will we let a vicious dictator slap the faces of the world's great and small powers and not be answered? How long will evil be perpetrated upon our people without recourse to the laws of human decency and international morality? When will the back-slappers of our government and others' stand up and put this modern Hitler in his place? How long will we refuse to make decisions not on the basis of oil interests or momentary expediency, but on what is right?

I am confident because I have witnessed in the past two weeks unprecedented public support for the State of Israel by Jewish and non-Jewish communities in this country. I am fairly confident because I now see very clearly how important Israel is to most of the people of this country. It makes me joyful to know that we have thrown our lot in with Israel, because we know that without her our life as Jews in this country will lose its cogency and its meaning.

It pleases me to know that the world is now, finally, giving recognition to the work that Jewish pioneers have been doing for eight decades. I am heartened to know that attention is being paid to the place where Judaism has found its home after two thousand years of exile, where the Jewish way of life is lived 24 hours every day, where the values of our people have taken root, and where the words of the Bible find their most faithful friends.

I am happy that we are able to help Israel, even though I am grieved that she needs this help. I am moved by seeing hundreds of American youth risk their lives by taking up the hoe and scythe while their fellow Jews man the borders. I am thrilled to see millions of dollars flow into Israel through the U.J.A. and its emergency fund, and more millions of Israel bonds purchased by American Jews. I am deeply moved by seeing thousands of Jews pray together for peace in Israel, and by their self-sacrificing devotion in praying, fasting, worrying, and giving to help Israel.

I am happy that we have the opportunity to help the Jewish people in the 1960s, because we did not have that opportunity in the 1940s. For that very reason, as well as for all the others, we must do everything within our power as human beings to lend assistance to our brethren in Israel. They are giving of their lives and their blood, and the least we can do is to give of our means—more generously than we ever have for any cause ever before.

I am pleased that we meet here this morning because we can think of nothing else but Israel. I am pleased that fifty of my colleagues volunteered in Washington to go to Israel this summer to work wherever they are needed. I know hundreds more will go, including myself, if the call goes out for us.

Most of all, I am confident, because this story is not a new one to me. I have read it in the Bible, and I have read it in the books of Jewish history. The names were different, but the events the same. It may have been Pharaoh, or Haman, or Hadrian, or Torquemada, or Chmielnicki, or Hitler, but the plot was the same. I am not alarmed, because I know that this crisis is only one in a long chain wherein power-hungry madmen thought they could win power through hatred and wickedness and greed. I am confident because I know they will lose, because the world can only be conquered with love, with responsibility, with mutual help, and with respect for the property and the rights of one's neighbor, and most of all with a dream of peace, such as our ancient Prophets hoped for and prayed for.

I am confident because I know that our Redeemer liveth, that God is on our side. The inexorable law of history shows us that this pharaoh will ultimately destroy himself by his greed the same as all the others have.

I am confident that Israel will do whatever she has to to maintain her self-respect and national dignity. If it is peace that the Arabs want, peace they shall have. If it is war, then war they will get, and I know that I, and I hope you too, will do whatever we can to prevent it, but once present, to end it. It may set us back twenty years, but we will be defending more than the work of two decades; we will be defending the dreams of four thousand years. To me, and I know to you, that heritage is worth defending, and our people are worth fighting for. We have great patience, and plenty of time. For we know that if these twenty years' work is undone, we will start afresh, as we have many times before. We know that ultimately the outcome will be on our side, and that right and justice must prevail. These are God's laws, and we are their bearers to the world. Our example must continue to show them that there is only one way to live in this world, and that is for justice and righteousness. To me, and I know to Israel and to the entire Jewish people, our way is to live by the ideals of our ancient heritage. For our brethren in Israel, some of them, it may mean to die by them.

The question that stands on the agenda of the world at this grave hour is whether a nation of two and a half million has the same right to live as nations of two hundred million. This is the question being decided now in the UN Security Council, and in the Congress of the United States, and in the White House on Pennsylvania Avenue in our nation's capital. Not whether Israel can send its ships through the Gulf of Aqaba, but whether only those who carry enough power to destroy their enemies can survive in the age of nuclear warfare.

I hope and pray, with you together, that America decides this question the way we think it should. For not only the life of millions of Jews and Arabs depend upon it, but millions of Americans as well.

To close, I would like to recall what Israel's ambassador, Avraham Harmon, said the other night to the Rabbinical Assembly.

At the end of Birkat HaMazon, we say the following line: *Adonai oz le—amo yiten, Adonai yevarekh et amo bashalom.* "May God give strength unto His people, may He bless them with peace." "I think he has given them strength, and I think they will be blessed with peace." To that we can only add, **Amen!**

21

Winning the Peace

LAST SUNDAY MORNING, EXACTLY ONE WEEK AGO TODAY, I
spoke before this distinguished congregation in prophetic
terms. Without knowing that in a matter of hours a major
war would break out, I presented a very dim and depressing
picture of the Middle East situation. Now, only seven days
later, I speak to you only a few hours after that war has been
terminated. My friends, we have just finished a week which
neither you nor I shall ever forget for the rest of our lives.

All of us are very proud and very joyful at this moment
of triumph over the forces of evil and violence. But our joy
must be tempered and our exhilaration only partial, for many
reasons. First of all because of the endless pool of blood that
has been spilled during these trying six days. I said last
week before we had knowledge of the war's inception, that
I was both depressed and confident. Depressed at the gravity
and potential danger of the situation—a concern that was
justified only too quickly. And confident that, if war did break
out, our side would emerge victorious. My confidence, too has
been justified.

Delivered Sunday morning, June 11, 1967, hours after the end of
the Six Day War.

Today, even after our great victory, I stand before you not as depressed as before, because the damage, we pray, is completed, and the achievements seem to have been worth the price. But neither am I as confident as I was last Sunday morning. For now the fate of the State of Israel no longer lies within its own hands. Its stake in the future will be determined, probably, if past history is any precedent, by the major powers in the world, the United States and Russia. I had the deepest confidence in Israel. This confidence was borne out. I cannot say that I have that same feeling of confidence either in the Soviet Union's sense of fair play, or in the square dealings of our own government.

As the news of victory began to come across the wires early this week, all of us were jubilant. Other than a few sorrowful hours early Monday morning, all of us were pleased with what we heard, saw, and read almost the whole week, though we were not pleased at the tragic loss of life on both sides of the conflict. Though we were pleased at the results of the battles, to my mind the greatest hour for Israel, and for the Jewish people everywhere, was when the world sat spellbound listening to the moving eloquence and brilliant oratory of Israel's Foreign Minister, Abba Eban, on Tuesday night in the Security Council. Eban has been compared to Churchill in his ability to articulate the cause of his people in reasonable and eloquent terms. Every Jewish head was raised proudly as we heard Mr. Eban defend his country's attempt to live in its ancestral homeland, speaking its ancient language, and live up to its ancestral moral principles.

What was violently disturbing to us was that Mr. Eban's brilliance and eloquence had to battle alone, as his country did in the fields of the Holy Land with its armed power. We were glad that Israel could fight its physical battle alone and come out supreme. We were not so glad to see Mr. Eban battle alone against a vast array of Communist and Arab nations who violated her honor, sullied her good name, insulted her dignity, and impugned her good intentions.

We would have wished that one nation—just one nation among the 128 in the council of nations—would come to her defense and act as her ally. We would have liked to see at least one other voice raised in defense of a tiny nation of two million fighting against eighty million enemies who encircled her borders with intent to destroy. We would have liked to see one other nation with the courage to stand together in spirit with Israel, even if they were not asked to stand together with her on the battlefields.

The nation that had the solemn moral obligation to defend Israel's good name was the nation that for twenty years has been making empty pledges and promises to stand by her in the hour of need, the United States of America. We are indeed grateful to God that America was not asked to redeem its express and solemn obligation to defend Israel militarily. I shudder to think what the results of this war would have been had Israel been required to rely upon the strong arm of the United States of America.

Our country was neutral this week. In word, in thought, and in deed. We were neutral to Egypt for the past twenty years. We were neutral when Nasser nationalized the Suez Canal. We were neutral when the American Information Service's Library was burned and the Egyptian government did nothing to prevent it. We were neutral when Israel invaded Sinai with Britain and France. Ten years ago, our neutrality expressed itself in asking Israel to pull back its troops and let the monster recoup his lost power. Yes, our government has been neutral—but to paraphrase George Orwell, sometimes the United States is more neutral than at other times.

There is no doubt in my mind that future generations will find the greatest moral failure of our day in a nation's being neutral when evil and aggression are being committed by a majority on a minority. We should no more be neutral in the Middle East than we are in Southeast Asia. We should no more be neutral than we are at home in fighting prejudice, discrimination, and poverty. One cannot be neutral in the face of evil. Either we destroy it or it destroys us! To fight the Communists in Vietnam and take a back seat in the Middle East is nothing short of moral schizophrenia!

If America learned nothing else during this agonizing and bloody week, it should have learned that we have *one* ally and *one* alone in the Middle East! In its cowardly diplomatic acrobatics, our country has refused to see that full implications of the East-West alignment in the Middle East which became so crystal clear these past few days. It has refused to admit that we cannot *buy* the affection of power-hungry nations bent on conquest and destruction.

Israel threw in her lot with the Western powers almost from the beginning. Yet we were blinded by the gold and the oil into thinking that we could befriend the Egyptian dictator who would rule in the Middle East. Israel stands proudly in the Middle East as an oasis in a desert. A vibrant, democratic nation, making some of the great social, medical, agricultural and scientific progress of any nation in the world, should have been recognized by us for its Western similarities. We should have recognized Israel as our only true ally, but we didn't. Perhaps finally our government will listen to Nasser when he says that Israel and America are allies, if they did not know it before—or listen to Russia. How ironic that our enemies are proclaiming a truth we should have accepted long ago on our own! How ironic it is that for thirteen years we have accepted and wooed the devil, and now it is he who rejects us when it should have been we who rejected him!

This week Israel did to Nasser what America should have done ten years ago, or at least let be done by others. We ought to be thrilled that a tiny nation of two million acquitted us of our own moral obligations when we were too cowardly to do it ourselves. But from yesterday's reports, Nasser seems to be back in power, as strong as ever politically. His defeated nation has rallied behind him. And unless the great powers force him to make peace with Israel, his belligerent voice may be yet heard in the years to come.

Nasser has played a very smart game. No matter how many wars he fights and loses, he still emerges victorious. He has nothing to lose. Time and time again he can lose, because his hands are quickly upheld by others. But tiny Israel stands alone. She can win three times in two decades, but should she ever lose only once, she is finished. All that it takes is one loss to be annihilated. When Nasser is losing, the UN quickly brings an end to hostilities. But let him once, God forbid, emerge on the winning side, and the Soviet Union would veto any move to bring a cease fire. And so we are left with the sorry and disastrous situation, where if Nasser wins, he wins, and if he loses, he wins!

That is why we are meeting here now, dear friends. We have been lulled into complacency by Israel's victories. But now that the war has been won, the greatest battle is yet to be fought. That battle will be fought between the United States and the Soviet Union. Here Israel's hands are not as strong as they can be on the battlefield. It will only be determined in the next weeks who really emerges as the winner. We can easily have won the war and lost the peace, as happened in 1957, unless the United States acts differently than it did then.

It is no secret that this blood bath of June 5 to 10, 1967, would not have been necessary were it not for the dastardly negotiations of Eisenhower and Dulles in 1957. Their neutrality then helped Egypt gain back its strength and put itself into a position of aggressor once again. They made this war possible even more than U Thant. Let it not be said ten years from now that the next war is the result of what Lyndon Johnson and Dean Rusk did in 1967.

If the terms of the settlement of this war are not firmly and unequivocally directed toward a permanent peace for the future, then all the damage and destruction and death shall have been in vain. This is our role now, and in the coming weeks. To be even more vigorous and firm in writing and wiring our national leaders to see that Israel's soul is not sold to the devil as it was once before. The vocal expression of Americans of all faiths and all parties will be required to see that Israel keeps at least that amount of territory which will insure its national security in the years to come, and that a strong and lasting peace agreement is thrust upon the defeated aggressor. The role of the individual American in this battle is far from insignificant.

The Israelis have seen to it that the fighting war was won. We must see, and the United States government must see, that the diplomatic war is won. Unless she achieves this solemn moral act, all the platitudes about defending Vietnam from the Communists will make us look morally and politically sick.

There is a second reason for our meeting here this mornin—a second thing we must all do if we are to discharge properly our moral obligation to our brethren in Eretz Yisrael. That is to help them rebuild their country and their economy.

We would kid ourselves if we thought Israel came away from this battle unscathed. Her young men now lie dead in their hundreds on the fields of battle. Her sick and wounded, civilian and soldier alike, overflow her hospitals and clinics throughout the country. Many of her tall buildings lie in rubble, and her farms are covered with the ashes of mortar shells. Despite her phenomenal and miraculous military achievements, her body is bent in sorrow and in grief and in pain over the depth of her human and material losses. Tel Aviv, and we hope, Haifa, emerged without too much damage. Jerusalem, however, came off much worse. So did many of the kibbutzim, whose buildings lie flat and whose fields are scorched and useless.

The full extent of the death and destruction may not be known for some time in this country, but we can be assured that the story, when fully told, will be a sad one.

The little information we have is staggering. When my wife and I lived in Israel for a year in 1962 and 1963, we lived one block away from the new National Museum in Jerusalem. When we arrived in the fall of 1962, it was just being built. Every day as we passed by on our way to the university we watched the workers lovingly raise the building from the foundations to the roof. When we left it was not yet completed. From the time of its opening some months after we left, it was the pride and joy of the State of Israel, a cultural oasis in a desert of ignorance and illiteracy in the lands of its Arab neighbors. Abba Eban announced in the Security Council already on Tuesday that the Museum had been shelled and severely damaged, only three years after its dedication.

The University City of the Hebrew University campus was

a model for universities the world over. Scores of buildings dotted its hilly campus and served as the place where Israel's youth were trained in the skills necessary for a growing country. The university too has undergone untold damage. One of its medical centers, the Shaarey Zedek Hospital, suffered from the venom and hatred of the Arab military machine.

These are the few facts we now know about. As I let my mind's eye run from city to city and from street to street throughout that wonderful land which I was so delighted to see with my own eyes, I cry as I wonder about which buildings now still stand to bear witness to the devotion and dedication of the young Israeli generation, and which of them lie in ruins bearing witness to their bloody struggle for survival.

And what of all the friends that we made in Jerusalem? Will we be able to sit and sip coffee with our friends Moshe and Rina Menachem in their Jerusalem flat and talk about their participation in this war, just as they told us of their exploits in 1956? Or do they now, God forbid, lie somewhere as yet unattended in the Sinai Desert or along the Jordan River, or in the hills of Syria? Were the young girls, Shula and Varda, our superintendent's daughters, able to withstand the scourge of war, or do their parents mourn them as they did their brothers and sisters in 1948?

I grieve when I think of these things and these people whom I love like brothers and sisters, and can only pray that they still remain in the land of the living.

I am embarrassed when I compare my life to the life of the average person my age living in Israel. Born and living in a land that has never seen war within its borders, my life has been totally free and devoid of the kind of pain and devastation experienced by my Israeli counterpart. While I have also known peace and security, he has known only war and strife. He was born probably in a Europe that sought to extinguish his life. It probably did that to his parents and cousins, and perhaps his brothers and sisters. He was lucky enough to escape that holocaust, only to have to withstand the onslaught of seven enemies when his nation was brought into existence. He had to fight to survive again in 1956 and in 1967—at least three times in two decades, after being plucked from the fires of a foreign land.

What good to me are the luxuries—the gold watches, and the fancy clothes, the sleek cars, and the plush convenience that surround my life, if my brothers in Israel have no food to put in their children's mouths. What good is living comfortably in the suburbs, when my heart and my mind are agonized by their suffering and their losses.

If we haven't learned this great lesson over the past four thousand sorry years of Jewish history, we haven't learned anything—that whenever one Jew anywhere in the world suffers, I must suffer along with him. When he is poor, I am poor. When he is hungry, I must be hungry. When his family dies, my heart dies.

My friends, if we do not feel that it is our homes and our cities, and our hospitals, and our museums, and our brothers that have been destroyed, then we too must bear the sin of neutrality. If we can stand by when Jews in Israel gave their homes and their cities and their farms and their sons for the sake of their national survival and their moral principles, and claim to be neutral and unaffected by the horrible deeds of this week, then the lesson of six million and more of our brethren has been lost upon us. If we do not give up some of our pleasures, and our luxuries, and our comforts in the days and months ahead, so that the Jews in Israel may begin the job of re-creating their homeland anew, then we have no right to call ourselves Jews. If we do not today give as generously as we possibly can to the cause of rebuilding our ancestral homeland, then we dare never utter another prayer for the welfare of Jerusalem and her inhabitants. We dare never enter a synagogue and never enjoy the privileges of belonging to the indestructible people of Israel.

For four thousand years we have stuck together as one nation and fulfilled the biblical command to open our hearts and our hands and our pockets to our brethren. At this very great hour of hope and promise, and of dire economic need, we dare not do less. God help us discharge our obligation proudly.

22

The Transformation of the Jewish People

ONE OF THE LESSER-PUBLICIZED SIDE EFFECTS OF THE SIX DAY War of June, 1967, is the transformation of the Jewish people.

No Jew today is the same Jew he was in early May of this year. The Jewish people are not the same Jewish people. The Jewish world is a new world. Jewish theology is a new theology. Jewish history, Jewish liturgy have been revivified and irrevocably altered.

The catalyst of the transformation was that part of the world Jewish family that swore political allegiance to the State of Israel. They accomplished the unbelievable and impossible acts which set off the chain reaction. They were God's instrument in this theophany, even as the ancient Israelites with Moses were in their own Egyptian confrontation.

The stuff of the transformation pre-existed. It was embedded in four millennia of sacred history. It burst out of its

Delivered Rosh Hashana morning, October 5, 1967.

hard shell and sprang, Pandora-like, into vibrant, life-giving spirit. The will to life was suddenly and unexpectedly actualized. The seed of Jewish creativity found sunlight and was fructified. The processes of nature pushed forward with unpredictable swiftness. The corporate life of the People of the Covenant received an impetus wholly new and energizing. Since June 5, life can never be the same.

In its own way, the Six Day War will ultimately have an effect on subsequent Jewish history (and therefore, on world history) as important and revolutionary as the Exodus from Egypt. Of the three fronts of the War, it was the battle for Jerusalem which transformed the Jewish people. This was not a battle against Arabs. It was a battle against the evil in man. Against smallness, hatred, xenophobia. Against anti-Semitism the world over. Against persecution of minorities. Against dictatorships everywhere. Against all the Nassers, Stalins, and Hitlers we have had to suffer for four millennia.

Furthermore, it was a battle against our worst selves. Against Jewish indifference. Against Jewish passivity—against Auschwitz.

In the holy city Jews fought hand-to-hand, inch by inch, with heavy losses. The Jewish people were fighting their way back into history. Pushing through centuries of exile, hatred, and persecution, they reached the pinnacle of their ancient glory: the Western Wall. Upon arrival at the roots of Jewishness, the sound of the ancient shofar rang out, shaking every Jew in the world to the quick. A prayer was whispered— *She-hecheyanu, ve-keeymanu, ve-higeeyanu, lazman hazeh*— "Who has kept us in life, and sustained us, and enabled us to reach this unique and unforgettable event in Jewish history."

The shrill blast of the ram's horn caused a spiritual tremor in the world. Its piercing notes crushed the walls of indifference, guarding the way to each Jewish heart, as if Joshua had sounded down the ramparts of Jericho. Few have recovered from this trauma. Some—perhaps most—never will. The transformation is irreversible.

Not only Jerusalem was made whole. The Jewish world was made whole. The Jewish soul mended its fissure. The

Jewish people became one, never to be divided again. All
Jews became statesmen and theologians at once, demanding
the eternal unity of their transnational peoplehood. No United
Nations resolution can undo this unilateral spiritual declaration. Furthermore, this reunification was not administrative,
but existential. What God has done, what mortal can undo?

Jerusalem the Golden. To understand what happened on
the 28th of Elul, 5727, Wednesday, June 7th, one must know
what Jerusalem has meant to our people. Jerusalem is not a
city. It is much more than that. It is an idea. It is not a place;
it is an event. It is a process. A symbol not only of what has
taken place, but what is yet to take place. The only meaningful
concrete description of Jerusalem is found in the haunting
melody that has pervaded the homes and schools of Israel
and elsewhere: "Jerusalem the Golden." Jerusalem is a fig-
ment of the Jewish imagination, but was only a visionary
imagination until June 7th. It is now a real dream, a golden
dream. It is the Jerusalem of David, of Solomon, of Ezra,
and Nehemiah, of Judah the Maccabee—all rolled into one
golden city of Jewish dreams.

If anyone thinks that the transformation of world Jewry
was sudden, he is wrong. June 7th was the climax of Jewish
history from Abraham to now.

It might seem strange at first to think of a military victory
as a great spiritual event. Yet, if we think of the Exodus
from Egypt in comparable terms, we can easily see how the
political, the military, the national, and the spiritual have
always been different parts of the same whole in Jewish history—the nature and destiny of our people, and our Faith.
In the Bible as afterwards, the Jewish people have never
failed to see the finger of God acting upon our lives in the
most seemingly unspiritual events. Yet our greatness has
been that in a physical world we have always recognized the
spiritual dimension of life.

This basic Jewish concept was grasped beautifully by, of
all people—and this emphasized the truth of the idea only
more so—Major General Yitzchak Rabin, commander of the
Israel Defense Forces. In a special convocation on the recap-
tured Mount Scopus, site of the pre-1948 campus of the

Hebrew University, General Rabin was awarded the honorary degree of Doctor of Philosophy. In the presence of Israel's President, Prime Minister, and a host of other government leaders, General Rabin explained why he thought an academic institution was honoring a military hero.

"These soldiers," he said, " were carried forward by spiritual values, by deep spiritual resources, far more than by their weapons or the technique of warfare.

"All of this springs from the soul and leads back to the spirit. Our warriors prevailed not by their weapons but by the consciousness of a mission, by a consciousness of righteousness, by a deep love for their homeland and an understanding of the difficult task laid upon them: to ensure the existence of our people in its homeland, to protect, even at the price of their lives, the right of the Nation of Israel to live in its own State, free, independent and peaceful."

All objective observers agree that Israel's fighting men acquitted themselves not only with military brilliance, but with spiritual splendor: Rabbi Eugene Borowitz, one of America's leading Jewish theologians, expressed it this way:

"They acted like real human beings in an area of the world where real human concern is still scarce. They won because of their human virtues and even in victory showed none of the fanaticism or vengefulness we all despise. The Israelis thus won a victory for humanity, for what it may still mean to be a man in our day."

Elie Wiesel had the same feeling, which he expressed in an article this past July:

"Do not tell me that they were moved by the will to power or materialistic domination. The urge that moved them was rooted in the spirituality of their past. Their experience was a mystical one. Even the unbelievers among them felt transformed by their own acts and the telling of them afterwards. The words on their lips had a strangely burning and distant sound.

". . . Mankind will never know victors less arrogant, heroes more modest, men more moderated and so thirsty for peace and purity."

The Response of the Individual Jew. A small minority of

Jews were able to participate in the actual fighting. The rest of us did our share in whatever way we could. All of us wanted to feel part of these great events, because we felt as though we were linking ourselves with a supremely worthy cause, and that we were living through a great historic moment, one that would never repeat itself in our lifetime.

The atmosphere among Jews the world over was even more charged than it was in 1948 or 1956, during Israel's first two wars. During the hundred-hour war to Suez in 1956, most visiting American Jews left Israel at the outbreak of hostilities. This time, not only did almost none leave, but thousands clamored to get there in time to take part, from America and all over the world. Over seven thousand arrived before the war.

Of the two hundred American students at Jerusalem's Hebrew University, only three returned, and two of those had sick parents. One student received a cable from home: "Am cabling money. Return home at once." His answer was flashed back immediately: "Am returning money. I am home. Suggest you use money to join me."

Suddenly, for American Jewry Israel became "home." Israeli soldiers were our fighters, and we referred to them as "we." "We took the Old City," "We reached the Canal," were phrases heard among Jews in the Diaspora. A people who for two millennia had no home, now had two homes: America and Israel.

At the end of May a teenage girl in Jerusalem, whose family had migrated to Israel from New York a few years before, received an urgent letter from her American grandparents to come back to New York, at least during the period of crisis. This is part of her answer:

". . . Please try to understand, WE ART NOT AFRAID and I know that personally I am ready for whatever the future holds for me. We will certainly not leave now. Did you leave the States when the Cuba crisis started? Please try to understand us though I'm sure it's hard for you. I know that I wouldn't be able to face myself or my friends, who have no relatives to worry about them abroad, whose fathers were called up or whose brothers and sisters are sitting on the

Egyptian border. Is it fair to take advantage of all the wonderful things this country has to give, but when my turn comes to give in return to run away and turn my back to other people's troubles?—It would be very selfish and cowardly.

"And besides, this is the JEWISH HOMELAND, not yet twenty years old. And as part of this people it is my home and my only real home and I love it. I wouldn't leave now and I *couldn't*. I want to stay and do whatever I can to help, even if I can't sit on the border. You should be proud of us even though I can understand your worry. After all, doesn't our family stand for honor and dignity and the good in man— to run away would prove the opposite." (*Reconstructionist*, July 7, 1967.)

This eloquent young lady expressed what all of us felt in our hearts during those trying days. For all of us it was a matter of honor. We knew that our people has always stood for "honor and dignity and the good in man." We wanted to be an active part of this extraordinary people at its greatest and finest hour.

And so we too pitched in. Between May 23rd and June 10th, we gave $100 million to the Israel Emergency Fund. We bought millions of dollars of Israel bonds. We emptied our savings accounts, sold our jewelry, even borrowed money from the bank, to be a part of what was happening.

We traveled to Washington in our thousands to let our government know how we felt. We marched, we sang, we danced, and we prayed in a moment of supreme self-sacrifice and altruism. The deepest feelings of Jewish solidarity sprang forth from the most seemingly assimilated Jew.

Those who couldn't give money gave of themselves in hours of labor, office work, campaigning, and collecting. Others, young people by their hundreds, signed up to go to Israel and replace the civilians now mobilized.

The Israel consulates and Hillel Houses throughout America were deluged with young eager faces begging to make the sacred pilgrimage to Israel at its time of deep peril. The word "volunteer" became a magic phrase in Israel, as Israelis learned of the great response of their brethren overseas. A high official of the Jewish Agency reported that as he reached the front door of his office the Monday morning of the outbreak of the war, a cab drove up with three men. The eldest of the three approached him and said, "I have no money to give, but here are my two sons. Please send them over immediately."

We gave in an unparalleled way, because we all knew that if events turned out other than they did, we—all of us— would share the blame, as we now share the joy. We knew that these High Holy Days would not be a time of spiritual rejoicing, but of black and dismal mourning had Nasser been permitted to complete Hitler's work. That is why we gave, and continue to give, and will give for the rest of our lives—of our money, our time, and our love.

We found that Jerusalem, Israel, and the Jewish people meant more to us than we have possibly imagined. Our Jewish roots went much deeper than any of us had ever dreamed.

At the same time, the Israeli who had tended to look down on his rich uncles in America suddenly gained a new respect for American Jewry. An Israeli tank driver who spoke in Philadelphia a few weeks ago reported that his morale and that of his comrades-in-arms was immeasurably boosted, because as he listened to his tiny transistor radio in the Sinai Desert, and heard of the unbelievable response of American Jewry to Israel's siege, he felt that he was no longer alone. His morale was so buoyed up that he could fight the next day with all the more vigor and passion and confidence.

We are here gathered on these Holy Days four months after the war to see if we can somehow capture the spirit we had then and see that it never dissipates. When we see a moving show, or read a profound book, or experience a deep emotion of love, we hope that that supreme moment will last forever. It can if we will it so. The spiritual reawakening and flush of religious emotion that all of us felt then somehow must be kept alive if the Jewish people is to continue to live on this high plane.

The year in Jewish history that went out yesterday evening must be more than a flash of lightning that shines for a moment but then is lost forever. It must make a permanent mark on our hearts, and on our minds and souls. We must capture its deepest reverberations on our Jewish being, and permit it to direct us to the most noble heights of Jewish life ever dreamed of.

When the skeptics among us speak of their religious experience, and the rationalists speak of miracles, and assimilationists talk of *Klal Yisrael*, we know something irrevocable has happened to us. We are once again brothers, and it is indeed pleasant and good for us to dwell together in peace and in purity.

If the people who were privileged to pray at the Western Wall felt as Moses speaking to God on Mount Sinai, then the rest of us must feel like the mass of Hebrews at the foot of the Mount, ready to do the will of our Maker—"We will do and we will obey."

The confrontation with ourselves and with our people and our God must lead us to even greater recognition of our past and responsibility ôf our future. Words like Torah, Israel, and God must take on a much larger role in our daily lives after June, 1967.

The distinguished Chancellor of the Jewish Theological Seminary, Rabbi Louis Finkelstein, prayed at the Temple Wall shortly after its redemption. In a letter to Conservative rabbis in this country he wrote, "Never, except perhaps on the Day of Atonement, have I participated in a more stirring service. All my life seemed a preparation for this great moment."

Our task as Jews today is to see that all our life is dedicated to re-creating the spiritual greatness of the year just ended, and to see to it, by our words and our deeds, that this great moment in Jewish history is a preparation for our future.

May it be Thy will. Amen.

23

A Stiff-Necked People

WE'RE A FUNNY PEOPLE, WE JEWS. WE'VE BEEN CALLED ALL kinds of names, cursed with all manner of curses, condemned with innumerable condemnations. One of the strongest things ever said about us was the epithet hurled at us by Moses himself, the great prophet and lawgiver, as he prayed to God for divine forgiveness after the sin of the Golden Calf. In the words of this week's Torah portion, "O Lord, let the Lord, I pray Thee, go in the midst of us, for it is a stiff-necked people; and pardon our iniquity and our sin, and take us for Thine inheritance." (Exodus 34:9.)

Moses' heart-felt words are filled with deep pity and love for this stubborn people, and he pleads with God to forgive them, and travel with them, and renew His covenant with them because they need His guidance desperately.

If we read between the lines, we can detect a slight strain of ambiguity in that charge that Moses hurls against us, his people, that we are stubborn and stiff-necked. It's not too different from the way any of us would talk about our own children. "That stubborn kid—he's just like his old man."

Delivered Friday night, February 27, 1970, Parashat Kee Tisa.

How often have we made the same remark, half in anger, half in love?

The ambivalence lies perhaps in the twofold nature of this quality in man's character, the quality of stubbornness. It has its good side and its bad side. Sometimes it's quite a positive attribute to be stubborn. When we sit down with a problem in math, unless we're stiff-necked and stubborn about it, we may never get it solved. Sometimes the crowd insists upon one path and we want to take a totally different one. If we have the strength of our convictions, we should walk our own path. That kind of stubbornness is wonderful.

Then there is a second kind of stubbornness, the kind that won't listen to reason, that won't bend with the times, that makes it impossible for a person to put himself in the other fellow's shoes. There is the stubbornness that keeps a man set in his old ways, and prevents him from progress and growth. That stubbornness is not a good trait to possess.

And so, without psychoanalyzing Moses, or putting words in his mouth that aren't there, I'd like to suggest that what Moses is thinking is something like this: These no-good pagans relapsed into their old idolatry while I was up on Mt. Sinai receiving the two tablets of the Law. They're a stubborn bunch, these stiff-necked Israelites! What can I do with them? However, were they not stiff-necked, would they ever have been able to withstand four hundred years of slavery? Would they ever have been able to endure exile from their homeland, cruel treatment in a foreign land? So, while I'm angry at this particular act of stubbornness, this reversion to their idolatrous behavior of many generations ago, I can see how this happened to them because it is the very same stubbornness which both led them to worship the Golden Calf and to survive the buffets of misfortune under a cruel, tyrannical Pharaoh.

The midrash seems to sense this ambivalence in Moses' charge as well. While a superficial reading of the Torah would suggest that Moses' charge is unmitigated castigation, one of the rabbis of the midrash sees another aspect to the passage. "You think that this is said disparagingly," said Rabbi Isaac in the name of Rabbi Ami, "but it is really in their praise, because they are a people prepared to give their lives to remain Jewish." (Exodus Rabbah 42:9, Soncino ed., p. 492.)

In the view of Rabbi Ami, Moses is describing the Jewish people as stubborn in a plea for their defense. He is saying, "Dear God, don't be too harsh with this brood. This slip into apostasy is a pure aberration. They're usually not like this. They are usually totally stubborn in their loyalty to Thee. Here, at Sinai, while their leader absented himself for a long period of time, they slipped from their usually fierce fidelity and faithfulness. Just because they committed this one sin, still count them among those who stubbornly and zealously guard Thy faith."

This is the typical approach of the midrash, which always attempts to whitewash the sins of our people and put them in the best possible light. And being somewhat of a chauvinistic and proud Jew, I can't say that I dislike the interpretation of Rabbi Ami. There is no doubt about it—we *are* a stubborn people, a *very* stubborn people, and had we *not* been a stubborn people, we never would have made it to this point in history. It's that stubbornness which has enabled our people to achieve what it has achieved, and to contribute what it has been able to contribute, and to survive in the face of centuries and millennia of forces that would have destroyed us.

I'm proud to be part of this fiercely stubborn people, and I hope all of us are. And furthermore, I hope we never surrender that stiff-necked posture, because we'll be the poorer without it, and so will the rest of the world.

The midrash also tells us that there are three stubborn traits about us which were so admired by the Almighty that when He saw these, He decided to redeem us from Egyptian bondage. One is that despite living in an Egyptian country, the Hebrew slaves stubbornly clung to the Hebrew language, and never gave up speaking it. The second is that despite the acceptable pattern of naming children in ancient Egypt, the Hebrew slaves continued the practice of giving their children biblical and Hebraic names. And thirdly, no matter what the level of morality was among their pagan neighbors, the ancient Israelites clung fast to their very high standards of moral behavior. These three acts of sheer stubbornness were what made God think us worthy enough to be redeemed.

Often this stubbornness in our customs and high moral standards caused other peoples to keep us isolated and persecuted. Nevertheless, this never deterred us. We remained stubborn and strong-willed. The Greeks and Romans wanted us to accept their manner of dress, their language, their love for sports, for art, for building, for cults of wine and sex— and in part we did accept some of these things. But we stubbornly kept aloof from the base character of these activities, and long after the end of their great empires we are here to tell the tale.

Antiochus and Hadrian wanted us to become Hellenized and Latinized, but we refused and it cost us our national independence. Torquemada insisted that we see the light of the official faith of Spain, and in our tenacity, we left the country we had become so familiar with and enamored by, and wandered all over Europe seeking a congenial host, rather than give up our stubborn clinging to being Jews. And in the worst tragedy of all our history, when the Nazi madman sought to break our spirit and crush our soul as well as our body, we marched with undying faith to the gas chambers, chanting *"Ani Ma-amin,"* "Despite the tragedy of today, I still have faith in God and in the coming of His messiah."

And just three years after this horrible, unspeakable massacre of one third of our ranks, when by all rules of logic and sanity we should have, after two thousand years of persistence in our stubbornness, given up the ghost, we then achieved the highest affirmation of our faith and national existence, and we dared to defy the laws of history by restoring our national homeland, and created an independent, sovereign Jewish State for the first time in two milennia.

This was undoubtedly the *height* of our stubbornness. What gall—what chutzpah—what temerity we must have had to take that daring step and tell the world we *insist* upon staying alive! We *insist* upon preventing Hitler from having posthumous success by not commiting suicide when any other people under these circumstances surely would have. Rather, we reaffirmed the eternal bond between the Land and the People, the eternal Covenant between the Creator and His Folk.

They told Eliezer ben Yehuda it couldn't be done. You can't revive a dead language after two thousand years of disuse. It's never been done. But our stubbornness did it!

They told Theodor Herzl it couldn't be done. You can't gather together thousands of people from all over Europe and Asia and expect them to live together in the same household. *But our stubbornness did it!*

When the British began to evacuate their troops from mandated Palestine in May of 1948, American Secretary of State George Marshall cabled David Ben-Gurion and pleaded with him as a friend not to declare the independence of the new Jewish State. Wait for better conditions. This isn't the right time. You can't create a State when seven hostile neighbor nations are poised on your borders ready to attack and destroy you. *But our stubbornness did it!*

But perhaps the greatest stubbornness of all is the firm, tenacious grip we have held in our own stiff-necked way, on the moral standards of our tradition, despite the brutalization our people has faced these many years.

We were forced into three bloody wars in the Middle East, and when the latest of these was finished the Chief of Staff of the Israel Defense Forces made a speech at the Hebrew University and told how profoundly affected his soldiers were by the terrible price the enemy paid in that war. "It may be that the Jewish people was never brought up, never accustomed, to feel the joy of the conqueror and the victor," said General Rabin in June, 1967.

And two and one-half years later, Prime Minister Meir, while visiting in London, said, "We can forgive the Arabs for killing our sons, but we will never forgive them for forcing our sons to kill theirs."

In our fierce, rigid stubbornness, we refuse to give up the values that have made us human while other people acted like animals.

The number one song on Israel's hit parade today is the product of the Nahal, Israel training youth corps. It is called "Shir HaShalom," the Song of Peace. It very closely resembles some of the peace songs being sung by the anti-war movement in the United States. It is a pacifist song, being sung by the army troops, and condoned with no reservations by the military authorities.

> Sing a song to love,
>   and not to victories
> Say not that the day of peace
>   will come,
> Bring that day on!
>
> Lift up your eyes in hope,
>   not through your gun-sights.

In the eyes of the Israeli authorities, the more love of peace there is in the military camps, the stronger will the army become. General Rabin has said that not hate makes good soldiers, but refined spiritual values.

We're so stubborn, we Jews, that we refuse to let war and murder of our people, civilians and soldiers alike, make us stoop to the enemy's level. We refuse to toss bombs into Arab markets, or machine-gun children's buses, or sabotage Arab civilian aircraft. Because we are stubborn!

The world can cut off their mail and their cargo to Israel.

The nations can boycott flights to Israel.

They can refuse to sell us their planes and their tanks.

They can mourn for Lebanese loss of planes and ignore Israel's loss of lives.

They can be as even-handed as they possibly can.

They can line their pockets with Arab oil.

They can tell us we're rude when we placard against France.

But we stubbornly want to survive, we stiff-neckedly want to live! We tenaciously want to cling to our faith in the God of Israel. For we know that we don't need large numbers of people, or large numbers of nations to justify our cause. We are a people by virtue of our Torah, not by the grace of Charles De Gaulle or Harold Wilson or Richard Nixon. Our values are not those of the political arena, but those of the House of Study, the Bet HaMidrash. We need only our own faith in the God of Israel who neither slumbers nor sleeps, who neither lies nor falters. As long as we maintain that ultimate faith in Him who chartered us and redeemed us, we need no other ally. May we always stubbornly adhere to that faith, and may God guard our path tomorrow as he did yesterday. If, then, we are a people born in stubbornness, matured in stubbornness, and reborn in stubbornness, then let that same ancient stubbornness guide us through the perils that await us tomorrow.

24

Israel the "Unreasonable"

IT'S DELIGHTFUL TO SEE JACKSONVILLE JEWRY TOGETHER TO-
night working towards a common cause. One of the things
for which we should be extremely grateful to Israel is that
the welfare of the State of Israel is one of the few causes
which unites all of the Jews in this city.

When I was in Israel last month Rabbi Mordecai Kaplan,
my former teacher at the Seminary, was one of the speakers.
Before he got up to speak—and you must remember that
Rabbi Kaplan is now ninety years old—he danced a hora
with another colleague because it was the Sabbath and we
were in Jerusalem, and there was a great spirit in the air.
Then, when Kaplan got up to speak, he said, "You know,
Rabbi Klein and I hold completely different ideas about
many things in Jewish theology—we have different concep-
tions of God, and yet we could dance together. The present
denominationalism in Jewish life is so foolish; what we need
is unity in American Jewish life. We must all dance together
for the sake of Israel and of world Jewry."

Delivered May 3, 1971, Jacksonville Civic Auditorium, Community
Observance of Israel Independence Day.

What I want to speak about tonight in the few minutes I have is this idea that Israel is so unreasonable, intransigent.

In 1967 when Israel was the underdog, and when bugles flared and drums rolled, and a little tiny nation of three million beat three countries, each of which was far larger and more numerous, Israel enjoyed quite a wide acceptance. But today the world is a bit bored with the Middle East on their TV sets, and the drama has disappeared, and the air of crisis isn't here, so everyone can point his finger and say, "Israel is being unreasonable."

That's the way it's been with our people over the centuries. Sometimes we're very popular—not often, but sometimes. But more often, the winds of popular taste are fickle and they are against us. Today they happen to be against us. But we have learned over and over again that as Jews we can rely on three things in time of peril: the Jews, the Jews, and the Jews. Not on international guarantees; not on good will of popes or pontificators; not on fragile self-serving promises that evaporate like water on a hot day; not on friendly nations whose hearts may bleed for us but who sit by and watch our enemies attack us; but only upon our own young boys who have given their blood for the welfare of our people.

So for this they say we are unreasonable. Because we have witnessed too many times our slow undoing through foreign apathy and anti-Semitism and isolationism.

That's why we are here tonight, paying allegiance to our people under siege—the siege of international opinion. We say to our brothers and sisters in Israel: *Do not yield!* WE STAND WITH YOU. Do not give up the land you were forced to conquer because of enemy aggression! In the name of every Jewish martyr of the past four thousand years, stand fast, and do not give in. This is not a Six Day War. This is a four-thousand-year war, in which Judah the Maccabee, and Trumpeldor and Ann Frank, and a child in a sabotaged school bus, all fought in the same war. And we too will do our share to support your efforts. We will build the schools, and the hospitals, and the roads, and the centers for new immigrants.

Indeed, we are a very unreasonable people! Golda Meir

recently said that she has been in Israel now for fifty years, and never during that half century has there been peace. The children of her generation fought in the Hagana; then came the Second World War; then the War of Liberation in 1948, and then Sinai in 1956, and then the War of June, 1967, and now the border wars. Is it so stubborn and unreasonable for a people who have gone through this for so many years to want a full and recognized peace with its neighbors? Are we so unreasonable?

The nations of the world stand by and preach from their high altars of morality and talk about not permitting occupation of territory by force. When the survival of Israel was in danger, what did the world do then? Is it so *unreasonable* to want to avoid being destroyed by your enemies, and to win the war which was designed to wipe you off the map?

Surely, we are an unreasonable people! A reasonable people would certainly not have survived four thousand years of destruction and persecution, of exile and pogroms; of annihilation and holocaust. A reasonable people would have given up the ghost.

The Greeks couldn't understand why this tiny people remained so unreasonable in not accepting their gods but insisted on being faithful to one God. And today, they are gone, but we continue to teach our idea of ethical monotheism to the entire world.

The Romans insisted that we were unreasonable, wanting to take off one day in every seven for rest. Their historians charged that we wasted one-seventh of our lives that way. But now the Romans are gone, and we unreasonable Jews are still here to teach the world about the concept of the Sabbath.

They said it was unreasonable to try to restore a language not widely used as a spoken tongue for two thousand years. Other peoples tried it and failed. But we're not reasonable. We did it, when others couldn't.

Other nations were exiled from their homelands and never returned. We were unreasonable, and we returned, not once but twice—and after a gap of two millennia.

And today again we're being unreasonable, when we won't

let Russia and other nations guard our borders. Well, we played the game their way too often before, and we know what happened! We watched the UN disappear overnight. We watched our friends sit by and leave us to our own defenses. Today we have the best defenses we ever had—a river between us and Jordan and a river between us and Egypt. And we're going to sit on those rivers until a peace treaty is signed—and be as unreasonable as we have to be in order to save our lives.

We can sit here tonight and observe Israel's twenty-third birthday because Jewish boys fought and saved our people and our homeland. Thousands of Russian Jews have a place to go because of Jewish boys' blood. We're not here because of anything that Dulles or Eisenhower did; nor because of anything Dean Rusk or Lyndon Johnson did; and we're going to be here again next year, despite whatever William Rogers tries to do. In two years from now we'll celebrate the silver anniversary of Israel because of the blood of Jewish boys and not because of international guarantees. If that's being unreasonable, then we are guilty as charged.

Would the United States government consider it reasonable to let Russia guard the border between North and South Vietnam? If it's good enough for Israel, then let's get out of Vietnam, and let Russia guarantee the peace there.

The prophet Hosea once said that the children of Israel are like the sand of the sea which cannot be numbered. The rabbis wondered why we should be compared with sand, since we were never so numerous—we have always been such a small people. And they decided there were two reasons why we were compared to the sand. First because sand is trampled underfoot. Our people has suffered so much and so often, that we indeed have been like the sand underfoot. But Israel was created to put an end to that! The existence of Israel means that never again will our people be trampled by others.

And the second reason was that sand, earth, is indispensable for life. Subsistence comes from the soil. Without the soil of Judaism there can be no life. Without the Jewish people, without the State of Israel, the world will not long exist. The world needs our people, our faith, it needs the State of Israel—because if Israel goes, we all go. Just as it needs the earth to survive, mankind needs the State of Israel, and her values and ethics and her example of a peace-loving people devoted to the cause of justice and righteousness and peace.

I can think of nothing in this world more important to celebrate than the continued survival of Israel. It is to this cause that we must earnestly dedicate our full selves on this great night.

25

Christian-Jewish Relations after the Six Day War

ANOTHER OF THE SIDE EFFECTS OF THE NOW-FAMOUS ISRAEL victory over Arab belligerents was the extraordinary response of Christians and the Church. I stated earlier that the response of world Jewry can be categorized in the area of phenomenal. Christianity's response, too, was phenomenal: a phenomenal failure.

Let me give you an example out of my own experience, and then present the national record as it appeared in print. In May of this year (1967), as, in Senator Clark's words, the apocalypse seemed to come upon the State of Israel, rabbis throughout the country received letters from the national office of the Rabbinical Assembly requesting that we try to interpret the events in the Middle East to our Christian colleagues.

Several days before the War I sent out a letter to one hundred Christian clergy in this area, explaining some of my views, and transmitting to them the necessity of their vocal

Delivered Rosh Hashana night, October 5, 1967.

support, as well as that of the entire Church in America, for an amelioration of Israel's lonely and tragic circumstance. In addition, I enclosed a statement, a "declaration of conscience," asking them to sign and return the declaration. I would then forward it to the New York office where a massive campaign was getting under way to publish ads in the national press with signatures of Christian clergy. The declaration was simple and straightforward. It declared Israel's right to live, rejected Nasser's illegal closing of the Straits of Tiran, and asked for protection for Israel against Arab threats.

The response was pitiful, to say the least. Some four clergymen returned the declaration signed. Three others offered their thoughts in letters, which were sent without enclosures. One distinguished gentleman, for whom I have a great respect, and with whom I have worked on other occasions, told me not to worry, that the UN would care for Israel, and that the Israelis could take care of themselves. Oh, yes, by the way, he added, let's not forget about the Arab refugees—we must worry about them too. As if their lives were suddenly being threatened by the convergence of massive troop movements and the outspoken promise to wipe them off the map.

Another gentleman, whom I had not met, kindly told me that he was praying for me. This was indeed a great comfort. It was as if someone held a knife at my throat, and after calling for help, he offered to mention my plight to the Almighty.

As I began to read the Jewish press, and the bulletins and releases of the various national Jewish defense and social action organizations in America, I saw clearly that my experience was far from unique. In fact, it reflected precisely the experience that Jewish leaders all over the country—even on the national scene—were discovering.

While Christianity was prepared to get deeply involved in civil rights protests, and in demanding American withdrawal from Vietnam, and to speak out on every other burning political issue of our day, they were not prepared to make known their position with regard to the existence of the State of Israel.

Such national Christian figures took their cue from people like Pope Paul, who could only concern himself with the holy places of Jerusalem. The bricks and concrete of the shrines of Christianity seemed to be far more important to him than two million Jewish lives. Nor was he interested in the fact that for nineteen years the Jordanians had desecrated and destroyed fifty-seven synagogues, bulldozed and desecrated the Jewish cemetery on the Mount of Olives while building a road through it for tourists, and defiled scores of other Jewish sites in old Jerusalem, Hebron, and elsewhere.

While Jewish Jerusalem was being rained upon on June 5 and 6 with shells and mortar fire and heavy artillery, the Kingdom of Jordan used Mt. David to launch its military barrages against the Jewish civilians in New Jerusalem. In striking contrast, the Israelis, who could have taken the Old City easily with its own heavy artillery and aircraft, decided to opt for the slower and more painstaking and costly path in terms of their own blood, of slow encirclement with foot soldiers, so as to protect the holy sites.

After the Israelis had conducted themselves with such dignity and restraint, in closely cooperating with President Johnson in letting the diplomatic world play out all its cards, all the official Christian leaders could do is to express their worries and concerns about the Arab refugees and the holy shrines.

One can imagine the shock and amazement and even horror felt by those rabbis who spent their entire lives painstakingly constructing bridges of ecumenical cooperation, and fostering dialogues and interreligious cooperation, only to find all their efforts undermined in an hour.

It is true that many individual Christians spoke up for the cause of the small David against the huge Goliath of Arabia, even as many of them condemned tiny David's audacity in daring to defend himself. However, as far as official Christianity is concerned, not a whimper of support came from any official, authorized body of the Protestant or Catholic establishments anywhere in the world. The churches of the world maintained a holy and studied silence.

One of the most outspoken and vicious attacks on Israel was made by the former President of Union Theological Seminary, the citadel of liberal Protestantism in Morningside Heights; Dr. Henry P. Van Dusen, in a letter on July 7 to *The New York Times,* insisted that all objective observers "stand aghast at Israel's onslaught, the most violent, ruthless (and successful) aggression since Hitler's blitzkrieg across Western Europe in the summer of 1940, aiming not at victory but at annihilation."

What a mouthful of hatred and malicious lies! To suggest that Israel's valiant fight for her life was embarked upon for purposes of annihilation is a crude and vile obscenity. Mimicking the anti-Semites in Russia, he linked Hitler's hordes with their victims. Said Abba Eban at the UN on June 19th, "There is a flagrant breach of international morality and human decency in this comparison. To associate the name of Israel with the accursed tyrant who engulfed the Jewish people in a tidal wave of slaughter is to violate every canon of elementary taste and fundamental truth."

And this from a leading Christian theologian, who had the power in his hands to mold and shape the thinking of scores of young theology students over the decades. Is it a wonder that his devoted students followed his suit?

Or perhaps we should point to the "humanitarian" observations of another of our so-called moral leaders of Christianity, Dr. Willard G. Oxtoby of Yale's department of religious studies. Writing in the *Christian Century,* Mr. Oxtoby called his article "Outright Disagreement with Israel's Planned Conquest of June, 1967 Is Required of Christians." Scoring Jewish leaders for muzzling Christian anti-Zionists, he wrote that "Besides caring for the hundreds of thousands of blamelessly suffering Palestinian Arabs . . . the churches must look towards the preservation of free speech in our nation in fact as well as in law. . . . For a time, virtually the only place in North America where the Arabs could be heard was the UN."

In fairness, we should say that one of the persons most appalled by such Christian anti-Israel stands was a graduate of Union Theological Seminary, Dr. A. Roy Eckhardt, professor of religion at Lehigh University. He wrote in a letter to *The New York Times:*

> If the world Jewish community has been shocked and disillusioned by the new Christian silence before Israel's plight, it must be driven to the verge of despair by the readiness of some Christian leaders to call black "white," to label as "aggressors" the targets of aggression, to identify as "annihilationists" those who barely escaped being annihilated by a foe pledged to turning them into corpses (and who are nevertheless prepared to deal righteously with their would-be slayers).
>
> There are elements of perversity, even insanity, in their identifications. Perhaps we will next be told that the death camps were actually protective measures created by the Nazis to keep Germany from being exterminated by Jews.

The scramble by Jewish leaders and rabbis to budge the church out of silence was not only a quiet diplomatic affair. Besides the many meetings in tension-ridden and smoke-filled conference rooms in ivory tower office buildings, certain brave Jewish figures made public their private disgust with organized Christianity in speeches and in articles. One such article, by Rabbi Arthur Hertzberg, Columbia University historian, appeared in the *National Catholic Reporter.* A sharp and bitter reply to him came forth from a close friend of Jewry, Monsignor George Higgins, who accused Hertzberg of trying to blackmail the church into supporting Israel by means of his ecumenical ties.

In a very perceptive communication distributed by the Social Action Commission of the Union of American Hebrew Congregations, four essential reasons were given to explain the silence of official Christianity in the face of Israel's threatening crisis.

First of all, many Christians are ignorant of the facts of the situation. They have not been following events there carefully enough to understand the dynamics and power plays going on.

This seems to me to be a poor explanation. Simple people all over the world felt strong currents of sympathy with the obvious underdog, tiny Israel, and antipathy towards the mammoth Arab enemy, often, in the case of Communist bloc countries, at the risk of their political security and personal safety.

The second explanation offered by this paper is that the churches have a huge financial and psychological investment in the Middle East missionary movement, which they were not prepared to jeopardize even if it meant letting Israel go down. Any Arab who knew of Christian support for Israel would not be a likely candidate for conversion.

A third explanation is deep and blinding sympathy with the Arab refugees. Christian groups have been collecting money and establishing relief centers for the refugees in Gaza and Jordan for years. Many Christian clergymen have spent time working in these camps. They have swallowed the Arab propaganda regarding the refugees and will not cease blaming Israel for allegedly driving out of innocent bystanders from their homes.

The truth of the matter is that the Palestinian Arabs were urged by the newly created State of Israel in 1948 to remain in their homes, but they were egged on by their Arab confreres on Arabic radio stations to flee the Jewish territory only to return shortly thereafter when the Jews had been driven into the sea.

The full truth, in addition, is that an equal number of Jewish refugees from Arab countries were driven from their homes in 1948, and have all been absorbed and settled in Israel long ago. Had the Arabs cared as much for their own as the Jews did, there would be no refugee problem now in the Middle East.

So the refugee problem, seen in isolation and in a false light, has blinded the eyes of many well-meaning Christians into sympathizing with the smooth dispensers of propaganda and manipulators of truth.

Lastly, explains the Commission, a degree of residual anti-Semitism takes its toll on Israel's call for world support against a threat on its existence.

Whatever the reasons, Christianity showed itself to be a miserable failure when her friendship and encouragement and justified support was required by the Jewish people.

Effect on Ecumenical Movement. The effect on the ecumenical movement in America has been disastrous. What has already been described by some detractors of this movement as "ecumania" has now ground to a slow crawl. There was a great segment of Jewry which had severe reservations about such dialoguing in the first place. Their answer since the events of these past months is now: "I told you so!"

A fierce debate had been raging in the Jewish community as to the propriety of such Christian-Jewish theological confrontation. Many eloquent and distinguished lights in American Jewry rejected outright the whole idea of subjecting the mother faith to the opinions of its disloyal daughter. It demeans Judaism, they argued, to engage in frank and open conversation with the church that carries an already great burden of guilt for historic Jewish suffering. Furthermore, they argued, to what point is such discussion? It can only be fruitless and pointless. Christianity will always demand the acceptance of Jesus as its price for negotiation, and Judaism will not accept it. Neither the members of the "Old" Covenant or the New Covenant will admit the legitimacy of its opponent. Christian-Jewish talk, they argued, should be strictly limited to working together on areas of mutual agreement: civil rights, achieving world peace, improving the cities, eliminating poverty, and the like.

Now, however, after the debacle of the Christian silence over the Arabs' planned genocide, even those who defended such dialogue have given up the ship. Rabbi Marc Tanenbaum of the American Jewish Committee, probably Jewry's leading advocate of Jewish-Christian relations, has declared that the ecumenical movement has suffered a serious setback.

The comments of Senator Hugh Scott in the Senate on September 21, 1967, bear out this apathy towards Jewish suffering. Said Senator Scott:

"One of the main problems which must be solved in order to secure peace is that of the Palestine refugees. Another is the brutal treatment of Jews in Arab countries. While world attention is focused on the plight of Arab refugees, there is shocking indifference to the fate of over 100,000 Jews who

remain in Arab countries and who are the target of savage
revenge."

Thousands of Jews in Egypt, Syria, Iraq, and elsewhere
today are being imprisoned, beaten, and despoiled. Thousands are incarcerated in inhuman conditions in these Arab
countries, and face ultimate annihilation. In Egypt several
hundred Jews of Egyptian nationality are imprisoned under
inhuman conditions, with former S.S. men and Gestapo officers, now residents of Egypt, acting as prison guards and
interrogators. Again, Christianity maintains its blessed silence. Echoes resound like a broken record through the world
out of the Vatican and elsewhere of pleas for holy places,
holy shrines, and Arab refugees . . . holy places, holy
shrines, Arab refugees.

A young and dynamic theologian and historian, Professor
Jacob Neusner of Dartmouth, who also happens to be a Conservative rabbi, about a year ago engaged in bitter dialogue
with an Orthodox rabbi regarding the advisability of dialogue
with Christianity. Writing in the quarterly journal *Judaism*
(Spring, 1966), Dr. Neusner wrote:

> Christians and Jews are talking together, and they are going
> to continue to talk together. If they are believing Jews and
> believing Christians, then their faiths are going to shape their
> interests in one another and the topics they discuss. These are
> facts of American life, and if they should change, it will not be
> for the better. Rabbi Berkovits may condemn them, but he can-
> not change them, nor should many equally serious and informed
> Jewish theologians *want* to change them.

Now, in the light of recent events, Dr. Neusner has again
written in *Judaism,* in the Summer, 1967 issue:

> I erred . . . in differing from Rabbi Berkovits' assessment
> of the promise of Jewish-Christian dialogue. . . . His judg-
> ment was correct, and that of his critics, including this writer,
> was completely false. His pessimism was merely realistic. Our
> optimism was wholly unfounded, as events have now shown
> with painful clarity. The way forward is likely to lead away
> from interreligious conversation and cooperation, except in
> secular, humanitarian ventures, on the one hand, and in schol-

arly inquiries into historical, literary, and philosophical issues, on the other. The middle ground of religious and theological conversation has, I think, been closed by the massive indifference and craven silence of those from whom some of us hoped for better things.

It is painful to admit one's error; it would be sinful not to admit but to repeat it, and, by silence in the face of consequential events, to lead others to suppose that nothing had changed. Much has changed for me, and I believe, for others as well.

Another distinguished thinker, Rabbi Eugene Borowitz, wrote of his loneliness and shock in the face of Christian apathy for Israel and Jewry. "I understand, but I felt lonely with that special sense one gets when one really needs his friend and he isn't there."

What's Next in the Dialogue Crisis? Where do we go from here? Will all dialogue stop? I hardly think so. Despite the pain and the agony, the frustration and the loneliness, the ecumenical age, though certainly administered a serious setback, is not yet moribund. The events of the past several months point mainly to a failure of achieving a goal, but not in choosing the wrong goals.

They show that we Jews have failed to convey to our Christian friends the indispensability of Israel in the Jewish scheme of things.

If the dialogue movement is to be revivified, we will have to make plain and clear the Jewish view of the centrality of Eretz Yisrael in our tradition, and of Kelal Yisrael, and to interpret these ideas to Christians in historical as well as theological terminology. We will have to enlighten them as to the real facts of the Arab refugee situation, and of the Jewish refugee situation, as well as of the plight of the Jews now living in Arab lands.

On the other hand, we will have to demand from them a just and moral view of the Middle East situation. Many distinguished Christians have accepted this position, and there is no reason why many more will not. Until that day we will be impatient and resentful, longing to heal the fissure that has been created by the aftermath of the war. We will have to suffer in our loneliness and frustration. But we cannot succumb to our bitter feelings, any more than the Israelis could succumb to the threat against them.

We must hope and wait—and talk and converse, and meet again and again face to face. We pray that ultimately, as prophesied in biblical times by Malachi (3:16) that "Those who revere the Lord will speak one to another."

26

Jewish Religion after the
Six Day War

TISHAH B'AV TRADITIONALLY MARKS THE ANNIVERSARY OF
Jewish tragedy—specifically, the destruction of the capital,
Jerusalem, the holy Temple, and the loss of national inde-
pendence.

What reasons were given by Jewish theologians of the past
for God's letting this destruction take place? What is the
Talmudic version of "After Auschwitz"?—or, shall we say,
"After Jerusalem"? How did the "radical theologians" of
yesterday deal with the fact that God permitted the destruction of holy Jerusalem, His own house, the Temple, and the
exile of His special people?

The ancient rabbis could only justify this evil by pointing
the finger of guilt at themselves. Not the death of God, but
the bankruptcy of morality on earth, caused this savage defeat of humanity. Not the impotence of the Deity, but the
perversion of man, is the rabbinic answer to radical theology.

We recite on each of the three pilgrimage festivals, Pesach,
Shavuot, and Succot, the following phrase in the Musaf Ami-

Published in the *Jewish Exponent*, August 11, 1967.

dah: "Because of our sins we were exiled from the Holy Land and removed far away from its sacred soil."

The Talmud goes further and gives many specific moral and spiritual failings as reasons for God's punishment of the Jewish people: the profanation of the Sabbath, carelessness in recitation of prayers, failure of children to attend school, lack of respect for rabbis, and the absence of trustworthy men.

One of the most interesting "sins" which the rabbis say were responsible for the Exile was that "no one reproved his fellow." One who does not criticize is not a friend, according to rabbinic thinking.

This attitude toward introspection and self-criticism always has been the hallmark of Jewish thought. It should be contrasted with the attitude of the Arabs during the Middle East war of June 5–10, 1967. Arabs were heard criticizing everyone under the sun but themselves for their disastrous defeat. The United States and Britain were guilty of complicity; the Russians were guilty for lack of support; the UN was guilty for not passing a resolution condemning Israel. In short, everybody was guilty but the Arabs themselves.

Many other thoughts enter one's mind on this first Tishah b'av after the war, the first time since the destruction of the Temple by the Romans that the Western Wall is contained within a sovereign Jewish State.

The first is that we should call the Wall by the traditional Jewish name—Kotel Maaravi—the Western Wall. It was given the name "Wailing Wall," according to some authorities, by non-Jewish travelers who witnessed there the daily prayer of pious Jews accompanied by sighing and sobbing over Jewish hardships in the Diaspora.

A second thought in reading the press is that our emotions have made more of that Western Wall than it really is. Not that sentimentalism is out of place in these exciting times— it is very much in place. No living Jew can fail to be thrilled to know that the historical institutions of ancient Jewish life are now protected by a Jewish flag.

The important thing about the Western Wall is that it was

part of the ancient Temple, whether Solomon's or not. It stood on the spot where Solomon's Temple stood. It bears all the hopes and yearnings of the Jewish people for millennia, and it stands as a monument to the indestructibility of the saving remnant of Jewry.

In that sense, it may be considered a shrine, even though the term "shrine" does not carry the same connotation in Judaism as it does in Christianity.

The return of the Wall to Jewish hands fulfills the midrashic oath that "The Divine Presence never departs from the Western Wall."

The restoration of the Temple mount to Jewish hands, and the reunification of the city of Jerusalem under Israeli rule, bring in their train many questions for scholars of Jewish law. We don't have answers to these questions, but they should be raised and discussed.

What is our position with respect to rebuilding the Temple? Even the Conservative movement, which has repudiated its hopes to resume the sacrifice of animals (the chief use of the ancient Temple), still includes in its liturgy, "O rebuild it speedily and enhance its glory."

What about the breaking of the glass at Jewish wedding ceremonies, which traditionally reminds us of the destruction of Jerusalem and the Temple? With a rebuilt Jerusalem will this custom fall into disuse? Or, can we still offer the traditional greeting of comfort: "May the Almighty comfort you among the mourners of Zion and Jerusalem."

What about the observance of Tishah b'av itself? Shall we continue to maintain it as a full day's fast, or does the restoration of the Holy City to renewed vigor offer us some opportunity to alter the second half of the day, as some have suggested, into a looking toward the future instead of into the past?

These are some of the questions. The answers will come only with time—perhaps Elijah will be the one who answers them. The skeptic might scoff at the thought of Elijah's second coming. But from our brethren in Israel we have learned to say, "Today you have to be a realist to believe in miracles."

27

Archeology and the Six Day War

THE INFLUENCE OF THE SIX DAY WAR ON SUBSEQUENT JEWISH history has been so tremendously significant that even now, one year later, we still cannot fully gauge all of its effects. Most people are aware of these changes in areas such as the Middle East power structure, the status of Soviet and Polish Jewry and of Jews in Arab countries, relations between Christians and Jews, Jewish philanthropy and Jewish self-respect and ethnic awareness.

One area in which the effects of the Six Day War have been highly important, and yet little has been said about it, is that of archeology, a particular field of interest of mine.

I have been an avid student of biblical archeology for some eight years, and have found it one of my favorite pastimes. It breeds excitement, it is full of challenge and mystery, resembling in many ways the work of a detective. The central task of biblical archeology, of course, is to illumine and clarify the period of civilization in the Near East in which the Book of Books was created. Thus, not only is archeology itself interesting to me, but the fruits which it produces—

Delivered Friday night, May 31, 1968, on the First Anniversary of the Six Day War. Published in *The American Zionist*, November, 1968.

namely, a fuller understanding of the Torah and the entire Bible—are often a great source of knowledge and inspiration to me.

Archeology not only helps us understand our past, but it clarifies our origins, and binds us ever closer to the earliest periods of Jewish creativity. Furthermore, since the present Middle East is such a fertile area for biblical excavation, it is a great source of pride to world Jewry that Israel is becoming the world center for biblical archeology, and its scholars the undisputed leaders in the field. No longer is it the case that biblical scholarship and archeological research is the sole domain of Christian scholars both in Europe and America.

War and Archeology Related. It is of particular interest to note that in Israel the great battles between the Arabs and the Jews have always been closely connected with important archeological finds. The first manuscripts of the Dead Sea Scrolls were acquired by Elazar Sukenik, Professor of Archeology at the Hebrew University in Jerusalem, on November 29, 1947, the same day that the United Nations voted to establish a Jewish state in Palestine. Ironically, one of the scrolls involved was the now-famous document known as "The War of the Sons of Light and the Sons of Darkness."

Now, after the Six Day War of June 5–10, 1967, we can see three major effects on archeology emanating from this brief but far-reaching military conflict.

I would like to touch on three main areas in which archeology in the Middle East has seen radical transformations as a result of the Six Day War.

The first is that since Israel's borders have expanded threefold, so has its available territory for archeological investigation and excavation. All or most all of the occupied areas are rich mines for the spade of the archeologist: the West Bank, the Gaza Strip, and the Sinai Desert. In the West Bank we have such significant sites as Samaria, Gibeah, Gibeon, Beth El, Bethlehem, Old Jerusalem, and hundreds of places of lesser importance. Gaza is the site of one of the five ancient Philistine cities, and the Sinai Desert is an unchartered elephant in archeological terms, with vast unexamined areas waiting for the modern scholar to come and uncover the path of Moses and the Israelites on their forty-year trek to the Promised Land.

For nineteen years Israelis have not been able to set foot on these territories, let alone examine them or dig there. Thus, the first thing that was done just days after the War ended was the organization of large teams of scholars to explore all of the newly conquered territories. Probably more work was done in these areas by Israelis than had been accomplished by Arab scholars in the entire period of Israel's existence.

The Rockefeller Museum. The second important effect resulting from the Six Day War has to do with the Palestine Archeological Museum in the Old City of Jerusalem. Built in 1929 with a two-million-dollar grant by John D. Rockefeller, and known popularly since then as the "Rockefeller Museum," this oasis in the Arabian cultural desert is very strategically located, and is, in fact, built to resemble a fortress. On its top is a large tower, with an eight-sided turret.

It was in this tower that the Jordanian armed forces mounted their gun emplacements on June 5, 1967, from which vantage point they attacked Israel and tried to defend the Old City.

Only an Arab country would so abuse a building wherein was stored priceless treasures collected during a period of almost four decades: the Samaria ivories, pre-biblical skeletons, Temple inscriptions going back two thousand years, a carved lintel from the door of the Church of the Holy Sepulchre, priceless collections of gold and jewelry from Roman times, and most important of all, the invaluable collection of Dead Sea Scrolls discovered over the past two decades beginning in 1948. Of the original thirteen scrolls, seven were in Jordan, in the Rockefeller Museum, and six were in Israel, and now housed in the "Shrine of the Book," in the Israel Museum complex in Jerusalem.

Since Israel would only fight in the Old City by hand-to-hand combat, avoiding any kind of bombardment that might have destroyed religious shrines or cultural repositories such as this museum, the Rockefeller Museum was spared bombing. But it did emerge from the War pockmarked with bullets, windows smashed, and Jordanian blood spilled on some of its exhibits.

When the museum was reopened to the public on July 11, 1967, after a month of clean-up and reorganization, visitors were greatly relieved to see that the only important changes were that the exhibits now had Hebrew as well as Arabic and English labels. However, one section of the museum was closed, that which stored the Qumran, or Dead Sea Scrolls. For weeks after the War it was feared that the Arabs had whisked the scrolls away to Amman at the start of the War. After an intensive search, the scrolls were discovered in a safe in a specially hidden compartment in a wall behind a display case. Israel demolition experts pried open the door so as not to destroy any of the scrolls, and found to their pleasant surprise all seven of the scrolls plus over four hundred scroll fragments.

Happily, all of the Dead Sea Scrolls are now in Israeli hands. Much to their shock and dismay, Israeli scholars found that the priceless treasures stored in the Rockefeller Museum had been very poorly treated. The cataloguing, general administration, display techniques, and security measures were sorely lacking in efficiency. The staff had carelessly permitted many important items be pilfered and sold in bazaars and antiquity markets. The staff was lacking in morale because they often went without pay, and had not been paid for a period of two months prior to the War. Hence their lackadaisical approach.

It is to the great credit of Israel that its own archeological museum, less than five years old, has standards vastly superior to the ones which obtained in the older museum.

The Jordanians have reaped their reward, not only for their general belligerency which brought them into the War and lost the Old City for them, but for their apathy and philistine attitude towards their archeological treasures. Not only that, but for their greed and ignorance as well. From 1948 to November, 1966, the Palestine Archeological Museum was governed by an international board of governors, since it had been decided by the UN that Jerusalem would become an international city. The city never saw its internationalization, but the museum did. Then, in November, 1966, Jordan unilaterally nationalized the museum, much to the objection and dismay of its board of governors. Thus, when the Israel government liberated the Old City, it became the legitimate successor of the Jordanian government, which had only six months before set the wheels in motion for Israel to take over the museum. Had they left things as they were, Israel would have to recognize the international status of the museum. Thanks to God's hardening of Hussein's heart, Israel now has both Jerusalem and the museum, and can now proudly say that all of the priceless Dead Sea Scrolls, written in the national language of Israel, are in the best possible hands.

To the world of scholarship the Six Day War has meant a new and higher level of research and achievement in biblical archeology because of the two facts described above.

The third archeological feat that came out of the Six Day War is perhaps the most amazing and important of all. It began on the fourth day of the War, Thursday, June 8, 1967. The son of Dr. Sukenik (who was responsible for bringing to light the first group of Scrolls in 1948), Professor Yigael Yadin, had been mobilized during the War and was serving in the War Room in Jerusalem in an advisory capacity. He had previously served as Chief of Operations during the 1948 war, and later as Chief of Staff. In the early 1950s, Yadin returned to win his doctorate and became an active member in the Hebrew University's Department of Archeology.

Yadin had had previous knowledge about another Dead Sea scroll of unknown contents, which had been harbored by the same Arab dealer in Bethlehem who had sold his father the earlier scrolls. For seven years Yadin had known something about this scroll, but could not make contact with the dealer.

When Yadin read the dispatch in the War Room which informed him that Bethlehem was now in Israeli hands, he immediately traveled there with a group of officers. The dealer was arrested, and a search of his house made. The exact details of this phase of the operation have still not been released by Yadin, obviously for political reasons, but he acknowledges that when all the facts of the story are made public, it will read like a tale from the Arabian Nights.

The scroll did eventually come into Yadin's hands. He found that owing to mishandling by the Arab dealer, it had deteriorated more in the previous seven years than during the two thousand years when it was hidden in the Judean cave. It had been preserved well in the hot, dry climate of the Judean wilderness, but in the hilly city of Bethlehem, where humidity in the winter reached up to 70 percent, it had deteriorated so much that part of it looked to Yadin like melted chocolate.

After a laborious process of humidifying and freezing, the brittle scroll was unrolled and found to be about three-fourths complete. The newest Dead Sea scroll is over twenty-eight feet long, four feet longer than the longest previously known scroll. It was written by an Essene scribe, some time during the first century B.C.E. The Essenes were a group of monklike ascetics, living in stern, rigid disciplinary conditions in the isolated desert.

The scroll was obviously meant to become part of the Bible —perhaps even the Torah—since it is the only Dead Sea Scroll, other than copies of books of the Bible, in which God speaks in the first person.

New laws, and Essene festivals are described, which are no longer observed today. A Feast of New Oil was observed fifty days after Shavuot, and a Feast of New Wine fifty days after that. Most of the scroll, however, describes the Temple, as seen in the mind of the Essenes, different in conception from that of the Jerusalem Temple, or from descriptions in other sources such as the prophet Ezekiel or the historian Josephus. Since most of the scroll is taken up with the description of how to build this Temple, Yadin has dubbed it "The Temple Scroll," and it is under this name that we shall certainly be hearing more about it in the months ahead.

Since the Essene sect was so preoccupied with Temple worship, Yadin feels that those scholars who look at the Essenes as the precursors of Christianity are far off base. One of the things that differentiated the early Christians was that Temple worship and animal sacrifice played no part in their religious life.

Probably the most startling thing about the scroll is contained in a section dealing with the laws of kings. If the king hears of a threat against "the land of Israel," he mobilizes one tenth of the people. If he sees that the enemy outnumbers him, he drafts one fifth for military service. If then, the enemy is seen advancing swiftly, he conscripts one third of the nation. Finally, when war erupts, one half of the people fight while the other half remains at home to defend the homeland.

Yadin says, and he would know, that these are precisely the stages of mobilization that took place in Israel during May and early June, 1967.

All of which proves that archeology is the handmaiden of history, and that in Israel archeology, the Bible, and history are re-lived again and again each year.

28
Soviet Jewry after the Six Day War

WE HAVE ALREADY DISCUSSED TWO MAJOR SIDE EFFECTS OF the Six Day War of June, 1967. First, the transformation of the Jewish people. Second, the implications of and effects on Christian-Jewish relations in America. Now we turn to the third major effect of the War: the intensification of anti-Semitism in the Soviet Union.

The Soviets are celebrating this month the fiftieth anniversary of the Bolshevik Revolution. You are all familiar with the name of Chaim Weizmann, first President of the State of Israel. In the year of the Bolshevik Revolution, 1917, Chaim Weizmann made the following prediction:

> We are an old nation and must not forget the warnings of history. Great hopes were raised by the French Revolution, also. The principles of equality may be decreed by law, but they take a considerable time before they become an integral part of the life of a nation. It is difficult to believe that anti-Semitism,

Delivered Yom Kippur Eve, October 13, 1967.

which has been systematically urged and cruelly practiced in Russia for so long, will suddenly disappear.

That was on the eve of the Bolshevik Revolution. Now, from the perspective of a half century later, his prediction has been sadly confirmed.

Soviet persecution of their Jewish citizens, numbering some three million, was serious enough before the Arab-Israel confrontation of June, 1967. Ten years after the denunciation of Stalin and Stalinism at the 20th Party Congress, all of Stalin's sins have been condemned except one: his savage treatment of the Jews. While there have been no outright purges of Jews as in Stalin's day, Russian anti-Jewish actions have been constant and virulent during the reign of Khrushchev, and continues under the new regime. Closing of synagogues to the point where only some sixty exist for the entire three million Soviet Jews, the ban on Jewish schools and publications, the absence of a rabbinical training seminary, the inhuman suppression of any kind of Jewish culture, religious, or social life all add up to a dismal and devastating picture of Jewish life in Russia. The half dozen rabbis still living in the U.S.S.R. are all in their seventies and eighties. Very little hope exists for any kind of Jewish continuity.

Besides the officially sponsored programs of anti-Semitism, a good deal of popular, or ethnic, anti-Semitism reigns throughout the major population centers of the Soviet Union. When the government-controlled press lets loose on one of its frequent attacks on Judaism and Jewry, this popular anti-Semitism is encouraged and given free reign.

This is what happened this past summer. The Soviet press had been violently condemnatory of Israel throughout the past ten years, but particularly so beginning in the weeks prior to the crisis of May of this year, and continuing up until now. Individual Soviet anti-Semites picked up the government line as soon as its colors were shown. Immediately following the Israeli victory in mid-June, a pogrom-like atmosphere prevailed in many Soviet communities. Reports of anti-Jewish atrocities, and of an intensified campaign of terrorism and vilification gradually filtered out of the U.S.S.R. through returning Western visitors.

In early July, the rabbi of the synagogue in Sukhumi was brutally murdered while on his way home from prayers. As he left the synagogue he was forced into a car, and later savagely abused and mutilated, and hanged in a Christian cemetery from a tree, upside down.

Other Jews were pressured at the threat of bodily harm into signing statements condemning Israeli "aggression." Forced meetings of Jewish people were held throughout the Soviet Union to arrange mass signings of such anti-Israel declarations. To the credit of the Jewish community there, which is becoming more and more resistant to government pressure, very few signed.

In the July issue of the only Yiddish publication in all of the Soviet Union, *Sovietish Heimland,* a purely government-sponsored mouthpiece, thirteen Yiddish writers were forced to denounce Israel. While we tend to be ashamed of such Jews, we are gratified that it was only this small number that signed it. Some one hundred Yiddish writers contribute to that monthly journal, and the other eighty-seven refused to bend to Soviet pressure. Not one Jewish scholar or intellectual put his name on the document. There were several conspicuous absentees, including Michael Lev, editorial secretary of the journal and a usually loyal party-line author.

It must be made perfectly clear that when the Soviets attack Israel, they are not only vilifying a sovereign political state thousands of miles way. To them Israel is merely the corporate Jew, the Jew of the nations of the world. They are therefore as much attacking their own Jews as those in Israel. To the Soviet way of thinking the State of Israel, the Zionist movement, and world Jewry, including, of course, Soviet Jewry, are all part of one world-wide conspiracy to take over the world, à la the forged "Protocols of the Elders of Zion."

Let me illustrate this. In an article in *Izvestia* dated July 2, 1967, one Yuri Ivanov wrote that "The nationalist clique of Israel, which should in no way be confused with the people of that country, preaches Zionism and is part of a New York-based international Zionist firm controlled by the U.S.A."

In other words, Jews who have ties to their ancestral homeland—Zionists—in every country in the world are mere puppets of an American group of imperialists who control world Jewry as well as the State of Israel. Because of Israel's victory over the Soviet-backed Arab states, Russia's Jews are being punished as part of the international clique based in New York which is responsible for this victory. It all ties together into a neat picture. The Soviet Jew is looked upon as a disloyal, politically dangerous, and alien resident, who has no rights and deserves none.

Khrushchev once remarked that he was not in favor of letting the Jews settle together in one Russian area, because in case of war they would act as a fifth column against the Soviet Union.

Immediately following the War, a flood of stereotypical anti-Semitic caricatures burst upon the Soviet press. Uncle Sam was made to look Jewish, reinforcing the popular image that the U.S.A. is controlled by Jews. So-called "eye-witness" accounts began to appear which testified to the brutal "Nazi-like" treatment by Israeli soldiers of helpless Arab prisoners. "Captive and wounded Arabs," reported *Izvestia* on June 17, "were stripped to the skin, deprived of their water flasks and abandoned under the blazing sun, in the sand. . . . The Sinai Desert has turned into a huge crematorium. . . ."

On July 5, Brezhnev himself said in Moscow: "In the atrocities against the peaceful Arab populations, it seems they try to copy the crimes of Nazi invaders. . . . The aggressors conduct themselves like the worst bandits and commit atrocities in the Hitlerite style."

On June 16, *Izvestia* wrote in an editorial: "The Israeli aggressors are murdering prisoners of war and peaceful peasants; they are arranging public executions, including women and children, and they are expelling residents from their homeland. Even Western correspondents are comparing these deeds to the crimes of the Nazis during World War II. . . ."

On June 18, *Pravda* wrote: "When one reads the reports of these crimes, terrible pictures of the recent past arise in the memory. The ovens of Maidanek and Auschwitz blazed. . . ."

On July 2, *Izvestia* said: ". . . Since both the Zionist and the Nazis elevated race and nation above all things, it was inevitable that a common bridge should arise between them."

On August 5, the Soviet news agency, *Novosti*, distributed a long article charging that Zionism is a world organization operating in sixty countries, and dealing in everything from religion to espionage. Some of the "Zionist" organizations listed in the article were B'nai B'rith, the Joint Distribution Committee, and HIAS. In August of this year, the head of the J.D.C., on a pleasure trip from his home in New York with his wife and nephew, was murdered, some report by the Soviet secret service, on a warm evening in Czechoslovakia. His body was found in the Moldau River.

In a frenzied anti-Semitic atmosphere such as this, one can understand that the position of the Jew is extremely precarious. Jews in Russia, like many non-Jews there, are overwhelmingly pro-Israel. The first day of the War they called the Israel embassy in Moscow in their hundreds wishing them good luck. The embassy was one of the principal guardians against anti-Semitism in the Soviet Union. Now that diplomatic relations no longer exist between the U.S.S.R. and Israel, and the embassy is shut down, the campaign against Jews is running wild with no one to stand guard.

Let My People Go. The world was given great hope last December, when Premier Kosygin announced in Paris that anyone who wanted to leave the Soviet Union to join his family abroad would have no problem. It was hoped that thousands of Soviet Jews would be able finally to spend "next year in Jerusalem." His statement was even printed in Moscow, giving great hopes to thousands of Jews who reported to emigration offices carrying with them the articles in the Russian press. The volume was so huge that, by mid-January, 1967, the press began a campaign charging anyone who wanted to leave the motherland with treason and disloyalty. In February a show case was made of an elderly

Soviet Jew, Solomon Dolnik, who was charged with spying for Israel by meeting Israeli embassy officials in the Moscow synagogue. By March of this year, synagogue officials in Moscow, Tashkent, and elsewhere were being summoned by Soviet secret police and under threats of retaliation were forced to organize letter-writing campaigns against Zionism. All of this was obviously directed towards discouraging emigration.

Then, of course, the War came, and while in the month of June those who had already received visas were permitted to leave the country, by the beginning of August all Soviet immigration to Israel ground to a total halt.

What a tragic ending to a story with such dramatic possibilities and great promise and hope. While Kosygin's December statement created sparks of great optimism in the hearts of many separated families, their lot today is bitter frustration. *The New York Times* reported on September 1, just six weeks ago, that some six thousand Soviet Jews had been prevented from emigrating to Israel because of the war in the Middle East.

All we can do is cry out in the words of the most ancient of liberators, *Let my people go!*

American Jewry's Silence. We in America must share part of the guilt for the fate of our brethren in the Soviet Union. We have not really even begun to organize the kind of worldwide protest campaign that is required under the present circumstances.

There is no question whatsoever that the leadership of the Soviet Union is extremely sensitive to such criticism. It has been deeply affected by the outcry of part of world Jewry, by the few protest demonstrations and letter-writing campaigns that have been organized.

However, we have not even scratched the surface here in this country in raising our voice over the spiritual and cultural genocide that is being committed against the second largest Jewish community in the world.

Professor Heschel warned us over a year ago that if we do not act quickly, future generations will spit on our graves saying, "Here lies a community, which, living in comfort and prosperity, kept silent while millions of their brothers were exposed to spiritual extermination."

Said Rabbi Heschel, "Over and above the noise of our banquets and testimonial dinners I hear the cry of Russian Jews: 'The Jewish people has forsaken us, the Jewish people has forgotten us.' Their dismay is mixed with disdain for those whose voice is loud but whose hearts are made of stone."

Last Yom Kippur eve I recounted a story about an American scientist who visited Kiev in the summer of 1966. That story is worth repeating. After speaking to an elderly Jewish man for about a half hour, the man arose, began to cry, and said: "Tell them at home we cannot hold out much longer here. Tell them at home we need help desperately—it is terrible, it is terrible."

And while they cry for help, American Jewry, despite the millions of dollars it spends, and scores of personnel it engages, in fighting the remnants of anti-Semitism in America, cannot afford to pay one full-time staff worker to deal with publicizing the problem of Soviet anti-Semitism. Several months ago, the American Conference on Soviet Jewry voted on a proposal that would create a sizable budget to pay for an office and a staff of people to devote themselves full time to organizing mass protests and publicity campaigns against Soviet maltreatment of Jews. The proposal was defeated.

Our response to the physical threat against Israeli Jewry was phenomenal. The threat against Soviet Jewry is a threat against an even larger Jewish population, not two million, but three million. We showed ourselves that we can mobilize our community and our resources to make a significant mark on world affairs.

Now is the time to do the same thing for Soviet Jewry— before it is too late! The threat is not physical, but spiritual. Does this mean we can disregard it, or treat it any the less seriously? It is a direct and vicious threat against Jewish life in one of the oldest and most creative centers of Judaism in this millennium. We must not let ourselves sit by while they perish.

Our silence up until now is incriminating evidence against

our slothful and apathetic complacency toward this problem. Only by drastic and dramatic and immediate efforts can we do anything about the destruction of this ancient and noble community of Russian Jews.

The Talmud has the following to say about the responsibility of the individual Jew in times of community crisis:

> Whoever does not join the community in time of danger and trouble will never enjoy the Divine blessing. When your brothers are in trouble, say not, "I have my home, my food, my drink. I am safe." If you were ever to think so, the words of the prophet would apply to you—"Surely this iniquity shall not be purged from you until you die." (Taanit, 11a.)

On this solemn and holiest night of the Jewish year, we must look into the mirror of our souls, and ask some very serious questions. Let me pose a hypothetical question: If for some reason a close relative of yours who had been living in the Soviet Union was suddenly released and migrated to America, and he came to visit you. Let us say, for argument's sake that he was your grandfather or uncle. And he said to you, "While I and three million other Jews were languishing under the yoke of a cruel dictator in Russia, what did you do to help me?" What would be your answer?

Last Kol Nidre eve, 1966, I spoke also about Soviet Jewry. After the sermon many people approached me and asked me, "What can we do?" And I made several concrete suggestions. In addition, in the congregational newspaper this past March I placed the address of the major organizations in America fighting Soviet anti-Semitism, suggesting that those interested might write and find out what more they could do.

Could you say to your grandfather from Russia, "I wrote one letter to a newspaper or a Congressman this year regarding Soviet anti-Semitism"? Could you tell him, "I inquired about what I could do to one Jewish organization this year"? Could you say that "I read one pamphlet sent to me by the Jewish organizations in America and educated myself as to the condition of Soviet Jews"?

If you cannot say even that, then Yom Kippur should be

a time for *Teshuvah*, for the deepest kind of repentance. For in truth, dear friends, your grandfather may not have asked you that question—but God himself is asking you that question tonight. "While three million of My people are languishing under the yoke of a cruel dictator in Russia, what are you doing to help them?"

I hope for the sake of all of us that when God asks us that question next Yom Kippur, we will have something to answer.

29

We Have Written Off Soviet Jewry!

CHAIM WEIZMANN, THE FIRST PRESIDENT OF ISRAEL, MADE A prediction fifty years ago, on the eve of the Bolshevik Revolution, when the Czar had been overthrown, and bright hopes of freedom and equality were being enthroned:

> We are an old nation and must not forget the warnings of history. Great hopes were raised by the French Revolution, also. The principles of equality may be decreed by law, but they take a considerable time before they become an integral part of the life of a nation. It is difficult to believe that anti-Semitism, which has been systematically urged and cruelly practiced in Russia for so long, will suddenly disappear.

Chaim Weizmann was too, too accurate in his prediction. The fact of the matter is that since the Six Day War in June, 1967, the Jews have suffered a government-sponsored program of cultural suppression and ethnic defamation far

Delivered January 3, 1968. Published in *American Zionist*, October, 1968.

worse than anything the czars could have conjured up.

The Failure of American Jewry. Responsible observers of the problems of Soviet Jewry have indicated that a conflict is now being played out in the hierarchy of Soviet leadership. The neo-Stalinists advise using the anti-Jewish campaign to cover up domestic and foreign setbacks, including the Vietnam crisis, the split with Red China, loss of control over Rumania, and the disastrous loss of face in the Six Day War. They point out that Stalin's harshest period of repression against the Jews came in the wake of Jewish apathy during the holocaust. He was encouraged, these observers point out, by the silence of the Jews and the rest of the world, to pursue his own policy of anti-Semitism.

All of this adds up to a very challenging situation for today's Jewish leaders. Conditions in the Soviet Union are such that the Jews there are in their greatest period of harassment and even greater potential danger since the black years of Stalin. How are our Jewish leaders meeting this problem?

There are today basically two kinds of Jewish leaders regarding the issue of Soviet anti-Semitism. One type of Jewish leader knows very little about the hard facts of Soviet Jewry, and the other type knows but does nothing about it.

Many well-informed Jewish leaders, while knowledgeable in every other area, are ignorant when it comes to an accurate assessment of the status of Soviet Jews. Far too many of them claim that the Soviet Jews themselves do not care about having Yiddish books and schools, prayerbooks, matzo, and other appurtenances of Jewish life.

The general press often portrays this view, reenforcing this widespread misconception. Most recently, the *New York Times* Moscow correspondent wrote that today Russia's Jews are Sovietized, and are not interested in their Jewish identity or Jewish heritage. Our own experience with many apathetic American Jews helps us to accept this view of things.

It is very true that there are many Jews, both in America and the Soviet Union, who have sold their souls to the devil of materialism, or Communism, as the case may be. Many Jews have relegated Judaism to the superannuated vestiges of medievalism, or of bourgeois nationalism, or of rootless cosmopolitanism, or whatever new term they may have for it today. And there are no Harris or Gallup polls to count these —they may even be majority, although I doubt it.

Does this mean that there is no interest at all on the part of Russia's Jews in any kind of Jewish life? Are we to dismiss with a flick of the wrist the Jewish community of Shalom Aleichem, Ahad Ha'Am, of Bialik and Peretz, of Mendele and Tchernikovsky, of Pinsler and Gordon? Is there not one community anywhere in the Soviet Union that wants to read a Yiddish paper or see a Yiddish show?

We must remember that Jewish life in Russia has roots reaching back over a millennium. Our own Jewish community has developed only within the last century. It is inconceivable that such a deeply rooted culture should suddenly atrophy and fizzle away, pouring down the drain the treasured accumulation of centuries.

The knowledgeable observer today sees definite signs in Russia that Jews there have a strong thirst for Jewish identity and Jewish cultural and religious life. How else can we explain the amazing phenomenon of Simchat Torah in Moscow year after year, when up to forty thousand young Russified Jews dance and sing in the streets: *Am Yisrael chai—* the people of Israel *lives!* How else do we explain the fact that on the morning of the Six Day War the Israel embassy in Moscow was deluged with hundreds of anonymous calls wishing Israel success in her fight for life? How else do we explain the fact that a recent visitor reports that hundreds of thousands of Jews were glued to their radios in June to hear the latest reports of the War, coming not from the Moscow radio stations, but from Kol Tzion Lagola, the Israeli station beamed into Russia, which broadcasts twice daily in Yiddish? How else can we explain the capacity crowds throughout the Soviet Union for Jewish cultural evenings, including performances by Jan Peerce and many Israeli folk singers?

There are several reports that Hebrew calendars are being circulated by hand in the thousands in some Russian communities. We know that the one Hebrew paper that reaches the

Moscow library, the Israeli Communist paper, is read and fondled every day by so many people that the print is rubbed off the pages by the end of the day. We know also that countless young Jews whose parents changed their nationality on their internal passports from Jewish to Russian, are now changing them back to Jewish.

There are legion stories of resistance brought out from behind the Iron Curtain with Western diplomats and tourists, about Jews who take dangerous risks in order to defy the program of cultural genocide taking place. Young people who don't even know what being Jewish is, are determined to wear their identity with pride, despite the dismal consequences awaiting them.

During the summer of 1966, Geula Gill, the Israeli singer, presented a concert series under the now-defunct Soviet-Israel cultural agreement. She was met with a tremendous outpouring of interest by Jews wherever she performed. In the city of Riga the crowds were so huge that police were called, and one of the policemen was overheard making anti-Semitic remarks. A fifteen-year-old girl, Naomi Gerber, boldly answered him, and was immediately arrested. Secret police later found a diary into which she had copied passages from books about the sufferings of the Jewish people.

An American scientist from Berkeley visited the Soviet Union in the summer of 1965 on invitation of the Soviet Academy of Medical Science. He tells of many experiences of meeting Jewish scientists who were extremely anxious to be identified as Jews. Once at a scientific meeting a colleague passed across the table a scientific journal, saying, "Here, you'll find this article very interesting." The American glanced at the page, and saw that penciled in between two lines of scientific data were two Hebrew words: "Ivri anochi" —I am a Hebrew. Other so-called assimilated scientists surreptitiously whispered in his ear, *"Shalom aleichem"* or *"Gut shabbas."*

Once while walking in the park this same Jewish scientist from Berkeley met an elderly man who engaged him in conversation. After a few minutes of chatting, it became obvious to the elderly Soviet Jew that the scientist was a young, observant Jew from America, even though he pursued a career in science. The elderly man could hardly believe his ears when he heard the young American say *"Im Yirtze HaShem"* —if God wills it. The climax came when the scientist pulled out of his shirt his inner tzitzit, or Arba Kanfot. At that point the old man began to cry, and when he couldn't control his sobs any longer, he arose and said: "Tell them at home we cannot hold out much longer here. Tell them at home we need help desperately—it is terrible, it is terrible." And he walked away.

All of these stories of heroic resistance, fifty years after the last Hebrew book was printed in the Soviet Union. Fifty years after the last class in Judaism. Fifty years after the last time a rabbi was ordained. Does that sound as if Soviet Jews are ready to give up the ghost? To me it sounds as though there is a deep thirst and a gnawing hunger for *Yiddishkeit*. For any tangible symbol of Judaism: to see a Jew from abroad, to touch a Hebrew newspaper, to hear a live voice from Eretz Yisrael.

A New York rabbi who visited four Russian cities in November, 1967, reported to a group gathered on Hanukka, "I am fulfilling the mission that was placed upon me by a Jew in the streets of Moscow just four weeks ago: 'Tell the Jews of America that Jewish religion and culture in Russia are not dying. They are being murdered.'"

The second count on which Jewish leadership is guilty is the crime of apathy. It is well known that the Soviet Union is very sensitive to public criticism. Why is it that prominent Soviet authors like Voznesenski, or public figures like Pavel Litvinov, grandson of Stalin's foreign minister, can publicly criticize the Soviet bureaucracy and the actions of the security police? They make their charges public because they know that publicity is the best defense against sanctions. It is only the writers who smuggle out their manuscripts and have them published abroad under pseudonyms whom the Soviets feel free to punish.

Many little rabbits have been devoured by the security wolves in the Soviet forest, with no one watching. When the wolf is brought into the courtroom of public opinion, however, his actions are severely restrained. If publicity and criticism are so important in determining Russian policy, why is there not in the United States a massive campaign of protest that would shake the world, including the immovable Iron Curtain? Why is it that the only noise we hear is an almost inaudible whisper!

I submit that we have written off the Jews of the U.S.S.R.! We have prematurely declared the patient dead. In the face of this gross moral lapse, the concept of Klal Yisrael becomes limp and empty. It is easy to care for Jews when they make us proud with their lightning victories. But the real test of Jewish responsibility is the undramatic care, the ongoing concern and the profound interest in the almost helpless Jews in the Soviet Union. They, too, are Jews.

We have played right into the hands of the Russian dictators. They are using a trick as old as Sennacherib and Nebuchadnezzar, who were even craftier than Hitler. They knew that to conquer the Jews one must conquer their spirit. They must cut them off from their roots, exile them far from their homeland, and strangle their religion and their culture. They must forbid them to make contact with Jews in other countries; prevent them from traveling abroad to rabbinical or Zionist conclaves; see that they get no matzo to remember their history of resistance to oppression; destroy their native language and prevent their children from studying Torah. This is the formula worked out in biblical days by Israel's archenemies that constitutes chapter one of the handbook of anti-Semitism employed by Stalin and his successors.

They have done everything in their power to cut off Soviet Jews from American Jewry, their only friend and ally, their only hope of survival. They know what we learned painfully in June, 1967, that, as one less-than-eloquent speaker phrased it, "nobody gives a damn about the Jews"—except other Jews.

We have permitted this program of isolating Soviet Jews to continue unchecked. While we spend millions on anti-Semitism at home, making studies of the number of Jews in industry, banking, and the professions; in fighting Christmas programs in public schools; in chasing non-Jews on whose chest we can pin a medal; we cannot find enough money in the overflowing coffers of American Jewry to support one full-time worker to fight Soviet anti-Semitism.

Jacob Neusner has written in another context that we are fighting the battles of the 1930's and 1940's, but ignoring the problems of today. "The present generation of Jewish leaders," he wrote, "was nurtured by the issue of that age and continues to respond to the questions of those days. Like an old war-horse, its ears prick up at the old battle-cries; the trumpets of ancient fighting ring in its head, and it marches to old tunes." In short, we are fighting the straw man of anti-Semitism at home instead of the real enemy of our people across the seas.

The historian of the future will brand our generation "the apathetic generation." They will look upon our generation of Jews as the first in history that stood by, knowingly, and watched the decimation of three million of our brothers, undergoing the cruel punishment of cultural genocide.

Rabbi Heschel has expressed his frustration with this situation in the following way:

> I do not want future generations to spit on our graves saying: "Here lies a community which, living in comfort and prosperity, kept silent while millions of their brothers were exposed to spiritual extermination."
>
> Over and above the noise of our banquets and testimonial dinners I hear the cry of Russian Jews: "The Jewish people has forsaken us, the Jewish people has forgotten us." Their dismay is mixed with disdain for those whose voice is loud but whose hearts are made of stone.

The one organization that is most equipped to do something, the American Conference on Soviet Jewry, has been largely an impotent, bureaucratic machine, slowly plugging along without staff, nor budget, spending most of its time on parliamentary hairsplitting.

Being concerned with American Jewry and Israeli Jewry, the first and third largest Jewries in the world, we have made a disastrous leap over a great and noble segment of our people. We have written off three million Jews by our apathy and our ignorance. We have sold our brother into Egypt, by abandoning him in the pit of despair and hopelessness. We must go now and seek our brothers, before it is too late.

The Talmud has the following to say about the responsibility of the individual Jew in the times of community crisis:

> Whoever does not join the community in time of danger and trouble will never enjoy the Divine blessing. When your brothers are in trouble, say not, "I have my home, my food, my drink. I am safe." If you were ever to think so, the words of the prophet would apply to you—"Surely this iniquity shall not be purged from you until you die." (Taanit, 11a.)

30
Imposed Anonymity

THERE ARE MANY WAYS TO DESTROY A HUMAN BEING. ONE OF the achievements, if we may abuse that word, of modern technology is that man has devised new and more efficient and more subtle ways to deprive his neighbor of his essential humanity. Gas chambers and crematoria are but a few of the more palpable examples of such humanity-destroying devices.

But the most subtle way of destroying one's sense of humanity is to tell someone he is not someone. To say to a human being he is not a human being. To force someone to think he is an animal, unworthy of the rights and privileges of mankind.

We do this in many ways. We do it by denying people a home in certain "pure," "undefiled" neighborhoods. By refusing to hire members of a certain group in jobs that demand white skin, or pure, red, American blood, or Christian birth, as admission tickets. By telling a person that a black hand has no right to put a ballot in a box.

One of the most subtle ways of destroying a person is to

Delivered Friday night, February 9, 1968. Published in *American Zionist*, March, 1968.

refuse to tell him who he is. By denying him the history and heritage that are rightfully his. By saying, implicitly or otherwise, "You were born today. You have no past worthy of recording, of teaching. Your ancestors were nonbeings. They accomplished nothing, and contributed nothing to civilization."

There are many victims to this kind of imposed anonymity. Negroes in America who know nothing of their past, who have never heard of their people's heroic figures, and have never been exposed to the proud pages of their ethnic history, are some of these victims.

Also victims are the Jews in the Soviet Union who are not permitted to know any of the achievements of Russian Jews in the past. Part of the campaign of cultural genocide in the U.S.S.R. is a campaign to tell Russia's Jews that they have contributed nothing to Russian civilization, history, or culture.

The Jews in Russia today suffer all of the penalties that being Jewish brings in its train, but none of the blessings. Government policy dictates that nothing about Jewish contributions to czarist or Soviet Russia be published.

Let me furnish some examples.

One of the truly great centers of Jewish culture in past centuries was Vilna. One of the greatest Jewish minds ever to create, Elijah the Vilna Gaon, who flourished in the eighteenth century, gave distinction to that city. Vilna was known in Jewish literature as "The Jerusalem of Lithuania" for its depth and breadth of Hebrew scholarship. Yet in the latest Guide Book for the city of Vilna, not a word is mentioned that Jews ever lived there, that there were Jewish writers, thinkers, poets and teachers. That there were Jewish publishing houses, theaters, museums, scholarly institutions, nor that a Jewish workers' movement existed there. All the history of the city of Vilna is given, but not a mention of Jews.

Textbooks throughout the U.S.S.R. avoid mention of Jewish contributions. A 1963 edition of a senior high school text on ancient history, published by the Soviet Academy of Pedagogical Sciences, omitted the chapter on Jews that had been included in previous editions.

Soviet encyclopedias give short shrift to Jews and Judaism. The so-called *Large Soviet Encyclopedia,* which originally devoted sixteen pages to the article on "Jews," has now reduced the article to two pages.

When a thirty-volume edition of the writings of Maxim Gorky were published by the Soviet Academy of Sciences in 1956, they carefully excised all passages relating to Jews, including one passage in which Gorky quoted Lenin as saying "There are few intelligent people among us. We are, generally speaking, a gifted people, but intellectually lazy. An intelligent Russian is almost always a Jew or a man with Jewish blood." Gorky's vehement condemnation of pogroms was omitted from his book *On the Russian Peasantry.* His lecture of 1906 "On the Jews" and his 1907 letter "On Zionism," and all the references to anti-Semitism are expunged in this so-called complete edition of the famous writer's collected works.

Recently an American scholar wanted to do research on the history of Jewish participation in the Second World War in Russia. He reports that he had great difficulty finding information, not because the Jews didn't make a contribution, but because it was carefully hidden from the public. After painstaking research he was able to find out that a half million Jews served in the Soviet armed forces. A high proportion of these were officers, including fifty generals and hundreds of colonels. One hundred and twenty-one Jews received the coveted Russian version of our Congressional Medal of Honor, the decoration called "Hero of the Soviet Union." Yet, in November, 1966, a Soviet history of the Second World War was published containing over six hundred pages, and mention was made of Jews in only two minor places.

Silence on the Holocaust. Perhaps the greatest insult to Soviet Jews is the complete ignoring of the tragedy of six million Jewish deaths under Hitler. While in every other Communist country the Eichmann trial was given full coverage, it was scarcely mentioned in the Soviet Union.

The play, *The Diary of Anne Frank,* based on *The Diary of a Young Girl,* was performed all over the world, but in Moscow it was presented only two evenings, after considerable struggle. Both performances, according to *Tass*, were well attended and well received. But the government refused to let it be performed more than twice, and nowhere else besides the capital.

In 1963 the twentieth anniversary of the Warsaw Ghetto Uprising was observed in Warsaw, where almost a thousand foreign delegates attended. Not one official Soviet delegate appeared.

We could go on and on giving instances of the planned and government-sponsored program of enforced anonymity for Soviet Jews, but none rankles the conscience more than the cause célèbre of this whole issue: the case of Babi Yar.

Babi Yar is a ravine outside of Kiev, where, in 1941, the Nazis machine-gunned 100,000 Jews to death. Jews were ordered by the Nazi invaders to report to Babi Yar at eight o'clock in the morning, September 29, 1941. They were then stripped naked and lined up in tight columns of a hundred, and machine-gunned into the ravine.

When plans were announced by the Kiev Town Council in 1959 to construct a stadium at Babi Yar, the Soviet novelist Viktor Nekrasov wrote in the Russian literary journal, "Is this possible? Who could have thought of such a thing? To fill a . . . deep ravine and on the site of such a colossal tragedy to make merry and play football? No, this must not be allowed!"

Almost twenty years to the day after the Babi Yar massacre, a young, outspoken Russia poet, Yevgeni Yevtushenko, wrote a poem which was to memorialize Babi Yar in the minds of all men everywhere for all time. Yevtushenko explained in an article in the French press that he had been interested in creating a poem on anti-Semitism, but was seeking an appropriate form. After a visit to the ravine at Babi Yar, he wrote his famous poem "Babi Yar," which begins:

> No gravestone stands on Babi Yar—
> Only coarse earth heaped roughly on the gash.
> Such dread comes over me; I feel so old,
> Old as the Jews. Today I am a Jew. . . .

He recited it for the first time at Moscow's Polytechnical Museum before some twelve hundred students on September 16, 1961. It was obvious from the response that many people among the intellectual class shared his contempt for anti-Semitism. In his own words he described his reaction: "When I finished there was total silence. I just kept folding the paper in my hands, scared to look up. When I did, the entire audience stood. Suddenly the applause began and continued for nearly ten minutes. People rushed up on stage and embraced me. My eyes were full of tears."

On March 8, 1963, Khrushchev attacked the poet for his immaturity. The poet was denounced by others for suggesting that the authorities had not erected a monument to the Jewish martyrs because of lingering anti-Semitism.

In 1966 the Ukrainian Architects Club announced that some two hundred designs for a monument had been placed on exhibit. On November 26, 1966, the London Soviet Information journal announced that "A large marble plaque has been ceremonially installed in the centre of Babi Yar. The inscription reads: 'A monument to the Soviet people, victims of fascism in the years of the temporary occupation of Kiev in 1941–43, will be put up here.' "

Just prior to the Soviet Fiftieth Anniversary celebrations declarations were made to foreign newsmen that a memorial would be built before the Fiftieth anniversary of the Bolshevik Revolution. Yet it is now almost a half year after the anniversary of the October Revolution, and no monument has been put up.

We pray that the day may soon come when every man everywhere will be free to know of his past, and thus be able to march proudly into the future.

31
An Exchange of Freedom

Use of Pulpit on Other Historic Occasions. Prime Minister Golda Meir gave the American rabbinate and the American synagogue the supreme compliment this week, by choosing them as the best vehicle by which to transmit an important message to the American Jewish community. By sending her Minister of Immigrant Absorption, Mr. Nathan Peled, on a special mission to United States Jewry, she declared her trust, confidence, and faith that the pulpit of the American synagogue can be the transmitter of her personal wishes to her fellow Jews on these shores.

Being a student of history, I could not help but think of two other occasions in recent history, when the synagogue pulpit was able to function as such a transmitting vehicle of communication when all other more official and openly available media were impossible to utilize. Both of these took place in the period of World War II, a time whose historical circumstances are in many ways so much parallel to the crisis in Jewry that we face today.

Delivered Friday, February 18, 1972. This address was printed and distributed to every American rabbi by the United Jewish Appeal.

One is the kind of sermon which must have been preached in many German synagogues in the late 1930's by men like Rabbi Joachim Prinz, now of Newark, New Jersey. Rabbi Prinz published one of his last sermons in Germany in 1938, in this month's issue of *The Jewish Spectator*. He warned his people of the impending doom on the Jewish horizon, and pleaded with them to act before it was too late to save Jewish lives. The other was the sermon given by Rabbi Marcus Melchior of Copenhagen, *erev* Rosh Hoshanah, 1943, when a German informant had told the rabbi about the coming danger to Jewish lives in Denmark, and he, in turn, brought this information to the knowledge of his congregants, and then organized an emergency underground evacuation of all of Denmark's Jews across the Kattegat to Sweden, before Yom Kippur of that year. That sermon saved seven thousand Jewish lives.

The number of Jewish lives that can be saved by sermons from American Jewish pulpits during this month throughout America can possibly be a hundred or two hundred times that number. I thus begin my heavy tale with a prayer to Almighty God that the words of my mouth and the meditations of my heart be acceptable this evening before Him, and before you, this holy congregation of Israel. For so much is at stake.

The Facts of Mr. Peled's Visit. But now, to the historic meeting I attended yesterday in Miami. Mr. Nathan Peled came to the United States this past Sunday night (February 13), expressly for the purpose of meeting with America's two thousand pulpit rabbis. On Monday, he met in New York, Tuesday in Chicago, Wednesday in Los Angeles, and yesterday in Miami. By now he is back in Israel. During these four meetings, he met with a large percentage of the American rabbinate throughout the country.

In order to fully understand what he said, it would be helpful to know something about Israel's Minister of Immigrant Absorption. He himself is a Russian immigrant, having been born in Odessa, and came to Palestine in 1933, to work on a kibbutz. Prior to his present post he was Ambassador to Bulgaria and Austria. In Bulgaria, he confronted Jewish life

in Eastern Europe firsthand. In Vienna, he would frequently
go to the Austrian airport to meet immigrants from Rumania, Russia, and from Eastern Europe generally. His
work also took him to the Soviet Union on several official
visits, during which time he made it his business to seek out
Jews and Jewish communities to talk to and meet with.
Thus, his background as a native Russian, and having had
direct personal contact with Soviet and East European Jews,
makes his work in absorption more than merely a political
task or a governmental obligation. It is *melechet hakodesh* to
him—a sacred labor, one of the great *mitzvot* of our day, to
save the remnants of Jewry, and to implement the biblical
vision of *kibbutz galuyot*, the Ingathering of the Exiles. His
task, in essence, is to prepare the State of Israel for the coming of the Messiah, before which time, we are told, all of the
scattered remnants of our people must be brought back home.

I cannot, of course, convey to you all of the stories, nor all
of the facts, presented to us by Mr. Peled. The important
facts which you must know will follow shortly. One brief
incident, however, must serve as a backdrop to everything
else I have to say.

During one trip in 1961 to a small Jewish community called
Gori, just outside of Tiflis in Soviet Georgia, Mr. Peled
asked his Intourist guides to take him to the synagogue in
that town. It was a Monday morning about 11 A.M., and of
course he expected to meet only the head of the synagogue, or
perhaps if fortunate one or two other people if they happened
to be there at the time. The communication system among
Jews in Russia is amazingly swift under the circumstances,
and word had reached Gori that an Israeli diplomat would
arrive Monday morning. When Mr. Peled walked into the
synagogue that Monday morning, the congregation was a
full one. Every Jew in town had come to greet him and see
him, and, hopefully, to hear him speak.

The *Rosh HaKahal*, the head of the community, got up to
speak. He warmly welcomed the Israeli dignitary, and proceeded to tell how wonderful things were for Jews in the
Soviet Union. However, knowing that the Intourist guides
would not understand Hebrew, he was able to slip in one

brief Hebrew sentence, and made it sound like a biblical quotation.

"Mr. Ambassador," said the Russian Jew, "everything here is wonderful. The government takes care of all our needs. Please convey to the Jewish people in Israel and throughout the world the feeling of how happy we are to be here in Russia. There is nothing that we need, or that our wonderful government does not do for us. As in the words of the Bible, *Matai yihye kibbutz galuyot?*—When will the Ingathering of the Exiles take place? God help us get out of this Soviet prison—we can't bear it any longer!" And he concluded his speech in Russian.

Mr. Peled responded in Russian, and during his speech, he too added a "biblical" quotation. *"Kibbutz hagaluyot yihye bimhayra beyamenu!* The Ingathering of Exiles will be soon, in our day! Please God!"

That was ten years ago. Even Mr. Peled could not know then that *kibbutz hagaluyot* would take place soon—in our day—and that by 1970 it will have begun, and that by 1971 and 1972 it would be going full speed ahead.

How Many Will Be Let Out? One of the major questions which is frequently discussed in connection with the issue of Soviet Jewry is "How many Jews will be permitted to leave?" This is a key question, and one that I had in mind in going to Miami, and one which you certainly expected and hoped to have answered in coming tonight. Now that I have heard Mr. Peled, and have spoken with him, I can only say: That depends largely upon us. But it also depends on other factors, some of which we can control, and some we cannot.

First of all, it depends upon the will of Soviet Jews. This is a crucial first step. All the international pressure in the world cannot do a thing unless the Soviet Jewish activists continue their brave and heroic program of protest and complaint. We have good reason to believe that the Soviet Jews will continue to do their part, if only we will continue to do ours—and I will explain what I mean by that shortly.

The Soviets have been following a two-pronged program in defusing their "Jewish problem," and in trying to reduce the number of applications for exit visas. One is to begin to let out the noise makers, the activists, in the hope that after their departure things will quiet down. The second is to intimidate those that remain through such acts as searching apartments, harassment, interrogation, prison sentences, and widely publicized trials such as those in Leningrad a year ago.

The reaction, to say the least, has not been what the Soviets expected. Apparently they never read the story in Exodus about the Egyptian enslavement of their Jews three thousand years ago. "The more they were oppressed, the more they increased and spread out, so that the Egyptians came to dread the Israelites." (Exodus 1:12.) Today as well, the more the Soviets oppress the Jews, the more their protests increase, and the more the desire to leave spreads among Soviet Jews.

Just by way of example, in the city of Kharkov five Jewish families arranged a "sit-in" in the office of a local official, demanding that they be permitted to go to their Homeland. The officials decided to localize the issue and nip it in the bud. Thus, they immediately gave permission for them to go. But the week after those five families left, fifty families applied for exit visas. This same chain reaction is taking place all over the Soviet Union, and it apparently is displaying no sign of abatement.

This is something completely new for the Soviets. They have had vocal minorities before, but they have always been able to deal with them rather easily. They merely apply their notoriously cruel suppressive measures, such as KGB harassment, incarceration, exile, and the like, and the sparks of freedom fizzle out. When the Soviets exiled the Tartar leadership to Siberia, no one paid any attention, and the uprising was quelled in short order. But with the Jews, this is not so easily done. The other hundred Soviet nationality groups are all concentrated in one geographic area. Furthermore, the Jews are influential people in Soviet scientific and cultural life. Even more importantly, however, the Jews have support outside the Soviet Union throughout the free world. Wherever Jews live, there have been demonstrations, letter-writing campaigns, approaches to the Soviet ambassador and other officials.

The number of Jews who can leave Russia in 1972 and after also depends upon a number of political factors—some of which we can influence. One is President Nixon's trip to Moscow this coming spring. If between now and May we can mount a successful pressure lobby on the President to make this question one of high priority on his agenda with Kosygin, then that will add a great deal of weight to the already increasing volume of pressure placed upon the Soviet authorities.

One thing we must be extremely careful to avoid is "compassion fatigue." Once it appears that American Jews are satisfied that Jews are now getting out, and once the pressure relents, that will be the day that the Soviets will begin to cut back the number of emigrées. And so, we must continue our campaign full speed ahead.

By now you probably know that the number of Jews leaving the USSR has dramatically catapulted from a thousand in 1970 to thirteen thousand in 1971, and if it continues on the present level, we hope between thirty-five and forty thousand during 1972. With the proper combination of lobbying on our part, other help which I will ask of you tonight in a few minutes, and a good political climate, this number could again dramatically climb to even greater proportions.

At the rate of fifty thousand per year, it would take, of course, half a century to get all the Jews out. Why the note of urgency, therefore? There is no urgency in the sense that if we do something now, in 1972, we will have finished the job, and can then sit back and relax. The critical urgency lies in the fact that if we *fail* in this crucial moment of Jewish history to meet the beginnings of this challenge, when the level is still fairly low, we will have created a lost opportunity which will preclude the future possibility of increasing the numbers and saving a large and great Jewish community from spiritual destruction.

To take advantage of this great historic opportunity, we must help solve many of the problems that now face Soviet Jews and the State of Israel.

What Dangers Face Soviet Jews and Israel? A Soviet Jew wanting to apply for an exit visa must endure a prolonged period of mental, physical, and emotional agony. Since the principle upon which the Soviets are permitting Jewish emigration is repatriation of families, every Soviet Jew making application to the office of OVIR must bring an affidavit from an Israeli relative. In 1971, forty thousand such affidavits were supplied by various sources, and relatives were "found," "discovered," and "produced" by various Jewish organizations. Thank goodness, there is no problem in this sphere, and that all Jews can be considered one large "family."

Next, the Soviet Jew must, after sharp and sustained interrogation, repudiate Soviet citizenship, and ask for repatriation to his true Homeland, the State of Israel. The Soviet officials at that point begin to treat this individual as a disloyal rebel, unworthy of Russian residence or benefits, and as one who is committing treason. Were the Soviet Jew able to leave within days or even weeks after application, that would present no major problems. However, often the waiting period goes into months and, in some cases, years.

Not only must this man without a country now find means of support for himself and his family (since in all likelihood he will have lost his job for his treasonous act), he must also pay the Russian government a huge fee for his education, for the exit visas, and for the plane ride to Vienna—all of which adds up to about 1,000 rubles per person, or several thousand dollars per family. A Soviet doctor earns about 150 rubles per month, so you can see what an impossible hardship this imposes.

Were this money not available to the Soviet Jews, which they themselves clearly do not have, the whole Operation Soviet Exodus would have to be aborted.

This does not begin to explain the needs of then getting these Jews from Vienna to Israel, housing them, settling them, feeding them, retraining them, and building schools, hospitals, and other facilities for them—which costs Israel about $35,000 per family—just for bare essentials.

All this at a time when Israel's social problems, problems of finding housing and providing education for Sephardic immigrants of ten and fifteen and twenty years ago, problems of an enormous budgetary drain for defense, have never been more critical.

The Challenge and the Opportunity. Just think to yourselves what will happen if Soviet Jews in Israel begin to write letters to their friends and relatives back in the U.S.S.R. that their problems are not being solved and that living conditions in Israel are impossible; that the dream of the great return to the Promised Land has turned out to be nothing more than a nightmare! What will happen then? What will happen to this long-awaited dream of restoring a huge segment of our people, cut off from us for over a half century, back into the main stream of Jewish life?

Just think to yourself what you would have done had you been able to save a Jewish life thirty years ago, when no price in the world could have kept six million Jews alive! What sacrifice would you make were we able to turn the clock back and say to ourselves, "If only we pay a certain price for each Jew, we could save one third of our people from gas chambers and crematoria"? Is there anyone in the synagogue tonight who would not sell his home, give up his car, wear old clothing, and eliminate all vacations and luxuries—if only we could turn the clock back and save six million Jewish lives?

Well, unfortunately we cannot turn the clock back. And I don't think the Jews in the U.S.S.R. will be shot if we don't ransom them. But there is something that is worse than physical death. And that is spiritual death—death not by gas but by shame; death by disgrace, death by purposelessness; death by humiliation; death by loss of pride, dignity, faith and hope. And if affluent American Jewry is not willing to ransom their brothers, why should they have hope, and faith? In whom can they trust, if not in us? If they give up their last source of deliverance in the world, then why go on fighting and struggling and endangering their lives and their jobs and risking separation and exile and imprisonment?

Unless we American Jews rise to the greatness of this unprecedented opportunity, we will have written a chapter in Jewish history that is far worse than the one written by the Nazis thirty years ago. For they were madmen, racists, power- and glory-hungry maniacs. If we lose these three million Jews, or two million Jews, or one million Jews—or however many want to escape the Soviet prison, then it will not be because of a deranged megalomaniac in Europe. It will be because of selfishness, and greed, and callousness and insensitivity. We will have done to our own brothers what Hitler never succeeded in doing to us.

We have now been protesting and demanding from the Soviets to let our people go for almost a decade. Finally, they have begun to listen to us. Now the ball is in our court. The Russians are saying to us, as it were, "Either put up or shut up. Here's your chance. Take it or be quiet, and stop all the noise." We cry out, Let My People Go! Now, we—yes, we, American Jews, must let our own people come by providing for them the wherewithall with which to make this Messianic pilgrimage, and to forge a new life in the Land of Promise when they arrive.

The sad fact is that half the members of synagogues in this country gave *zero* to UJA last year. Our Board of Directors passed a resolution last year asking that *all* our members make a contribution to the United Jewish Welfare Fund. This year I hope we will implement that resolution. I personally will want to know of any Jew in my congregation who commits the obscene act of ignoring the desperate plea of his brothers. In my opinion, the most vulgar expression in the English language is not any four-letter word, but "so what!", "I don't care!"

An Exchange of Freedom. In conclusion, I want to read to you a letter written by a gentleman from Orange County, California, to his children, last month. The author of this letter was a participant in a UJA mission to Israel in January, 1972, and he describes in it what happened to him when he met a plane of arriving immigrants from Russia at Lod Airport.

Two Jews met this morning.
Two Jews met this morning at Lod Airport, outside of Tel Aviv, shortly after the sun came up.
One arrived on a luxury jet from Austria.

One arrived on an air-conditioned bus from a luxury hotel, just days after he, too, arrived on a luxury jet . . . from California.

Two Jews met in Israel, and for each it was the first time his feet had touched the land of his ancestors.

Two Jews met in Israel, and embraced, and shed tears without shame, and exchanged only one word:

"Shalom."

These two Jews embraced for several minutes, and wept together.

One was sixty and dressed in black and wore a hat and cried.

The other was fifty and dressed in double knit and cried.

The man dressed in black carried a small package . . . personal to him.

The man in double knit carried a small package . . . an expensive camera.

Both cried, and exchanged only the one word.

The man in black, three days before, left his home in Russia.

The man in double knit, three days before, left his home in California.

. . . these two Jews met this morning.

For the man in black, freedom became his, the dignity to live and worship (if he so desires) and work . . . and be free for the rest of his days.

For the other man, that which was his freedom—his personal, selfish freedom—was circumscribed, for the rest of his days, and his activities and his heart were no longer his alone.

I do not know the name of the man in black, nor did I see him after the embrace and the tears, nor do I know from what city he came nor to what home he went.

I am the other man, and I say to you that when two Jews met this morning shortly after the sun came up, they met as brothers and as kinsmen and they exchanged freedom.

I now have less.

I wrote this to you, my children, because I want you to know what happened to your father this day, January 12, 1972.

My dear friends, we too must give up some of our freedom, in exchange for theirs. Every Jew in this synagogue tonight must give up some of his freedom, because his treasure, his activities, and his heart are no longer his alone. We are all of us prisoners with the Leningrad nine, and with the Soviet three million. And we will not be truly free until every Russian Jew who wants to can go to Israel!

When Mr. Peled concluded his address, he said, "We demand from you, on behalf of Soviet Jewry, Israel, and the world Jewish people, to give us the ability to face and to solve our problems." I believe that our bearing the name Jew means that he has the right to make that demand upon us. I hope we will be great enough Jews to rise to the challenge of this historic hour.

32

The Lessons of Munich

TWO DAYS AGO, WHEN ALL THE BRUTAL, HORRIFYING FACTS OF
what happened in Munich became known, a taxi driver in
Paris summed up the feelings of many of us when he said:
"The world is going crazy!" James Reston echoed the same
thought when he wrote in his column last Wednesday: (*New
York Times*, September 6, 1972) "The tragedy at the Olympic
Games is just the latest reminder that there is now a kind
of madness in the world, a lunatic strain of anarchy that
hinders the peace and order of mankind."

From all walks of life, from almost all the nations of the
world, even including an Arab monarch, came expressions of
shock and dismay, disbelief, and revulsion at this unspeakable, inhuman act of twentieth-century barbarism perpetrated by insane terrorists—I won't dignify them by calling
them guerrillas or commandos—last Wednesday in Munich.
The grief and nausea, the fear and the disillusionment will live
with us, all of us, Jews and Germans, athletes and spectators,
Easterners and Westerners, for many years to come. This

Delivered on Rosh Hashanah morning, September 9, 1972.

month, indeed, will go down in history as a Black September recognized as such by all the world.

There is a general recognition that not against Israel or the Jews alone was this act of madness directed, but against all civilized men. Even in war and crime, there are certain barriers of decency, so fundamental to the concept of humanity, that no one, not even the lowest of our kind, dare cross without threatening the deepest and most profound cords of civility within man. As we gather in our synagogues in prayer and repentance, asking God's blessings for life and peace, for tranquility and harmony during the coming year, we are shaken to the very quick at the thought that we have not yet emerged from the century or from the climate that saw one-third of our people butchered to death. It almost renders our prayer futile in advance, rendering our annual High Holy Day period an exercise in verbosity and hypocrisy, knowing that this is the kind of world in which we live, and that our feeble words and thoughts can hardly change events such as these.

And though the world shudders and shakes at the tragedy, how do we feel, we who are the cousins, the brothers and sisters of those who perished so violently? Those of us who have suffered the loss of a parent or other close relative know that while all of our friends and neighbors may be kind and charitable and sympathetic in their condolences, no one feels the grief as deeply as the mourner himself. And as we listen to Willy Brandt and Richard Nixon and George McGovern and Pope Paul, and all the leaders and followers of countries across the globe, and appreciate their kind remarks, we know that no one feels the pain as do we who are Jews. We who are flesh of their flesh, bone of their bone, members of the Household of Israel.

At a recent memorial service in Israel for the soldiers who fell in 1948 and 1956 and 1967, Golda Meir rose to speak to the throng of parents and widows who lost their dear ones in the wars for Israel's survival. After a few hushed moments of staring into the crowd of tear-filled eyes, Golda at last composed herself and said: *"Mishpacha g'dola achat anachnu*—we are one big family." Indeed, we are one big family, who, even though the Law commands us to interrupt our mourning for the Festival, feel as though our own garments are rent and we are still in the period of *Shiva* for those whose graves are still fresh in the soil of the Homeland.

And not only we mourn, but God himself, who chose our People for moral advancement and instruction to the nations, mourns with us as a number of His chosen sons end their lives in so untimely and unjust a way. The Hebrew Nobel Laureate Shmuel Yosef Agnon wrote an introduction to the kaddish which points up the dearness of each soul in Israel both to God and to our fellow Jews.

> A king of flesh and blood who goes out to war against his
>   enemies
> Brings forth his force to kill and be killed.
> There is doubt whether he loves his soldiers
> Or whether he does not love his soldiers,
> Whether they are important in his eyes
> Or whether they are not important in his eyes.
> And even if they are important in his eyes,
> They are no more important as corpses.
> But our King, the King of kings, the Holy One, Blessed be He,
> Desires life, loves peace and pursues peace,
> Loves Israel His people and has chosen us from all the
>   nations,
> Not because we are greater in number,
> For we are the least in number.
> And because He loves us and we are few in number,
> Each one of us is as important in His eyes as a whole
>   regiment.

> Therefore we pray after the death of each Jew
> Yitgadal, v'yitkadash, sh'may raba. . . .
> And if we pray thus for each one who dies;
> How much the more so for our dear brothers and sisters,
> The children of Zion,
> The slaughtered ones of the land of Israel,
> Whose blood was spilled for the glory of His name
> And for His people
> And for His land
> And for His inheritance. . . .

Part of the atmosphere of disbelief during these past several days was created because of the many ironies that conspire to make all of the past week one of the blackest in recent memory. Munich, the city whose very name conjures for us an era of surrender and world apathy and bitter war whose chief victim was our people. The Olympic Games, designed by a French nobleman in the nineteenth century to enable the nations of the world to compete on the sports field instead of the battlefield, and to thereby create harmony and foster international brotherhood and peace. The Twentieth Olympiad will go down in history as the one which was ushered in with a memorial service for Jews at nearby Buchenwald, and ended with another memorial service for Jews, the pariah people of history, the world's scapegoat, and whipping boy. The victim nation of Israel sent one of the smallest delegations to Munich because, in the words of one team member, Israelis don't have time or resources to send young, virile men out of the country for games. They are needed too desperately for more serious needs: to defend their Homeland. And all of this at the Olympiad in which the star athlete, who broke seven world records and won seven gold medals, the highest number ever won, was a Jew, a symbol of the return of our people to the cultivation of the body as well as of the spirit, and a source of not a little pride and joy, if only temporary, to our people the world over. All of these bitter ironies help make the tragedy of Munich even more difficult to swallow and more impossible to believe.

There is, of course, no doubt about the responsibility of the tragic events of Munich. Yigal Allon said it in his speech at the Israeli memorial service. Newspaper editorialists made it quite clear. Diplomatic spokesmen for many countries candidly pointed to the Arab nations who harbor the terrorists, who give them repeated encouragement, overt and tacit, who support their activities and grant them comfortable sanctuary.

And there is also little doubt about whose responsibility it is to remove this ugly blemish from blackening our globe. The editorial in Wednesday's *New York Times*, September 6, 1972, made that very clear when it said: "The primary challenge of the Munich crimes is to the international community. The fundamental issue is whether there can be effective common action against fanatics and criminals who recognize no boundaries or limits to their depredations. Any nation willing to tolerate or condone such outrages by word or deed deserves outlawry by the civilized world."

It seems as though the Soviets and the British and French cannot even grant their consent to a proposed international anti-hijacking treaty which would require signatory nations to suspend air service to any nation that did not punish or extradite air pirates. I am afraid that the kind of attacks on innocent Israeli citizens, in countries throughout the world, which we saw this past week and which we have seen countless times in other European countries during the past several years, will continue unless Russia and these other nations come to their senses and to the realization that if Israelis are not safe, then no one is safe.

As Jews, we must do all in our power to see that the international community meets its responsibility in abiding by the universal standards of justice and morality and human decency which were bequeathed to the world by our people three millennia ago. Only if we can assure the survival of our people, can mankind assure its own survival. As Eric Hoffer once put it, "As the fate of Israel goes, so goes the fate of all the nations. Israel is a barometer of the humanity of the world."

This question of Israel's survival leads me to a comparison between the events of this past week and the Torah reading of the second morning of Rosh Hashanah. On both mornings of this Festival, we read of the great patriarch Abraham, and in the second day's lesson, of Abraham's command from God to kill his only son Isaac as a sacrifice. One wonders whether the sacrifice of our people is really the desire of God, to help bring the nations of the world to the realization of the dire consequences of slaughter and violence.

As the drama of last Tuesday morning, afternoon, and evening played itself out, we anxiously awaited the denouement, waiting to see, as one who reads the story of the Akeda, whether Isaac would indeed be sacrificed, or whether in the last moment his life would be spared. The Munich story did not end on as optimistic a note as the Akeda story. No ram appeared in the thicket at the last moment to take the place of the helpless Jew who lay strung to the altar awaiting his sacrifice. But there is a different version of the Akeda story which appears in a medieval midrash, which resembles our story more directly. In this embellished account, Abraham actually kills Isaac, and then, seeing what he has done, he pronounces the blessing *Mechayay Hametim*—He who brings life to the dead—and Isaac's life is restored, only to have the drama played out once more, when Abraham sets out a second time to slay Isaac, realizing that he had not fulfilled God's original command.

When Israelis went to bed Tuesday night, after having feared the worst, they pronounced the blessing *Mechayay Hametim,* and their wish came true. Rumors circulated that the Olympic contestants had escaped their fate, and were safe in police hands. Even the Wednesday morning papers helped this myth to receive wide credence. But then the radio reports came and verified that the final word was the worst we could expect. The Israelis met their death, as it were, a second time.

In the midrashic version, when Abraham is about to raise his hand the second time, it is then that the angel calls out and tells Abraham: Stop! Scholars inform us that this midrashic account can be traced to the period of the Crusades when Jews were killed in masses and their bodies piled heaps upon heaps. The Crusaders would go through the piles of Jewish corpses and if there were any still gasping for breath, they would kill them again. Kill them again? Is it crazy, is it impossible? Could Abraham kill Isaac and then after bringing him back to life try to kill him again? Could the Crusaders have tried to kill the Jews twice in the same day? Did the foolish and naïve optimism of German government authorities permit us to think the Israeli Olympic team was saved from death and then killed again? It all sounds so crazy, as it did to the cab driver in Paris.

But isn't this really the theme of Jewish history? This is

what the midrash meant, and this is what happened this week in Munich. Jews aren't killed once, as other peoples. They have to be killed again and again and again. They killed us in the Crusades. And then they killed us in 1492 at the Inquisition. And then in 1648. And then again in the 1940's. And now again at Munich—they killed us again and again. This is Jewish history—the world has to kill the Jews again and again and again.

Two members of the murdered Israeli Olympic team escaped the tortures of Soviet Russia—one just three months ago. In Russia they were killed once—killed spiritually. Their Jewish heart and soul were ruthlessly murdered. But then we pronounced the bracha, *Mechayay Hametim*, and we brought them to Israel, and they were saved from the fires of the spiritual and cultural inferno of the U.S.S.R. And now these remnants of Russia, and of the holocaust of Europe, are gathered together in Munich, Germany, to be killed once again.

And what will happen if this pattern repeats itself, if the nations of the world stand by and let it happen again? Will we watch the people who are remnants of Hitler and Stalin, who died a thousand deaths in their persecution and torment, on the verge of death as a people, and who then miraculously pronounced *Mechayay Hametim*, and created a Jewish State to enable them to survive, will we watch them be killed again?

It is our task on this first day of the New Year to make it known in the world that we will not watch this happen again—anywhere, any time! Not in Munich, not in Lod, not in Tel Aviv, not in Geneva, not in Kiev, not in Leningrad, not in Sinai, not in the Golan—nowhere and at no time! WE WILL NOT LET THEM KILL US AGAIN. Not our children, not our athletes, not our soldiers, not our teachers, not our university students, not our school bus drivers, not anyone!

On this New Year's day, among the three holiest of the Jewish year, we think of the martyrs of our own time. In the spirit of the Martyrology, the *Eleh Ezkerah*, in which we read of the *asara harugay malchut*, the Ten Ancient Jewish Martyrs, we now pay our highest tribute to these *achad asar harugay malchut*, the Eleven Modern Jewish Martyrs, who gave their lives for the sanctification of the name of God and Israel.

There is a midrash that tells us that one of the ancient ten martyrs, Rabbi Ishmael, was being tortured by the Romans, and twice he let out a deep cry of agony that reached the heavens themselves. God spoke to Rabbi Ishmael and warned him that if he cried out once more, He would turn the world back to primordial chaos. Rabbi Ishmael gnashed his teeth and held back the third cry. One asks himself why Rabbi Ishmael did not let out that third cry, and damn the whole world. What a heavy burden he had on his shoulders, balancing the universe on the tip of his finger. Why didn't he just say, Let it all end now. Let this world, so full of brutality and violence and hatred and barbarism, let it go down, and let the human story come to an end. Elie Wiesel has suggested that he did cry out but nobody heard, nobody cared. Another writer has suggested that the "real wonder of the story is that Rabbi Ishmael, who got so little compassion from the world, nevertheless loved it so much that he gritted his teeth and did not cry out and thereby saved it from destruction." That Rabbi Ishmael acted "out of love for a world that was not worthy of his love." These are some of the mysteries of Jewish history and Jewish existence that plague all of us after the Munich tragedy. Can we still love the world that is so unworthy of our love?

One of the grand themes of Jewish history is that no matter how many times they kill us, and no matter how often they demonstrate that they are not worthy of our love, we defy them. We defy them by our will to survive, our will to go on, and to affirm life, and to say, *Zochrenu lechaim, Elohim chaim,* Remember us unto Life, O thou who art the Source and Creator and Guide of all Life. *Lo amut ki echyeh v'asaper maasay yah.* I shall not die but live and bear eternal witness to the deeds of God.

33

What We Can Learn from Israel

FOR THE PAST FIFTEEN YEARS ISRAEL HAS BEEN OFFERING help to eighty small nations in the so-called Third World which model themselves after a tiny nation that has proved she can do it.

The program began in 1955 after a visit to Israel by Ben-Gurion's friend, U Nu, who was astounded at the amazing results of the border kibbutzim in both agriculture and defense realms. A short time after the Burmese leader's visit, a crew of experienced Israel kibbutzniks went to Burma and set up a Burmese "kibbutz" in part of the vast wasteland on Burma's border with Red China. Soon after, forty Burmese families spent a year on an Israeli kibbutz, and later began a movement to build such border cooperative farming settlements in their own country.

In 1957 the program spread to Ghana, when Israel and that tiny nation formed a shipping firm in partnership, with Zim Lines operating a fleet of ships and at the same time training Ghana crews and officers. By 1967 Ghana herself was able to take over a fleet of more than a dozen vessels,

Delivered Friday night, February 16, 1968. Published in *National Jewish Monthly*, May, 1969.

with their own internationally qualified captains and crews.

By 1960 so many requests deluged Israel that she created a special Department for International Cooperation in the Ministry for Foreign Affairs. In the period 1958 to 1966 over eight thousand men and women from the developing nations received technical training in Israel in courses designed especially for them, with Israel providing generous scholarship for these students. During the same period, over fifteen hundred Israelis were on special missions in the small nations of Afro-Asia and Latin America giving courses and training indigenous leadership skills in a multitude of fields, including agriculture, engineering, education, medicine, pioneering youth military preparation, vocational training, administration, and trade unionism. Today in Israel there are more students from Africa than from any of the other continents.

Israel today helps nations as far and as different from each other as Burundi, Cameroun, Central African Republic, Ethiopia, Gabon, Ghana, Ivory Coast, Nigeria, Swaziland, Uganda, Ecuador, Iran, and even Vietnam. Anyone traveling to Israel today inevitably sees in the streets of the capital cities and in the farms visitors from Africa as well as Asia and South America.

Israel provided training to help Kenya create its police force even before it declared independence. It trained the Congo's paratroop corps, introduced scientific dairy farming into Chad, created an eye clinic in Liberia while training ophthalmologists at Hadassah Hospital to return and man the clinic, paved highways in Nigeria, and built the leading hotel in Liberia.

Why Israel? Why Israel? Why do all these tiny developing nations turn to little Israel for technical assistance? Why not go to the superpowers? There are several reasons.

First of all, Israel has faced many of the same problems that these other small countries have: small population, few natural resources, an inhospitable climate making irrigation a necessity, and a desperate need to develop techniques for large and small projects in a short space of time.

Secondly, Israel has shown amazing ingenuity and creativity in solving her numerous problems with a pioneering spirit born of necessity that larger powers never had to face. In a period of two decades Israel has redeemed and rejuvenated vast stretches of semi-arid land that had been abused and neglected and laid waste for two millennia.

The President of Mali expressed the feeling of every leader of the emerging Afro-Asian mini-states when he summed up Israeli's achievement in this way: "Israel has become an object of pilgrimage for African peoples who seek inspiration on how to build their own countries. Israel has become a human approach to building a new society of two hundred million Africans."

The third reason for turning to Israel is that there are no political strings attached. There is no worry about colonialism, no threat of communist or capitalist subversion. Unlike the American foreign aid program which runs into $3 billion, the Israeli program costs only $5 million annually, and yet has none of the corrosive aspects of rich-uncle giving. It is not so much money as know-how, not so much material gifts as setting an example, not so much foreign aid as mutual aid, giving a different hue to the relationship of the two nations involved which lifts both countries in morale and stature.

While there are other small nations giving aid to developing nations, no program of mutual assistance compares to Israel's. It has been the model for much larger states—even for America. Israel looks upon its assistance program as a mere extension of her own pioneering devotion which built Israel from 1948 to 1968.

Israel has reaped many benefits from this program. Of most recent import, a tabulation of votes by Afro-Asian states on UN resolutions after the Six Day War shows that besides being a great humanitarian venture, Israel's international cooperation program has had great political advantages.

At the UN last June (1967), while fifteen Afro-Asian nations voted for the pro-Arab resolution, twenty-two Latin American countries, seventeen African nations and two Asian states voted for the Western resolution demanding an end to Arab belligerence before Israel's withdrawal from the occupied territories of Sinai, the West Bank, and the Syrian Heights.

Lessons for American Jews. There are four lessons to be drawn by Americans from Israel's Program of Technical Assistance to emerging nations.

First of all, we must redouble our efforts to support Israel as a channel for the growth of the Third World nations. As Americans interested in the emergence of enlightened, educated, and peaceful governments of tomorrow, we have an excellent opportunity to bring about a world of peace by helping Israel help others. Our own government's prestige abroad has been steadily waning and consequently has less and less moral influence on the small nations.

Just as in the days of the Prophets, the people of Israel are setting an example to the world of how a tiny nation, among many giants, can be the moral and spiritual model for all the world. In smallness of size and at the same time greatness of spirit, our people in its Homeland can influence the entire course of moral history for generations and millennia to come.

The second lesson is that Israel's assistance program has within it the seeds of a peace settlement for the Middle East. What Israel has done for fifteen years for a multitude of Afro-Asian and Latin American states, she can do for her Arab neighbors who live in filth, poverty, disease, and ignorance. If only the Arabs will agree to make peace with Israel, their scientific, medical, economic, and social growth can spiral to great heights with the help of tiny Israel.

The third lesson is that Israel deserves the support, both financial and moral, of not only American Jews, but all Americans, *especially* black Americans.

In a spiritual and moral sense Israel has, through her spirit of pioneering devotion to re-creating a homogeneous national spirit, become the symbol for the yearnings of the black people of Africa for black nationalism. We might say that Israeli power has been a model for African power.

It is all the more shocking, therefore, to witness the support that SNCC and other extremist groups have given to the Arab side in the recent June, 1967, war, and the frenzied anti-Israel attacks such groups, which by no means represent a majority of black Americans, have made upon Israel.

The fourth and last lesson, and perhaps the most important in America today, is that American Jews must emulate the spirit of selfless devotion demonstrated by their Israeli brethren right here on our own frontier.

We American Jews must do for the American blacks what Israeli Jews have done for African blacks. Israel did not sit and twiddle her thumbs and self-righteously cry "anti-Semitism" when African nations condemned Israeli "imperialism and neo-colonialism" at Bandung in 1955 and at Casablanca in 1961. They began to win the support of these nations by helping to bring them out of ignorance and poverty into self-respecting nations.

This is what American Jews must do for the black American today. Not cry "anti-Semitism" and succumb to the backlash movement, that finds easy excuses for further repressing the black man and ignoring his cries and his needs. But set an example and lend assistance, to end poverty, disease, ignorance, discrimination and racism of any kind.

Just as tiny Israel set an example of a young, dynamic, pioneering and forward-looking nation, so American Jews, who have already set an example of a small, industrious, ethnically-cohesive American minority, must share what they have learned with other minorities in this country, and not sit back and criticize them for not following our example. Let us go out and teach them how to follow our example. Let us work together with them hand in hand, shoulder to shoulder, in a program of mutual assistance, lifting the spirit and raising the morale of Jews, blacks and all America.

Then both Israel and American Jewry shall have set a noble example for the world.

34

Israel: A Tiny State, a Great Nation

WE ALL KNOW THE STORY OF PESACH, AND THE ORIGIN OF
the word "Pesach," or "Passover." During the tenth plague,
an angel of death "passed over" the houses of the children
of Israel when he saw the blood on their doorposts, and their
firstborn sons were spared. This morning's Torah reading
begins with the following command, given to our ancient
forebears in Egypt:

"And you shall take a bunch of hyssop, dip it in the blood
that is in the basin, . . . and apply some of the blood to the
lintel and to the two doorposts." (Exodus 12:22.)

Why was the hyssop chosen to be the marker of the Jewish
doorposts? The midrash has the following explanation (She-
mot Rabba 17):

> There are things which appear lowly in human eyes and yet
> which God uses for His good deeds. Consider the hyssop bush.
> It is the lowliest of all plants. Nevertheless, with so small a
> thing, God worked miracles and freed Israel.*

Delivered Saturday morning, April 10, 1971.
* I am grateful to the late Rabbi Milton Steinberg for this midrash.

Of the many wonderful messages Passover has to offer us, this one is not the least important: the importance of small, lowly things which are chosen by God to work His miracles.

Dear friends, the State of Israel is one example of this exalted idea. A tiny little State that has shown herself to be a great nation. A little hyssop bush, chosen by God to fulfill His purposes in human history. You remember what God said to Moses in Deuteronomy: "It is not because you are the biggest of peoples that the Lord set His heart on you and chose you—indeed, you are the smallest of peoples; but it was because the Lord loved you and kept the oath He made to your fathers that the Lord freed you with a mighty hand and rescued you from the house of bondage, from the power of Pharaoh, king of Egypt." (Deut. 7:7–8.)

This tiny people, that has survived pharaohs from Moses' time until ours, is still performing miracles like those we read about in the Torah lesson this morning.

I can best summarize the mood and spirit of the people of Israel today in a brief story I heard while there on my recent trip to Jerusalem on the historic occasion of the first convention in history of Conservative rabbis in the Holy City. (March 14–24, 1971.)

It seems that two Israeli soldiers were told during the Six Day War to go to the Sinai Desert and bring back Egyptian prisoners, and for every one they brought back they would receive six Israeli pounds. They went and searched, and weren't able to find any enemy soldiers. So they went to sleep in the Sinai Desert, and when they awakened, one of them opened his eyes and there was a pair of Egyptian boots staring him in the face. When he got up he looked around and saw thousands of Egyptian soldiers with tanks and guns as far as the eye could see. Whereupon he turned to his comrade, and said, "Yaakov, we're rich."

Here is a people plagued with war since its birth twenty-three years ago, with enemies on every border, having sent its sons to battle on three occasions, and facing the prospect of another war any day, and having the courage and confidence and character and inner strength to trust in the Rock of Israel, and in the biblical promise that "God will give strength to His people, and will bless His people with peace."

On the very first day we were taken to an Israeli air force base in the Galilee, and addressed by the commander of the base, a man who reminded me very much of General Yitzchak Rabin, Commander of Israeli forces during the recent war. In the introduction we were told that this tough yet gentle commander took a two-year leave from military duty to study Talmud in an Orthodox yeshiva outside of Tel Aviv. If we want to know how can Israel's army be so humane and compassionate, and so filled with human values when they should be filled with hate and lust for revenge, then here is the answer. Because there are commanders like this colonel who care enough about Jewish tradition to investigate what wisdom and insights the classic Hebrew books might have for him, an Israeli air force colonel in the twentieth century.

That is why it is hard for me to pity Lt. Calley and to sign petitions making a martyr and a hero out of a man who murdered women and children in cold blood, when I see the type of people in Israel's Defense Forces who are so different in character and action.

Another story I heard about the Six Day War while I was in Israel will serve as a useful contrast to the atrocities we have been hearing about in Vietnam. An Israeli soldier found himself in a narrow cobblestone street in the Old City of Jerusalem, with shells bursting on all sides, when he heard an Arab call out to him from a nearby house. "I need a doctor," the Arab called out, "my wife is having difficulty in childbirth. Please, quickly, get me a doctor." What an absurd request during war! With so many Israeli soldiers wounded, lying in pools of their own blood, maimed and torn, waiting for medical aid, he should send the Jewish doctor to care for a woman and her newly-born son who might one day grow up to shoot the Israeli soldier's own son in another war. You might have guessed his decision: He sent an Israeli doctor to help the Arab woman.

The contrast of the Israeli soldier and the actions of the Lt. Calleys make it very hard for me to have pity for some of our American soldiers when brought to trial for war crimes.

Herbert Butterfield wrote that "Even in time of war, when passions can hardly be kept from rising high, all sanity depends on our keeping, deep at the bottom of everything, some remembrance of that humanity which we have in common with our bitterest enemies."

That is why this tiny state, God's little hyssop, is so deserving of my praise. Because above all, Israelis are human beings with souls, and consciences, and feelings, and moral standards.

One of the highlights of my ten-day visit was a military tour of the Old City of Jerusalem with General Uzi Narkiss, the commander of the forces which liberated Old Jerusalem on June 6 and 7, 1967. This two-hour tour was as exciting as anything I have ever done in my entire life, hearing directly from the mouth of the person responsible for our lightning victory in Jerusalem, how he accomplished it, pointing out from the vantage point of Mount Scopus, with the view of the entire range of the Judean hills before us, the strategic significance of each step in the battle, how it began and how it was finished.

One thing especially stuck in my mind. General Narkiss told us how on Monday morning, after war had broken out in Sinai, on the Egyptian front, he had contacted the General Staff and pleaded with them to let him move his troops into the Old City and capture it. The reply came back immediately: No! We will not open a second front in the war. We are notifying King Hussein that we will not fire a bullet on one inch of the Kingdom of Jordan as long as he doesn't. Narkiss was tremendously disappointed, but Israeli officers obey orders, and he had no choice but to listen. A few hours later he pleaded again, "Who in the world ever heard of Sharm el-Sheikh? The world doesn't care about some little insignificant outpost on the Gulf of Aqaba, nor who has control over it. But imagine what it will mean to the Jewish people if Jerusalem, the city of David, city of the Prophets, city of visions and dreams and peace, were again to revert to Jewish hands? Just think of the excitement, the exaltation of Jews all over the world if we were able to take Jerusalem and

restore it to become a Jewish city as it has been all throughout history until 1948! Never until twenty-three years ago
had there been less than a Jewish majority in the Holy City!"
   "No," said the General Staff. "Hands off!" But then, as
with so many other Israeli problems that seem insoluble, the
Arabs themselves provided the solution to this agonizing
dilemma. King Hussein shelled New Jerusalem, and sent his
troops to take over the UN House near Mount Scopus. This
endangered the tiny enclave of Israeli guards on Mount
Scopus which had been guarded for twenty years, and the
lives of Jewish men were now at stake. Jerusalem had to be
taken! And it *was*, within a matter of hours. The rest is
history.
   Typical of the Israeli's unassumed modesty, General Narkiss, after relating to the rabbis this dramatic personal tale
of his confrontation with fate, told of his arrival at the
Western Wall, *HaKotel*. Standing there facing the *Kotel*, he
confessed he didn't know what to do. His instincts informed
him to turn to the Wall and to salute—to salute Jewish history, Jewish tradition, to salute the Jewish past. And then
a moment later, he turned to his men and said, "Come on,
what are we standing here for? There's a war to fight!"
   I can't describe to you my own feelings the first time I
stood at this Wall. No poetic description, no eloquent portrait
of the event could possibly convey the feelings one has at his
first encounter with the Wall. All I can say is that I hope
and pray that every Jew will have the same privilege I had
to stand, to pray, to be at the Wall. Our convention began
with a very moving *Maariv* service at the *Kotel*, and I returned there every day while I was in Jerusalem, not wanting
ever to leave it.
   On Friday night, about thirty minutes before sundown,
we gathered again at the Wall and watched the young
yeshiva *bachurim*, from the Yeshiva of the *Kotel*, or from
the B'nai Akiva Academy, march down the hills to the plaza
before the Wall, and sing and dance prior to Kabbalat Shabbat. And dozens of us rabbis, including myself, joined in
their circle, and sang and danced in front of the Wall. And
every foot or two a different group of Hasidim had their

own minyan, their territory firmly staked out, shuckling and praying and singing to God of their joy at being at the Wall on Layl Shabbat.

And as I stood there at the Wall, I thought to myself, How could Jordan deny us, the Jewish people, the privilege, the high honor and noble privilege of being at the Wall, experiencing the religious thrill of a Sabbath or a Festival at the core of Jewish history, the very center of the Jewish world. How cruel and barbaric it was, for twenty years, for anyone to keep us away from this Wall, this symbol of our past glory and of our future rebirth and renaissance, to deny us the privilege of singing to God at the site of God's own House.

And today, Israel is building housing developments on every hill and slope of Judea in and around Jerusalem, to see to it that Jerusalem will be secure and safe for Jews for now and forever. Never again will the heart of our history and our faith be unjustly stolen from us. Despite whatever the U.S. State Department says, despite whatever vapid resolutions that are passed by the UN Security Council, the houses I saw going up on the hills of Judea are the symbol of Israel's willingness to face the wrath of the world in standing firm for the sake of her security and her right to be a people like all other peoples.

A careful search of the record shows that U Thant, in all his "great" moral sensitivity, never once protested when Jewish tombstones from the cemetery on the Mount of Olives were used to build Jordanian military latrine floors. Nor did any of the religious orders whose churches overlook the Mount of Olives. But now the world watches and complains while Israel carries out what it has a right to do. After hearing how Israel refused to attack Jordan first, and of how our men lost their lives and limbs in capturing the Old City in hand-to-hand combat, no Jew anywhere in the world would stop at anything to prevent the Jordanian army from setting foot in the Old City ever again!

The destruction of the Jewish quarter, and its houses and synagogues and yeshivot, are all there for the tourist to see, as a record of not only Jordanian inhumanity, but of world-wide indifference to Jewish rights.

On Shabbat afternoon, Zev Vilnai, master of tour guides in Israel, took us for a walking tour of the Old City. He told us of a request made to him by Golda Meir to find the location of the Jewish houses before the Jewish population was forced out in 1948. He then demonstrated how he was able to locate each former Jewish residence. Jewish custom dictated that residents of Jerusalem must carve out an indented space in the stone doorpost on the side of their door in which the mezuzah was inserted. All Vilnai had to do was find the indentation and the telltale mark of where the mezuzah was affixed to know where the Jewish homes were. This will help the government restore this important section of Jewish residences. It was a great thrill to know the mezuzah on the door of a Jewish home gave a sense of immortality to that home, that the mark of a Jewish home, together with the values it symbolizes and contains in the parchment inside it, helped to give a sense of permanence to our people in a world in which we are buffeted around from pillar to post, from generation to generation.

This feeling of being an immortal people, with deep religious values, was also brought home to us in the beautiful tale related to us on the last night of the convention by the Prime Minister herself, our Golda, as she is known in Israel —*Ha-Golda shelanu.*

She makes it a habit to go to Lydda Airport whenever a new planeload of Russian Jews arrives to settle in their Homeland. Just a few days before she spoke to us, she went into the arrivals lounge, and repeated the emotional scene that takes place there every time she goes to greet the new group of immigrants. They run and kiss and hug her. What a way to end a period of bondage and begin a new life in freedom—to have Golda Meir greet you at the airport! There is something unique and exciting about this pattern of a busy Prime Minister, worried about enemies and security, taking time out on a regular basis, to greet Russian Jews at the airport. Only in Israel could this happen!

On this particular visit, a little five-year-old boy rushed up and hugged and kissed the Prime Minister, and then proceeded to take off a Magen David from around his neck and gave it to her. She remarked that it would be a natural thing for an Israeli child or an American child to wear a Magen David, but how does a five-year-old Russian child, four generations after the Russian Revolution, and fifty years after Judaism stopped functioning in the Soviet Union, have a Jewish Star hanging around his neck? She asked him, "What is this?" and he answered, just as one of the kids in our own day school kindergarten might answer, "A Magen David." This particular Magen David was carved out of a Russian coin. And as the little five-year-old gave it to Golda he said to her, "A Jewish friend of mine who lives near me, and who wanted desperately to go to Israel but wasn't given permission, gave me this Magen David, and said to me, 'Take this to Israel. If this Magen David gets to Israel, then I know that I'll come after it.' "

This secularist Prime Minister, this woman who claims not to be a religious Jew, said to us after this experience, "This is *Yemot Ha-Mashiach*—this is the time our ancestors referred to as the Days of the Messiah." "This is Kibbutz Galuyot. We have a great *zekhut*. We're alive now when it's all happening, the Ingathering of the Exiles." Then I knew that I had come home, and had discovered what Israel was all about.

35
Jerusalem—God's City

TO THE JEW THERE CAN BE ONLY ONE HOME. HE MAY HAVE been born in New York, or London, or Morocco, and may live there all his life. In fact, he may never leave that city all his days on this planet. Yet, these cities are not his home. They may be the place he lives in. They may be his native country; they may demand his utmost and undivided loyalty politically, nationally, ethnically, and culturally. Yet, a hundred times and more every year of his life, a devout Jew reminds himself of the one city in the world that can never take second place, even to his place of birth.

I speak, of course, of Jerusalem. Jerusalem, the city that tradition has granted seventy various and sundry names and titles, but which is more than anything the city of God.

A Jew can never forget Jerusalem. He has pledged not to, as have his father and his father's father and all the fathers going back from King David four thousand years ago to our own day. "If I forget thee, O Jerusalem, may my right hand wither; may my tongue cling to the roof of my

Delivered Friday night, May 24, 1968; in celebration of the first Yom Yerushalayim, 5728. Excerpts were published in the *Jewish Spectator*, April, 1972.

mouth if I don't place you above my highest joy." (Psalm 137.)

When I am happy, I remember Jerusalem, and she shares my joy. When I am sad, I also cry over Jerusalem, her destruction at the hands of the Babylonians, and later the Romans—her desolateness, her emptiness.

While Jerusalem was in ruins, deserted by humanity since her real masters were driven out of her gates ages ago, the heart and mind of every Jew was desolate and empty. How can we be truly happy, Jerusalem, when you are treated with disdain and apathy? Can a bride rejoice when the groom is saddened? Can a Jew be glad when his spiritual mistress is barren and imprisoned by strangers who care not?

A Jew without Jerusalem—and Jerusalem without the Jew—is like a poet without pencil and paper, a musician without his instrument, an artist bereft of canvas and brush.

Three times daily we have prayed, with sobbing hearts and tear-laden faces, for our bride to return to us. "Return, O God, in mercy, to Jerusalem, Thy city, and dwell therein as Thou hast promised. Rebuild it in our own day as an enduring habitation." Morning, noon and evening, we cast our heart's glance to the East and eagerly look to see if she is returning. Maybe today, maybe soon. Your name is on our lips in every prayer, at every meal, at every religious service.

At weddings, we break the glass in her memory. At funerals, we place some of her earth in the grave. At the seder we say, "Next year, in Jerusalem." On Yom Kippur we utter, may our fast be held, "Next year in Jerusalem." Each summer on Tishah b'av when we relive the horror of her destruction twice on the same day six centuries apart, we ask God's comfort on her mourners:

> Comfort, O Lord our God, the mourners of Zion
> and the mourners of Jerusalem and the city which
> is in mourning, laid waste, despoiled and desolate,
> in the mourning that she is bereft of her children,
> laid waste as to her dwellings, despised in the down-
> fall of her inhabitants. Legions have devoured her: they
> have put thy people Israel to the sword. (Prayerbook.)

Whenever a pious Jew would build his house, Jewish law required of him that he leave a bare spot on the wall unpainted, or unplastered, in memory of Jerusalem. When he served up a banquet of delectable foods, he must omit at least one or two items, in memory of Jerusalem (Baba Batra 60a).

In short, Jewish life could not be complete while we are separated from our bride, our spiritual home, the central point of our religious universe. God himself is in exile from His own Holy City, and only when the days of redemption come will He return with His people.

You and I were alive when it happened. You and I were there, with the helmeted soldiers of the Israel Defense Forces when they broke through St. Stephen's and Zion Gates, and fifty hours later reached the Wall. You and I kissed its stones as we were finally reunited with our past, with our history, with our universal people, and with God.

I, for one, would not trade places with anyone who marched with Moses through the Red Sea. I would not trade places with anyone who watched the sun stand still for Joshua. I would not trade places with anyone who came back to Judea with Ezra. No moment in Jewish history can be as exciting, as inspiring and as exhilarating as that day one year ago this Sunday, 28 Iyar, when the dreams of kings and prophets and sages was realized.

Every word uttered by the Psalmist millennia ago jumped off its page and received a new spirit by God Himself.

> When the Lord restored the fortunes of Zion,
> We were like dreamers.
> Our mouth were filled with laughter,
> Our tongue with shouts of joy. (Psalm 126.)

There were five great historical holidays on the Jewish calendar before 28 Iyar, 5727, celebrating the Exodus from Egypt, the giving of the Torah, the dwelling in booths, the victory of Judah Maccabee and of Mordecai and Esther. Now there are six. This Sunday we celebrate it officially, and this entire weekend, our joy mounts gradually until the day itself when Jerusalem officially begins the second year of its re-unification.

The Psalmist says that Jerusalem was built as a City which is bound firmly together (122:3). Never again shall she be divided. This new holiday on the Jewish calendar, Yom Yerushalayim, as officially proclaimed by the Chief Rabbinate of Israel, has not, and will never be celebrated in vain.

Our Psalmists and Prophets and dreamers have been looking forward to this day too long for its greatness to be undone by any mortal or nation or group of nations.

On the third of the famous Six Days last June, Isaiah himself could have been resurrected and would have shouted out to the City of God,

Awake! awake! Clothe yourself with strength, O Zion.
Put on your beautiful garments, O Jerusalem, the holy city;
For there shall no more rule you the stranger, the unfit.
Shake yourself from the dust, Arise! O captive Jerusalem,
Loose the bonds from your neck, O captive daughter of Zion.

And as the news spread from the commanders who first reached the Wall, back to General Rabin and General Dayan, and then to all Israel, and finally, to all the world, we could have heard Isaiah himself listening to the good news, and proclaiming aloud:

How beautiful upon the mountains are the feet of him who brings good tidings, who announces peace, who brings good tidings, who proclaims salvation, who says to Zion: Your God reigns.

Hark, your guardians lift up their voice;
Together they sing for joy.
For eye to eye they see the return of the Lord to Zion.

Break forth into singing, you waste places of Jerusalem;
for the Lord has comforted his people.
He has redeemed Jerusalem.

The Lord has bared his holy arm before the
eyes of all the nations;
and all the ends of the earth shall see the
salvation of our God. (Isaiah 52:1–10.)

Yet, while our joy is indescribable and overwhelming,
while it grips us beyond our power of words, still a small
measure of sadness finds a corner in our hearts. Even though
we soon will celebrate the first anniversary of this sacred
event in Jewish history when the City of God was reunited
with the People of God, voices are raised around the world
in protest.

Only three days ago thirteen nations voted to have Israel
undo what fate and history demanded that it do. Where were
these nations, and where their loud protests for the past
twenty years when Jews were denied access to the Western
Wall, to Rachel's Tomb, to the Cave of the Patriarchs
(Machpelah), to the cemetery on the Mount of Olives?
Where was their indignation then, after Jordan had agreed
on April 3, 1949, in the Israel-Jordan Armistice Agreement
to provide "free access to the Holy Places and cultural institutions and the use of the Cemetery on the Mount of
Olives . . . ?"

Where was the wrath of these thirteen nations when Jews
were driven from the ancient Jewish quarter, and each of
the seven great main synagogues was destroyed and defiled?
Where was the United Nations while Jordan bulldozed a
road through the Mount of Olives for its tourists? Where
was international opinion when sacred Jewish tombstones
were used as floors for Jordanian legions barracks and for-
tifications? Where were the voices of those nations who
voted against Israel's occupation of Jerusalem last Tuesday
(May 21, 1968) when the Tomb of Simon the Just and the
Sanhedrin cages were littered with muck and filth?

The resolution that should have been passed this past
Tuesday was one which would congratulate Israel on bringing peace and harmony to a city that has been filled for
twenty years with barbed wire and gun emplacements; for
making its jungle-like no-man's-land into a garden of beauty;

for reconstructing dozens of synagogues which had been brutally assaulted and razed to the ground during the occupation of the foreigners; for restoring the great educational center of the Middle East, the Hebrew University, to Mount Scopus; for transforming Hadassah Hospital from a hollow ghostlike frame of a building to a center for rehabilitation for Jews and Arabs alike; for creating a showcase where Jews and Arabs can live in peace and harmony; where cultures, faiths and separated brothers live together once again; where a city divided has become one, whole, and lives its name again: City of Peace, Ir Shalom.

Were that the case, we should respect the United Nations Security Council. Instead we pity it, and laugh at it, if not scorn it.

No people in the world deserves to possess Jerusalem more than the people who built it under David, who built its central shrine on its highest hill, who loved it and prayed for its welfare, and who have mourned its loss for two millennia.

No people in the world deserves to have Jerusalem a part of its national homeland more than the people whose Prophets walked its streets and taught the world the concepts of justice and decency.

It is only fitting and natural for the religious capital of the world to belong to the people who gave religion to the world. It is only fitting and natural for the city where Hebrew was spoken by King David, and all the Kings, Prophets, and Sages who followed him, to belong to the people that now speaks Hebrew once again in its capital city, in its restored land. When scrolls are found near the Dead Sea in the Judean caves each year, they are written in Hebrew, the language of Israel, of the Jewish people, the language spoken in Jerusalem centuries and centuries before there was an Arab nation, before there was a United Nations.

A thousand years before there was a Paris, or a London, Jews walked and talked in the streets of Jerusalem. How dare any nation tell us to leave a city that has been ours for four millennia?

Would France consent to make Paris an international city?

Would England consent to make London an international city? Would Egypt agree to let Cairo be claimed by the world?

Then why should the Jewish people let Jerusalem become public property?

We demand from the nations of the world once and for all, that the same standards of justice be applied to our people as are applied to all other nations. We shall not accept less.

In the words of the ancient Statesman-Prophet of Jerusalem:

> For Zion's sake I will not keep silent,
> and for Jerusalem's sake I will not rest,
> until her vindication goes forth as brightness,
> and her salvation as a burning torch.
> Give Him no rest until he establishes Jerusalem
> and makes it a praise in the earth. (Isaiah 62:1, 7.)

Index

Eliot, George, 71
Esau, 29
Evers, Medgar, 120
Ezrat Nashim, 157

Fackenheim, Emil, 76
Finkelstein, Louis, 193
Fulbright, Senator William, 125

Gabriel (angel), 58 f.
Gandhi, M., 32
Gardner, John W., 39
Gaylin, Dr. William, 33
Ginzberg, Louis, 59
Golden, Harry, 67
Gordis, Robert, 9–11, 87
Gorky, Maxim, 245

Haggadah, 27
Halacha, 22
Harmon, Avraham, 177
Harrington, Michael, 103
Hebrew language, 196
Hertzberg, Arthur, 210
Herzl, Theodore, 198
Heschel, Abraham Joshua, 32, 76,
    111, 128, 171, 231 f., 241
Higgins, Msgr. George, 210
Hillel, 23 ff., 36, 66, 91, 118, 159
Hirsch, Richard, 82
Hoffer, Eric, 263
Holocaust, 71 ff., 184
Honi the Circle-Drawer, 36
Humphrey, Hubert, 171

Ibn Gabirol, Solomon, 73
Intermarriage, 66

Jackson, Jesse, 54
Jacob (patriarch), 29 ff.
Jewish Theological Seminary, 31,
    110, 150, 158, 193
John XXIII, (pope), 123

Johnson, Lyndon, 94, 172, 174,
    182, 204

Kaplan, Mordecai M., 201
Kennedy, Edward, 31, 136
Kennedy, John F., 48, 120
Kennedy, Robert F., 54, 57, 116 ff.
Kimche, Jon, 124
King, Martin Luther, Jr., 32, 54,
    99, 110 ff., 120, 143
Kissinger, Henry, 34
Koestler, Arthur, 45

Lang, Brian, 47
Leeser, Isaac, 139
Levinthal, Israel, 144
Levi-Strauss, Claude, 37
Lipchitz, Jacques, 41

McCarthy, Eugene, 171
McGovern, George, 260
McGuire, Brian, 48
McNamara, Robert, 93 f.
Maimonides, Moses, 30, 82, 128
Marshall, George, 198
Marx, Gary T., 101
Maslow, Abraham, 63
Maslow, Will, 101
Meir, Golda, 149 f., 154, 198, 202,
    248, 260, 278
Melchior, Marcus, 249
Messiah, 26 f., 123, 129
Mishna, 35
Mondale, Senator Walter F., 39
Moore, Cecil, 102
Moses, 58 ff., 65, 114–15, 147, 157,
    186, 193, 194 f., 273, 282

Narkiss, General Uzi, 275 f.
Neusner, Jacob, 213, 241
Nixon, Richard M., 34, 35, 39,
    200, 253, 260

Quotation Index

Index to
Rabbinic Literature

About the Author

DOV PERETZ ELKINS was born in Philadelphia in 1937. He has degrees from Gratz College, Temple University and the Jewish Theological Seminary. After ordination in 1964, he served as a military chaplain and in pulpits at Har Zion Temple, Philadelphia and Radnor, Pennsylvania, Jacksonville Jewish Center, Jacksonville, Florida, and is presently spiritual leader of Temple Beth El, Rochester, New York, one of America's leading Conservative synagogues.

He is passionately committed to a free pulpit, and to making Judaism relevant to the modern world and its complex social, political and moral problems. He views his role as guiding people toward the fulfillment of Judaism's mandate "to perfect the world under the Kingdom of the Almighty."

Along with his deep commitment to social justice is his boundless love for the Land of Israel and the Jewish People. He was one of the early activists for the freedom of the three million oppressed Jews locked behind the prison walls of the Soviet Union.

Rabbi Elkins has edited, co-authored and authored many books, including *Worlds Lost and Found, Treasures From the Dust, So Young to Be a Rabbi,* and *Rejoice with Jerusalem.* He and his wife, Elaine, have three children, Hillel, Jonathan, and Shira.